G.I. JOE
HOMEFRONT

IDW

Special thanks to Hasbro's Aaron Archer, Derryl DePriest, Joe Del Regno, Ed Lane, Joe Furfaro, Jos Huxley, Heather Hopkins, and Michael Kelly for their invaluable assistance.

IDW founded by Ted Adams, Alex Garner, Kris Oprisko, and Robbie Robbins |

ISBN: 978-1-61377-705-3

16 15 14 13   1 2 3 4

Licensed By:

Ted Adams, CEO & Publisher
Greg Goldstein, President & COO
Robbie Robbins, EVP/Sr. Graphic Artist
Chris Ryall, Chief Creative Officer/Editor-in-Chief
Matthew Ruzicka, CPA, Chief Financial Officer
Alan Payne, VP of Sales
Dirk Wood, VP of Marketing
Lorelei Bunjes, VP of Digital Services

Become our fan on Facebook **facebook.com/idwpublishing**
Follow us on Twitter **@idwpublishing**
Check us out on YouTube **youtube.com/idwpublishing**
www.IDWPUBLISHING.com

Originally published as G.I. JOE VOLUME 3 issues #1–5.

WRITER: FRED VAN LENTE
PENCILLER: STEVE KURTH
INKERS: ALLEN MARTINEZ WITH PHYLLIS NOVIN,
MARC DEERING, AND JUAN CASTRO
COLORIST: JOANA LAFUENTE
LETTERERS: NEIL UYETAKE, SHAWN LEE,
TOM B. LONG, AND CHRIS MOWRY
CONSULTING EDITOR: CARLOS GUZMAN
SERIES EDITOR: JOHN BARBER

COLLECTION COVER ARTIST: STEVE KURTH
COLLECTION COVER COLORIST: KITO YOUNG
COLLECTION EDITORS: JUSTIN EISINGER AND ALONZO SIMON
COLLECTION DESIGNER: SHAWN LEE

CHAPTER ONE

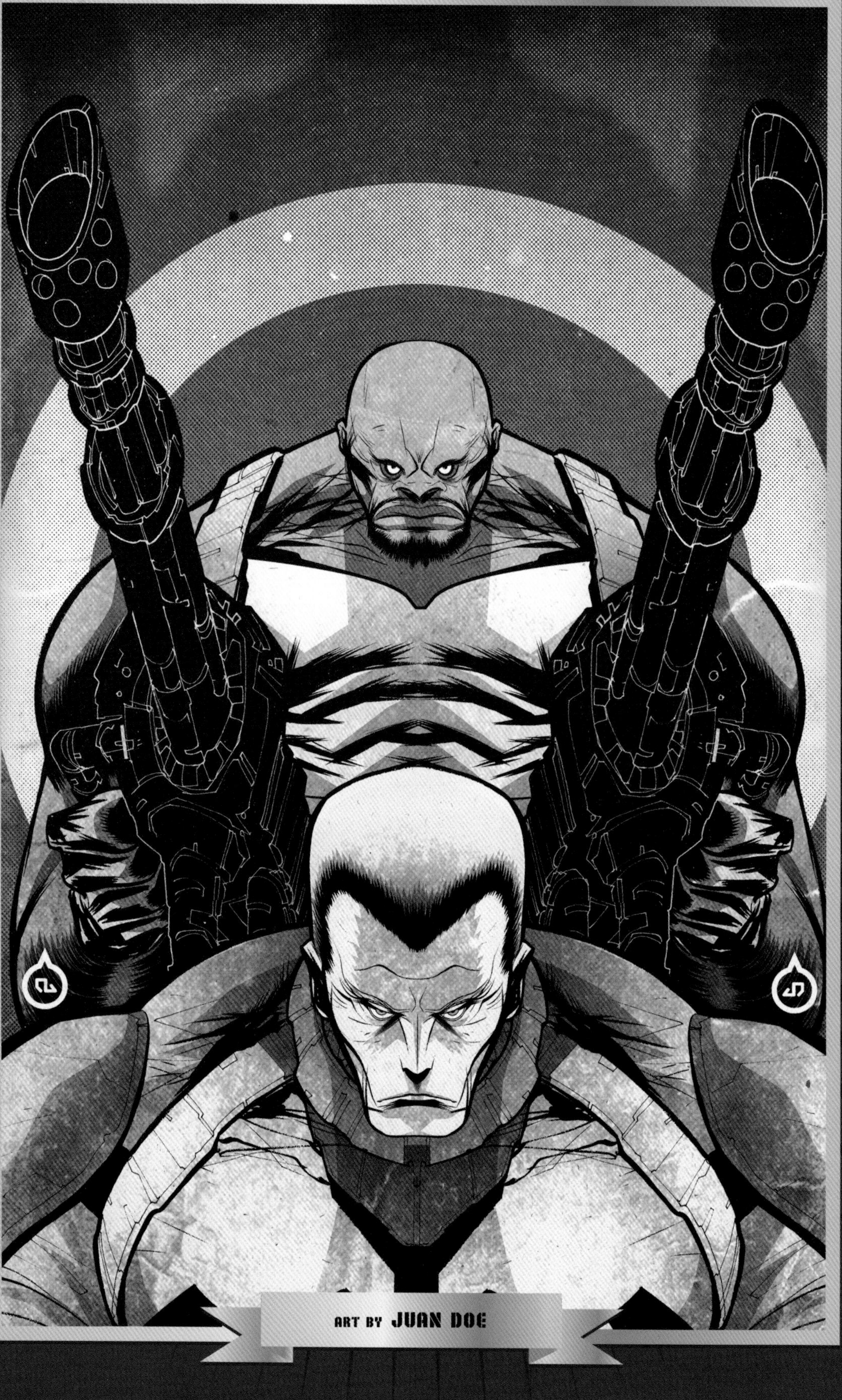

ART BY JUAN DOE

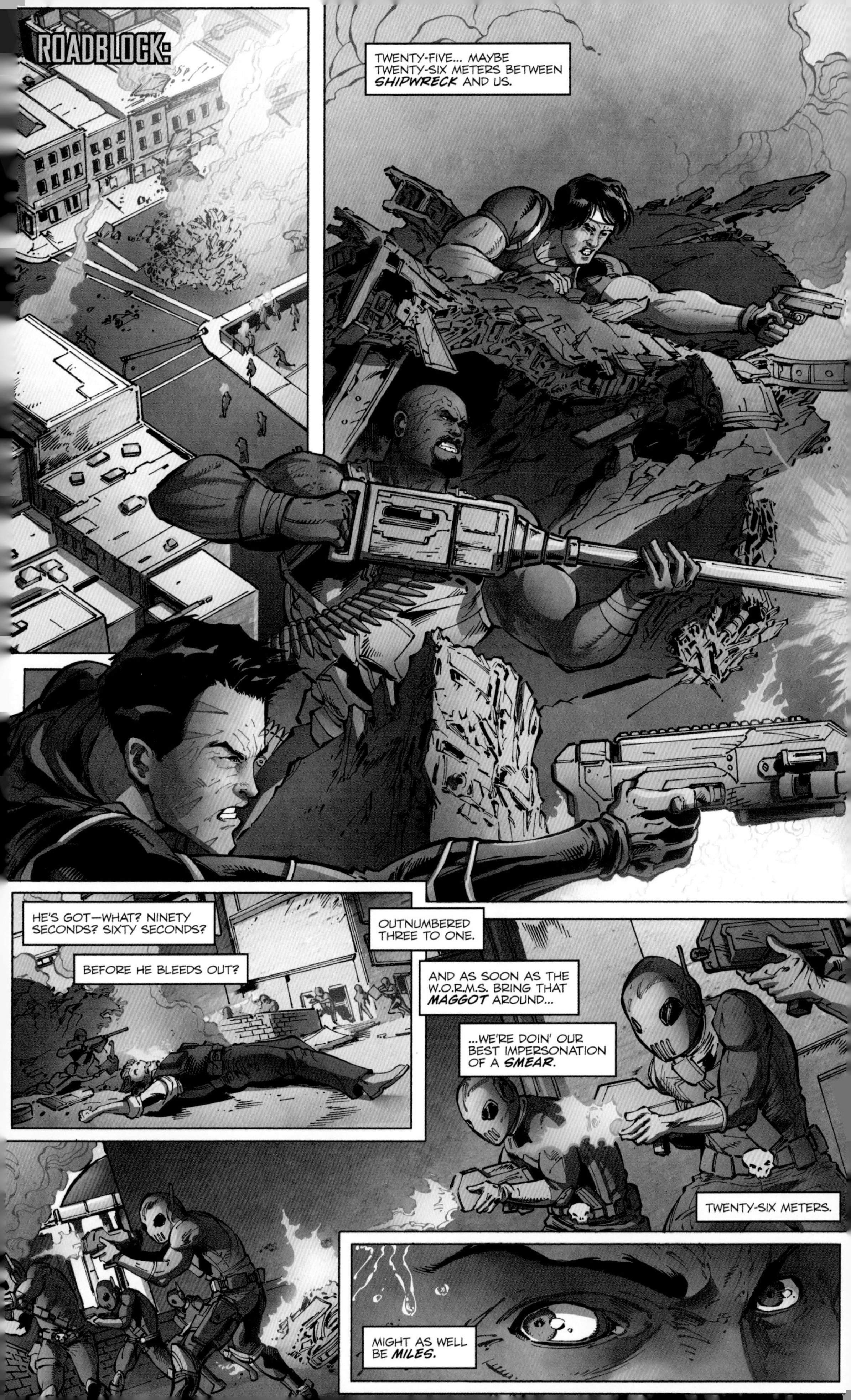
ROADBLOCK:
TWENTY-FIVE... MAYBE TWENTY-SIX METERS BETWEEN SHIPWRECK AND US.
HE'S GOT—WHAT? NINETY SECONDS? SIXTY SECONDS?
BEFORE HE BLEEDS OUT?
OUTNUMBERED THREE TO ONE.
AND AS SOON AS THE W.O.R.M.S. BRING THAT MAGGOT AROUND...
...WE'RE DOIN' OUR BEST IMPERSONATION OF A SMEAR.
TWENTY-SIX METERS.
MIGHT AS WELL BE MILES.

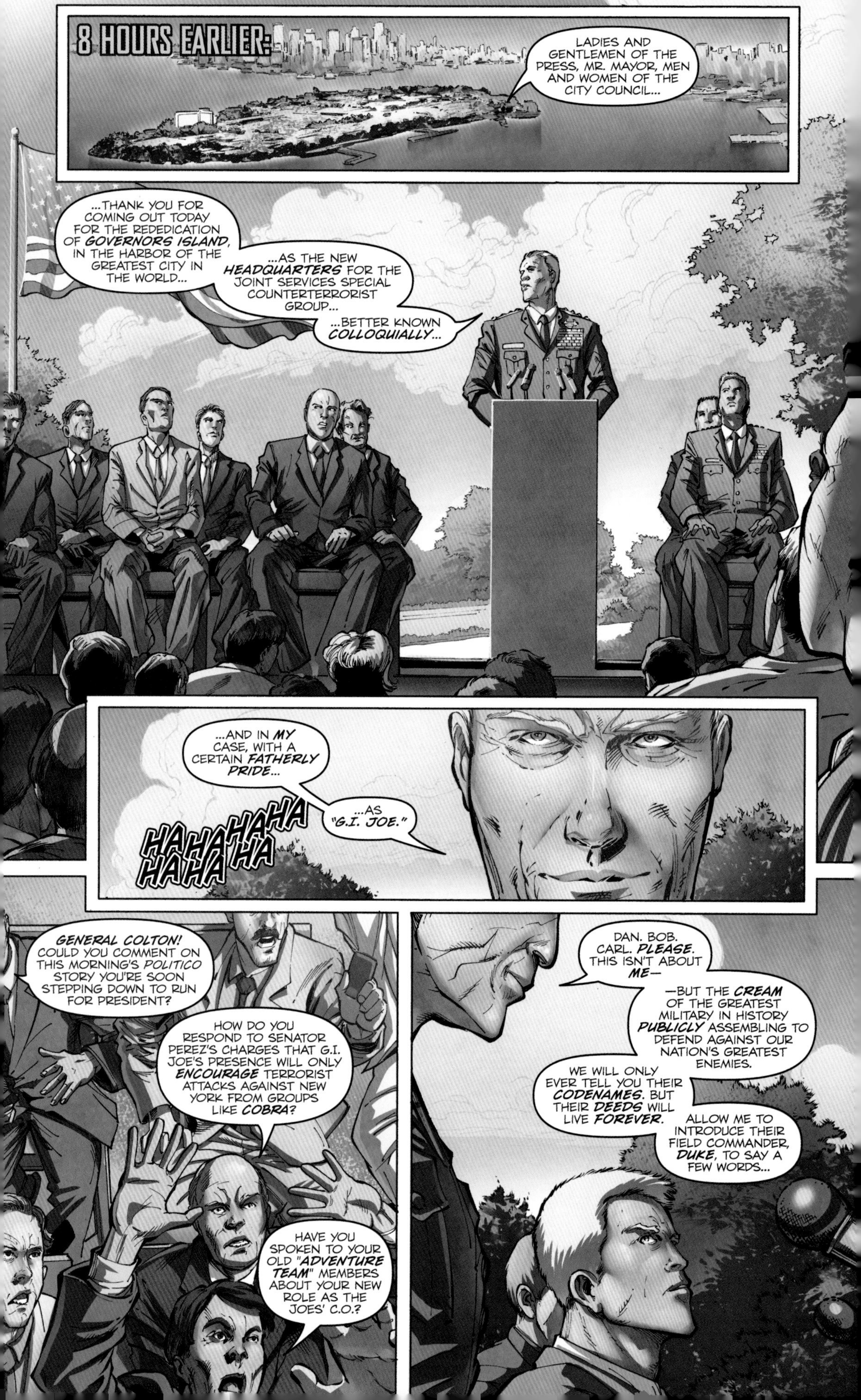
8 HOURS EARLIER:
LADIES AND GENTLEMEN OF THE PRESS, MR. MAYOR, MEN AND WOMEN OF THE CITY COUNCIL...
...THANK YOU FOR COMING OUT TODAY FOR THE REDEDICATION OF GOVERNORS ISLAND, IN THE HARBOR OF THE GREATEST CITY IN THE WORLD...
...AS THE NEW HEADQUARTERS FOR THE JOINT SERVICES SPECIAL COUNTERTERRORIST GROUP...
...BETTER KNOWN COLLOQUIALLY...
...AND IN MY CASE, WITH A CERTAIN FATHERLY PRIDE...
...AS "G.I. JOE."
HAHAHAHA HAHAHA
GENERAL COLTON! COULD YOU COMMENT ON THIS MORNING'S POLITICO STORY YOU'RE SOON STEPPING DOWN TO RUN FOR PRESIDENT?
HOW DO YOU RESPOND TO SENATOR PEREZ'S CHARGES THAT G.I. JOE'S PRESENCE WILL ONLY ENCOURAGE TERRORIST ATTACKS AGAINST NEW YORK FROM GROUPS LIKE COBRA?
HAVE YOU SPOKEN TO YOUR OLD "ADVENTURE TEAM" MEMBERS ABOUT YOUR NEW ROLE AS THE JOES' C.O.?
DAN. BOB. CARL. PLEASE. THIS ISN'T ABOUT ME—
—BUT THE CREAM OF THE GREATEST MILITARY IN HISTORY PUBLICLY ASSEMBLING TO DEFEND AGAINST OUR NATION'S GREATEST ENEMIES.
WE WILL ONLY EVER TELL YOU THEIR CODENAMES. BUT THEIR DEEDS WILL LIVE FOREVER.
ALLOW ME TO INTRODUCE THEIR FIELD COMMANDER, DUKE, TO SAY A FEW WORDS...

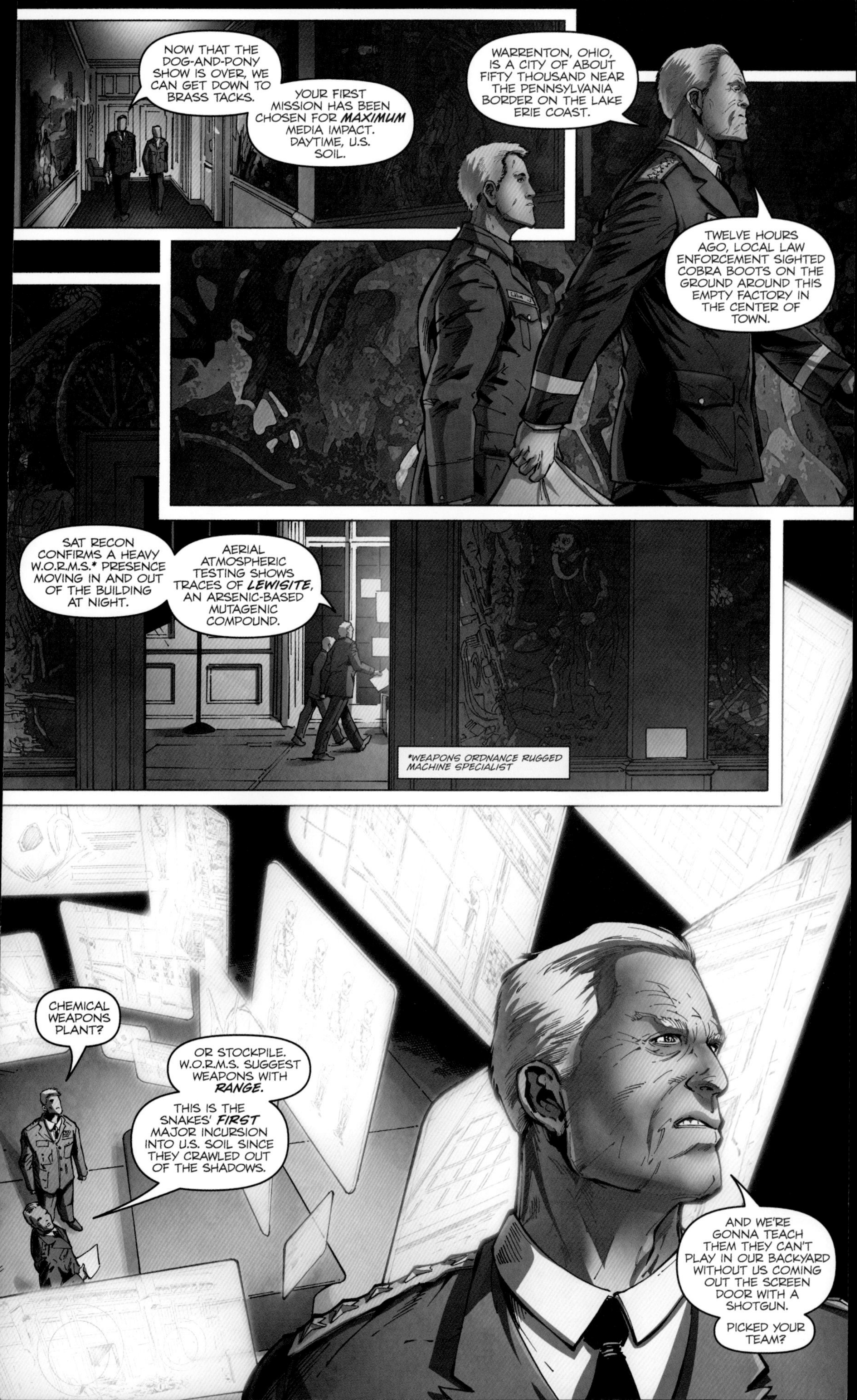
NOW THAT THE DOG-AND-PONY SHOW IS OVER, WE CAN GET DOWN TO BRASS TACKS.
YOUR FIRST MISSION HAS BEEN CHOSEN FOR **MAXIMUM** MEDIA IMPACT. DAYTIME, U.S. SOIL.
WARRENTON, OHIO, IS A CITY OF ABOUT FIFTY THOUSAND NEAR THE PENNSYLVANIA BORDER ON THE LAKE ERIE COAST.
TWELVE HOURS AGO, LOCAL LAW ENFORCEMENT SIGHTED COBRA BOOTS ON THE GROUND AROUND THIS EMPTY FACTORY IN THE CENTER OF TOWN.
SAT RECON CONFIRMS A HEAVY W.O.R.M.S.* PRESENCE MOVING IN AND OUT OF THE BUILDING AT NIGHT.
AERIAL ATMOSPHERIC TESTING SHOWS TRACES OF **LEWISITE**, AN ARSENIC-BASED MUTAGENIC COMPOUND.
*WEAPONS ORDNANCE RUGGED MACHINE SPECIALIST
CHEMICAL WEAPONS PLANT?
OR STOCKPILE. W.O.R.M.S. SUGGEST WEAPONS WITH **RANGE.**
THIS IS THE SNAKES' **FIRST** MAJOR INCURSION INTO U.S. SOIL SINCE THEY CRAWLED OUT OF THE SHADOWS.
AND WE'RE GONNA TEACH THEM THEY CAN'T PLAY IN OUR BACKYARD WITHOUT US COMING OUT THE SCREEN DOOR WITH A SHOTGUN.
PICKED YOUR TEAM?

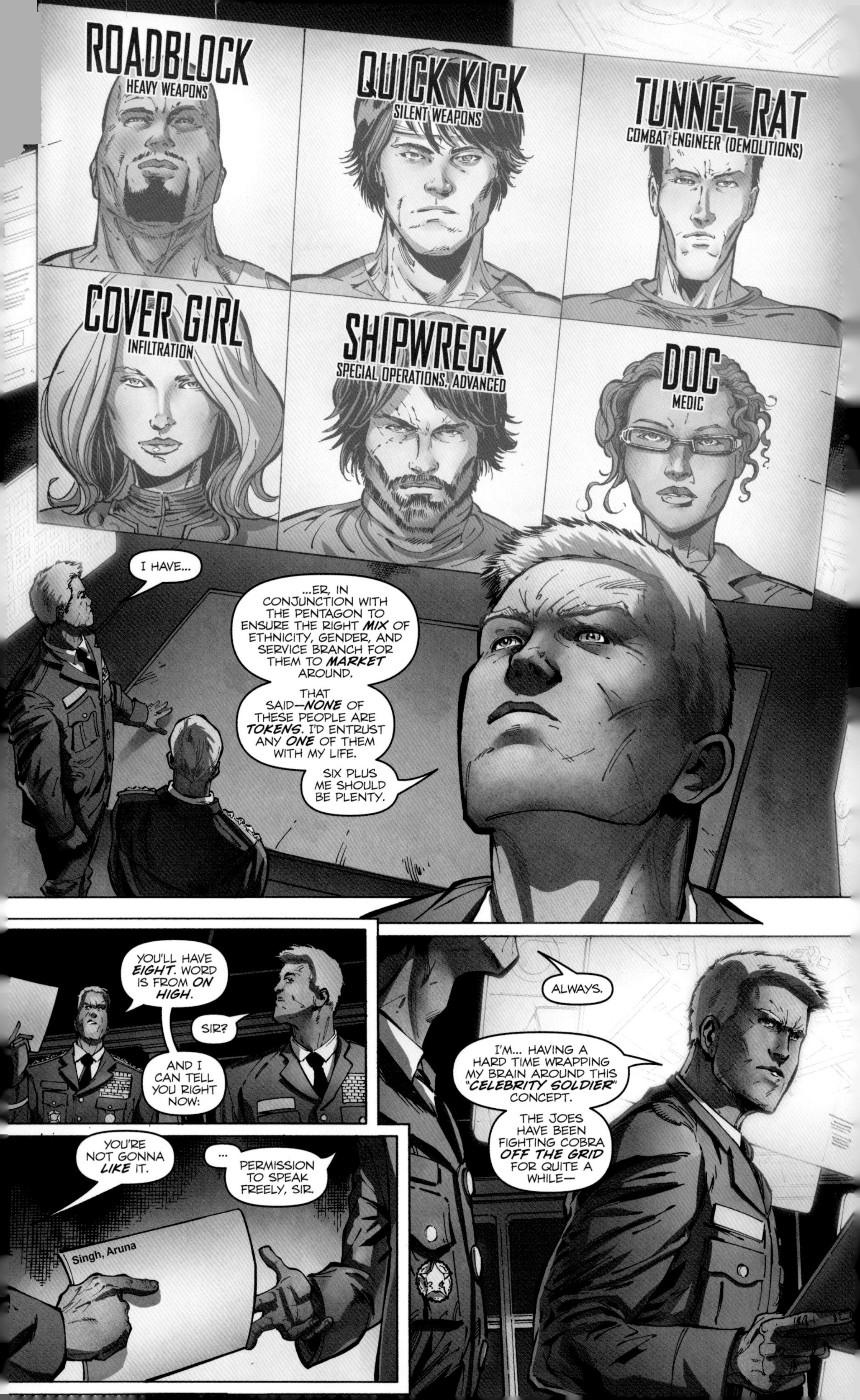
ROADBLOCK
HEAVY WEAPONS
QUICK KICK
SILENT WEAPONS
TUNNEL RAT
COMBAT ENGINEER (DEMOLITIONS)
COVER GIRL
INFILTRATION
SHIPWRECK
SPECIAL OPERATIONS, ADVANCED
DOC
MEDIC
I HAVE...
...ER, IN CONJUNCTION WITH THE PENTAGON TO ENSURE THE RIGHT MIX OF ETHNICITY, GENDER, AND SERVICE BRANCH FOR THEM TO MARKET AROUND.
THAT SAID—NONE OF THESE PEOPLE ARE TOKENS. I'D ENTRUST ANY ONE OF THEM WITH MY LIFE.
SIX PLUS ME SHOULD BE PLENTY.
YOU'LL HAVE EIGHT. WORD IS FROM ON HIGH.
SIR?
AND I CAN TELL YOU RIGHT NOW:
YOU'RE NOT GONNA LIKE IT.
...
PERMISSION TO SPEAK FREELY, SIR.
Singh, Aruna
ALWAYS.
I'M... HAVING A HARD TIME WRAPPING MY BRAIN AROUND THIS "CELEBRITY SOLDIER" CONCEPT.
THE JOES HAVE BEEN FIGHTING COBRA OFF THE GRID FOR QUITE A WHILE—

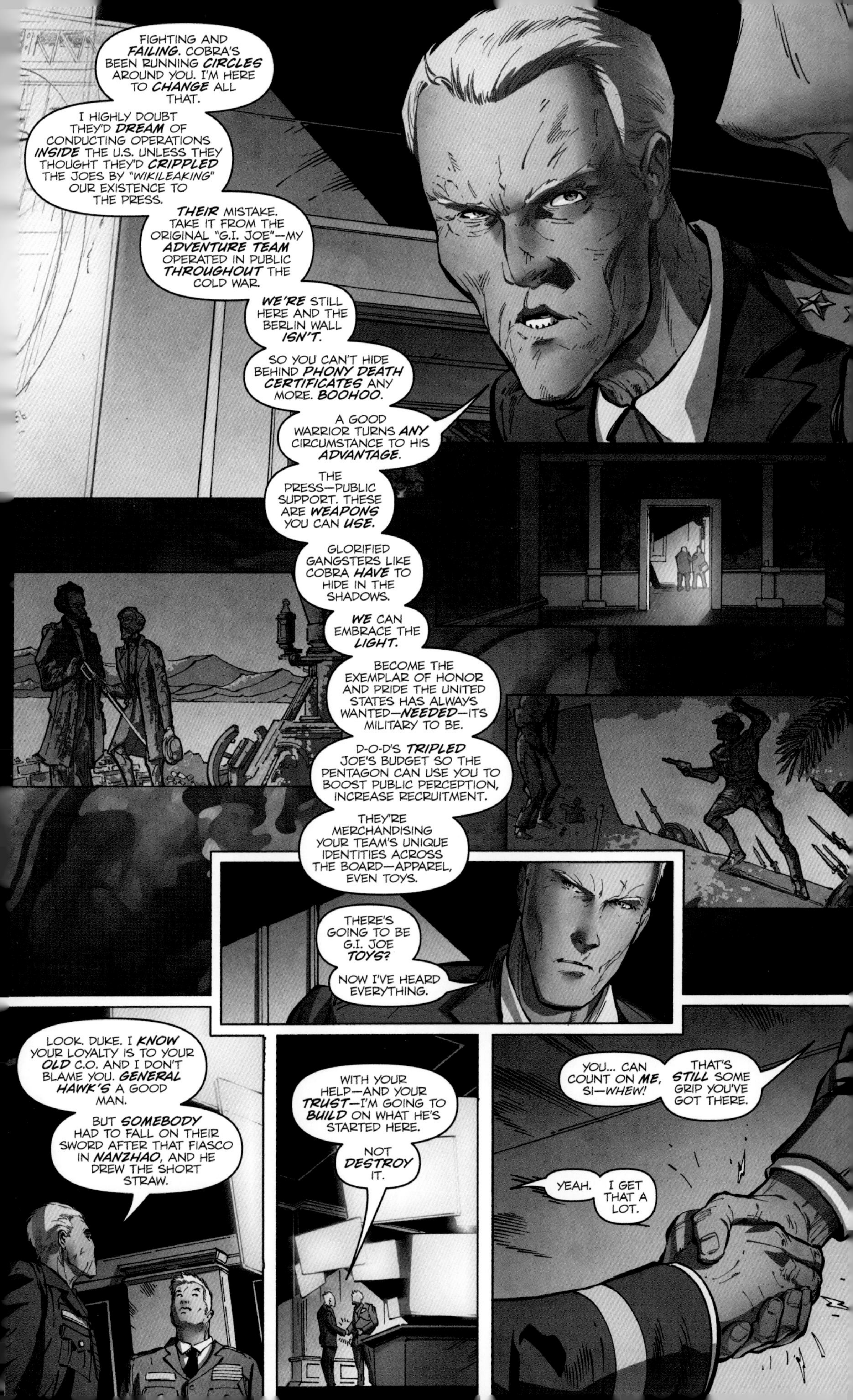
FIGHTING AND FAILING. COBRA'S BEEN RUNNING CIRCLES AROUND YOU. I'M HERE TO CHANGE ALL THAT.
I HIGHLY DOUBT THEY'D DREAM OF CONDUCTING OPERATIONS INSIDE THE U.S. UNLESS THEY THOUGHT THEY'D CRIPPLED THE JOES BY "WIKILEAKING" OUR EXISTENCE TO THE PRESS.
THEIR MISTAKE. TAKE IT FROM THE ORIGINAL "G.I. JOE"—MY ADVENTURE TEAM OPERATED IN PUBLIC THROUGHOUT THE COLD WAR.
WE'RE STILL HERE AND THE BERLIN WALL ISN'T.
SO YOU CAN'T HIDE BEHIND PHONY DEATH CERTIFICATES ANY MORE. BOOHOO.
A GOOD WARRIOR TURNS ANY CIRCUMSTANCE TO HIS ADVANTAGE.
THE PRESS—PUBLIC SUPPORT. THESE ARE WEAPONS YOU CAN USE.
GLORIFIED GANGSTERS LIKE COBRA HAVE TO HIDE IN THE SHADOWS.
WE CAN EMBRACE THE LIGHT.
BECOME THE EXEMPLAR OF HONOR AND PRIDE THE UNITED STATES HAS ALWAYS WANTED—NEEDED—ITS MILITARY TO BE.
D-O-D'S TRIPLED JOE'S BUDGET SO THE PENTAGON CAN USE YOU TO BOOST PUBLIC PERCEPTION, INCREASE RECRUITMENT.
THEY'RE MERCHANDISING YOUR TEAM'S UNIQUE IDENTITIES ACROSS THE BOARD—APPAREL, EVEN TOYS.
THERE'S GOING TO BE G.I. JOE TOYS?
NOW I'VE HEARD EVERYTHING.
LOOK. DUKE. I KNOW YOUR LOYALTY IS TO YOUR OLD C.O. AND I DON'T BLAME YOU. GENERAL HAWK'S A GOOD MAN.
BUT SOMEBODY HAD TO FALL ON THEIR SWORD AFTER THAT FIASCO IN NANZHAO, AND HE DREW THE SHORT STRAW.
WITH YOUR HELP—AND YOUR TRUST—I'M GOING TO BUILD ON WHAT HE'S STARTED HERE.
NOT DESTROY IT.
YOU... CAN COUNT ON ME, SI—WHEW!
THAT'S STILL SOME GRIP YOU'VE GOT THERE.
YEAH. I GET THAT A LOT.

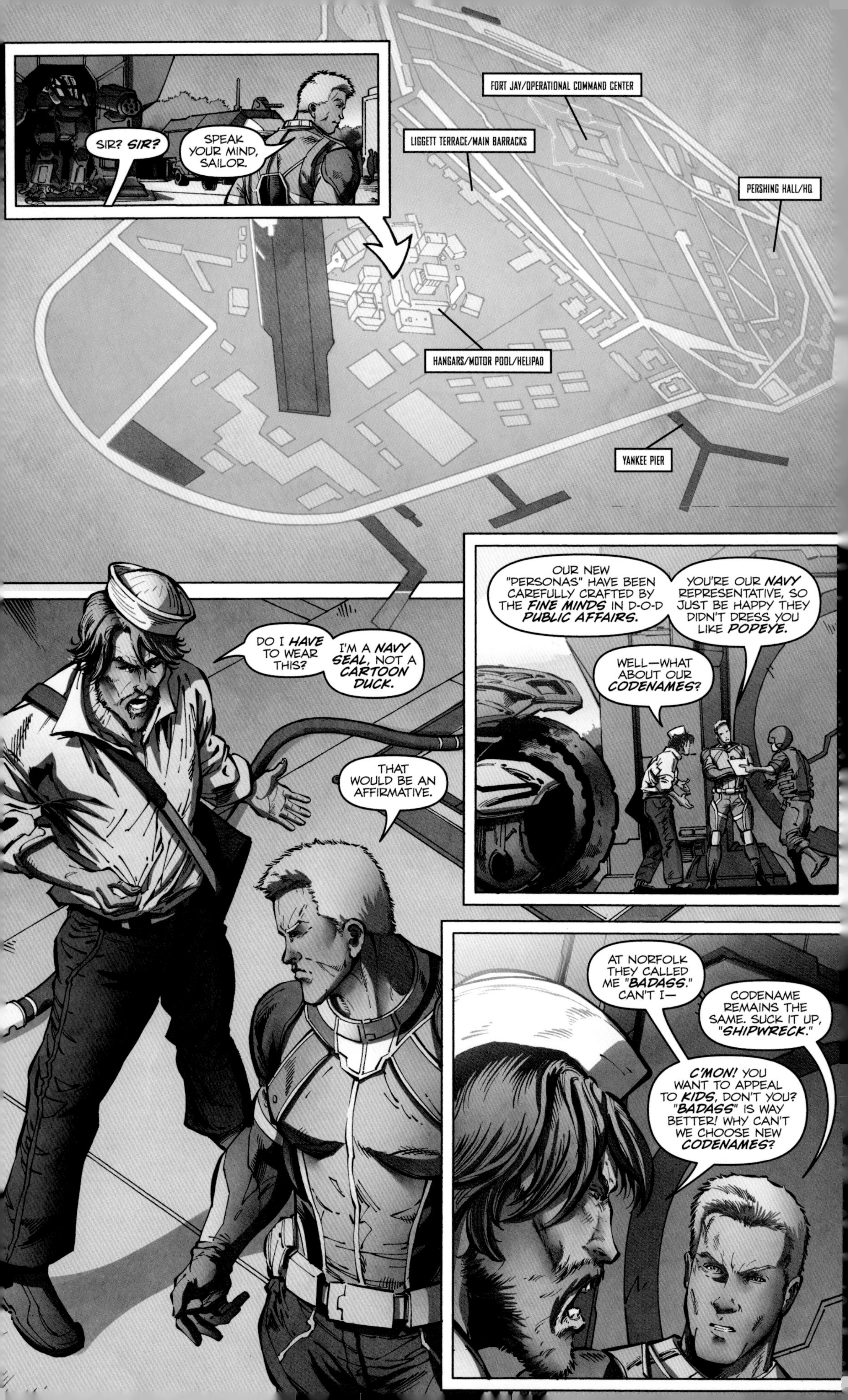

SIR? SIR?
SPEAK YOUR MIND, SAILOR.
FORT JAY/OPERATIONAL COMMAND CENTER
LIGGETT TERRACE/MAIN BARRACKS
PERSHING HALL/HQ
HANGARS/MOTOR POOL/HELIPAD
YANKEE PIER
DO I HAVE TO WEAR THIS?
I'M A NAVY SEAL, NOT A CARTOON DUCK.
THAT WOULD BE AN AFFIRMATIVE.
OUR NEW "PERSONAS" HAVE BEEN CAREFULLY CRAFTED BY THE FINE MINDS IN D-O-D PUBLIC AFFAIRS.
YOU'RE OUR NAVY REPRESENTATIVE, SO JUST BE HAPPY THEY DIDN'T DRESS YOU LIKE POPEYE.
WELL—WHAT ABOUT OUR CODENAMES?
AT NORFOLK THEY CALLED ME "BADASS." CAN'T I—
CODENAME REMAINS THE SAME. SUCK IT UP, "SHIPWRECK."
C'MON! YOU WANT TO APPEAL TO KIDS, DON'T YOU? "BADASS" IS WAY BETTER! WHY CAN'T WE CHOOSE NEW CODENAMES?

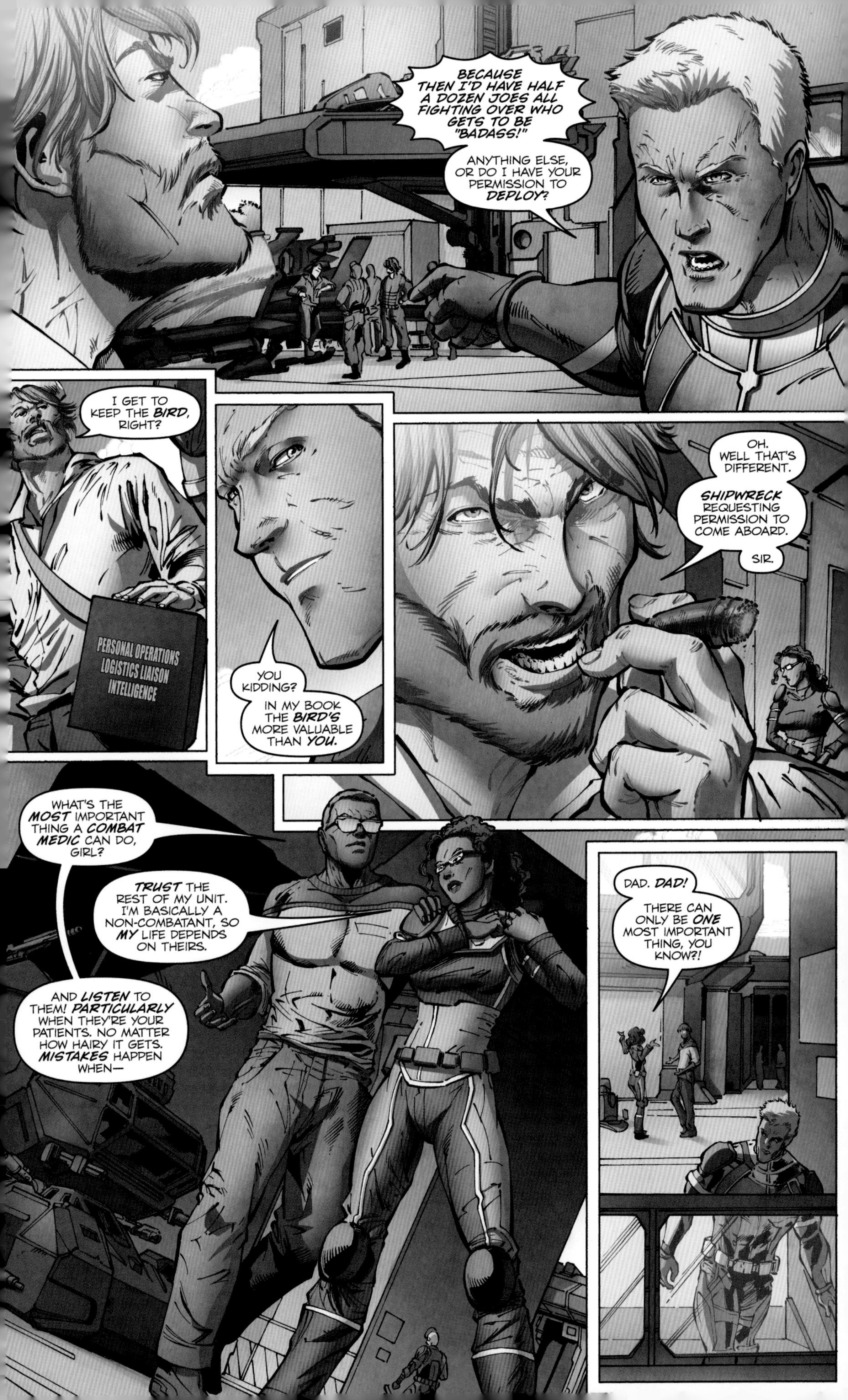
BECAUSE THEN I'D HAVE HALF A DOZEN JOES ALL FIGHTING OVER WHO GETS TO BE "BADASS!"
ANYTHING ELSE, OR DO I HAVE YOUR PERMISSION TO DEPLOY?
I GET TO KEEP THE BIRD, RIGHT?
PERSONAL OPERATIONS LOGISTICS LIAISON INTELLIGENCE
YOU KIDDING?
IN MY BOOK THE BIRD'S MORE VALUABLE THAN YOU.
OH. WELL THAT'S DIFFERENT.
SHIPWRECK REQUESTING PERMISSION TO COME ABOARD.
SIR.
WHAT'S THE MOST IMPORTANT THING A COMBAT MEDIC CAN DO, GIRL?
TRUST THE REST OF MY UNIT. I'M BASICALLY A NON-COMBATANT, SO MY LIFE DEPENDS ON THEIRS.
AND LISTEN TO THEM! PARTICULARLY WHEN THEY'RE YOUR PATIENTS. NO MATTER HOW HAIRY IT GETS. MISTAKES HAPPEN WHEN—
DAD. DAD!
THERE CAN ONLY BE ONE MOST IMPORTANT THING, YOU KNOW?!

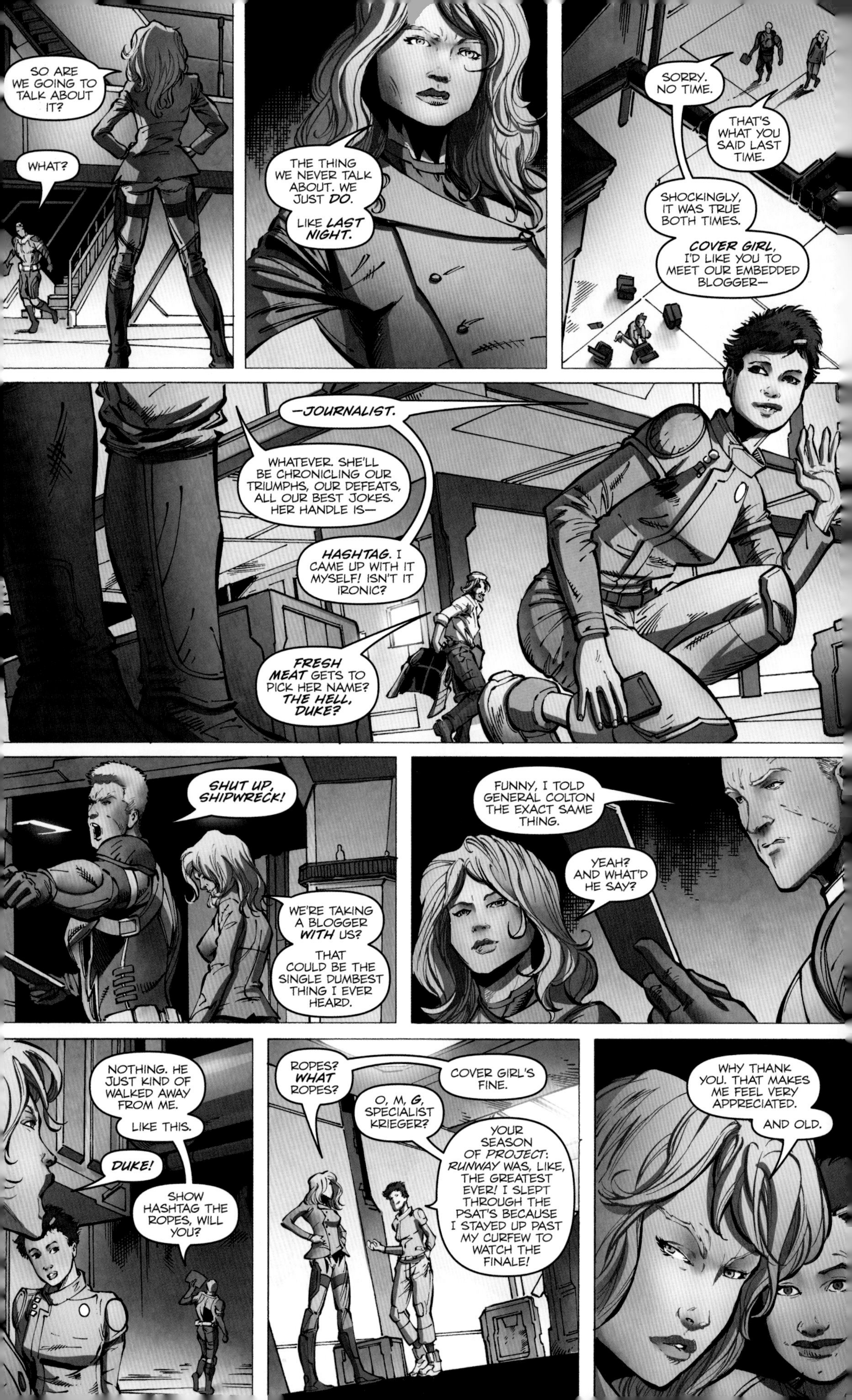
SO ARE WE GOING TO TALK ABOUT IT?
WHAT?
THE THING WE NEVER TALK ABOUT. WE JUST DO.
LIKE LAST NIGHT.
SORRY. NO TIME.
THAT'S WHAT YOU SAID LAST TIME.
SHOCKINGLY, IT WAS TRUE BOTH TIMES.
COVER GIRL, I'D LIKE YOU TO MEET OUR EMBEDDED BLOGGER—
—JOURNALIST.
WHATEVER. SHE'LL BE CHRONICLING OUR TRIUMPHS, OUR DEFEATS, ALL OUR BEST JOKES. HER HANDLE IS—
HASHTAG. I CAME UP WITH IT MYSELF! ISN'T IT IRONIC?
FRESH MEAT GETS TO PICK HER NAME? THE HELL, DUKE?
SHUT UP, SHIPWRECK!
WE'RE TAKING A BLOGGER WITH US?
THAT COULD BE THE SINGLE DUMBEST THING I EVER HEARD.
FUNNY, I TOLD GENERAL COLTON THE EXACT SAME THING.
YEAH? AND WHAT'D HE SAY?
NOTHING. HE JUST KIND OF WALKED AWAY FROM ME.
LIKE THIS.
DUKE!
SHOW HASHTAG THE ROPES, WILL YOU?
ROPES? WHAT ROPES?
COVER GIRL'S FINE.
O, M, G, SPECIALIST KRIEGER?
YOUR SEASON OF PROJECT: RUNWAY WAS, LIKE, THE GREATEST EVER! I SLEPT THROUGH THE PSAT'S BECAUSE I STAYED UP PAST MY CURFEW TO WATCH THE FINALE!
WHY THANK YOU. THAT MAKES ME FEEL VERY APPRECIATED.
AND OLD.

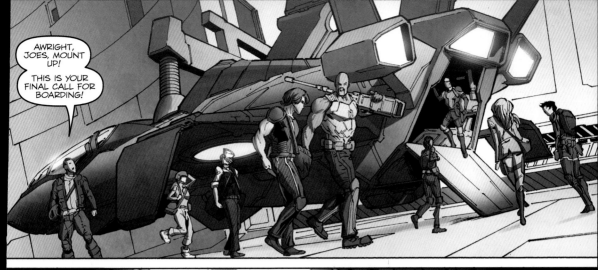

AWRIGHT, JOES, MOUNT UP!

THIS IS YOUR FINAL CALL FOR BOARDING!

SERGEANT LEE?

TUNNEL RAT.

IS IT TRUE *YOU* FOUND THE HIDDEN BUNKER OF THE PRESIDENT OF *AL-ALAWI?*

I CAN NEITHER CONFIRM NOR DENY THAT...

...BUT THAT HOLE *DID* REEK OF DRAKAR.

YOU'D THINK A DICTATOR OF HIS MEANS WOULD HAVE BETTER *TASTE.*

TWEETING IT!

SKYSTORM X-WING, THIS IS FORT JAY.

YOU ARE CLEARED FOR TAKEOFF.

SKIN US SOME SNAKES, *WINDMILL.*

ROGER *THAT,* GENERAL JOE.

ALL SYSTEMS...

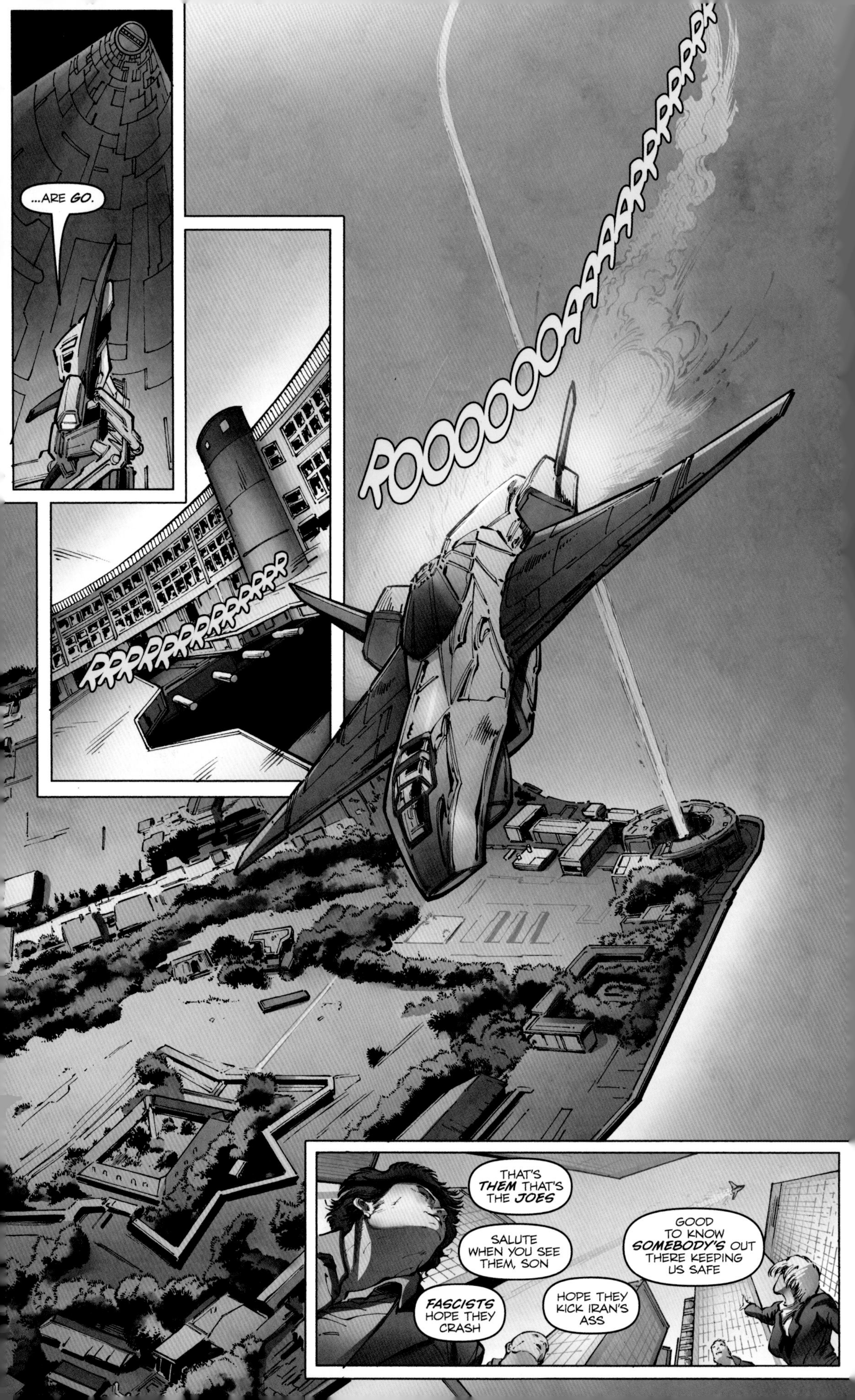

...ARE GO.
RRRRRRRRRRRRRRRR
ROOOOOOAAAAAARRRRRRRR
THAT'S THEM THAT'S THE JOES
SALUTE WHEN YOU SEE THEM, SON
FASCISTS HOPE THEY CRASH
HOPE THEY KICK IRAN'S ASS
GOOD TO KNOW SOMEBODY'S OUT THERE KEEPING US SAFE

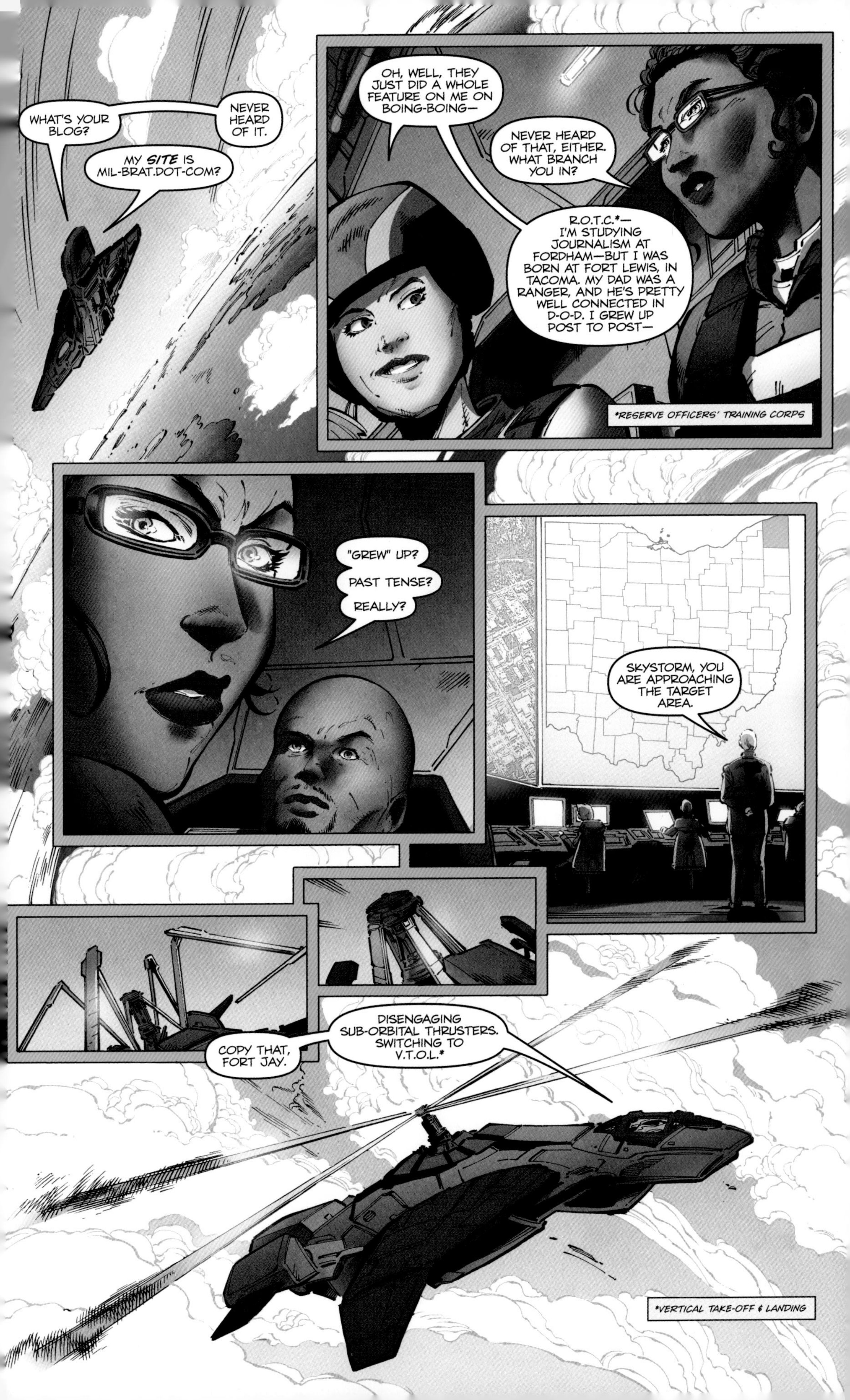
WHAT'S YOUR BLOG?
NEVER HEARD OF IT.
MY SITE IS MIL-BRAT.DOT-COM?
OH, WELL, THEY JUST DID A WHOLE FEATURE ON ME ON BOING-BOING—
NEVER HEARD OF THAT, EITHER. WHAT BRANCH YOU IN?
R.O.T.C.*—I'M STUDYING JOURNALISM AT FORDHAM—BUT I WAS BORN AT FORT LEWIS, IN TACOMA. MY DAD WAS A RANGER, AND HE'S PRETTY WELL CONNECTED IN D-O-D. I GREW UP POST TO POST—
*RESERVE OFFICERS' TRAINING CORPS
"GREW" UP?
PAST TENSE?
REALLY?
SKYSTORM, YOU ARE APPROACHING THE TARGET AREA.
COPY THAT, FORT JAY.
DISENGAGING SUB-ORBITAL THRUSTERS. SWITCHING TO V.T.O.L.*
*VERTICAL TAKE-OFF & LANDING

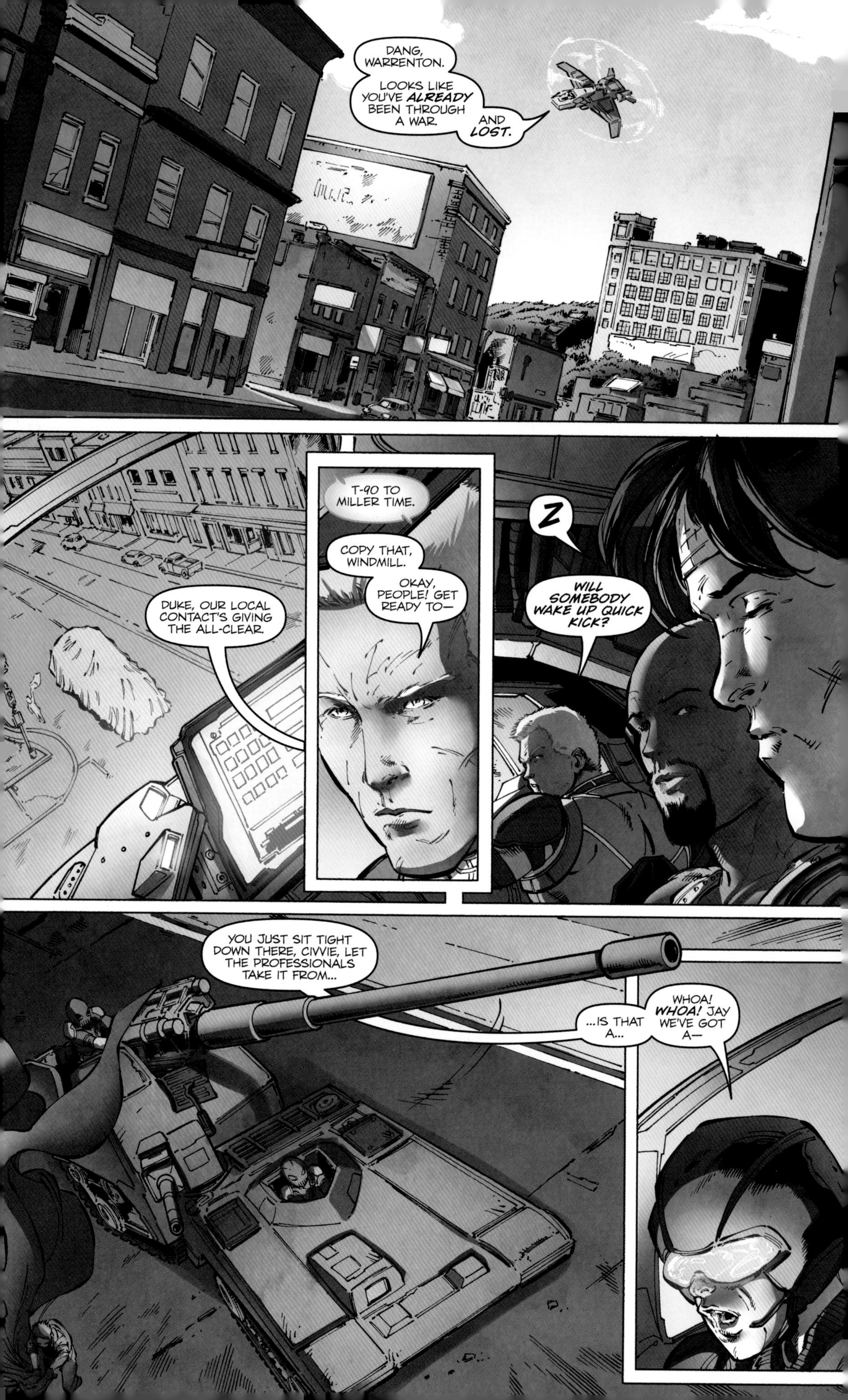
DANG, WARRENTON.
LOOKS LIKE YOU'VE ALREADY BEEN THROUGH A WAR.
AND LOST.
DUKE, OUR LOCAL CONTACT'S GIVING THE ALL-CLEAR.
T-90 TO MILLER TIME.
COPY THAT, WINDMILL.
OKAY, PEOPLE! GET READY TO—
Z
WILL SOMEBODY WAKE UP QUICK KICK?
YOU JUST SIT TIGHT DOWN THERE, CIVVIE, LET THE PROFESSIONALS TAKE IT FROM...
...IS THAT A...
WHOA! WHOA! JAY WE'VE GOT A—

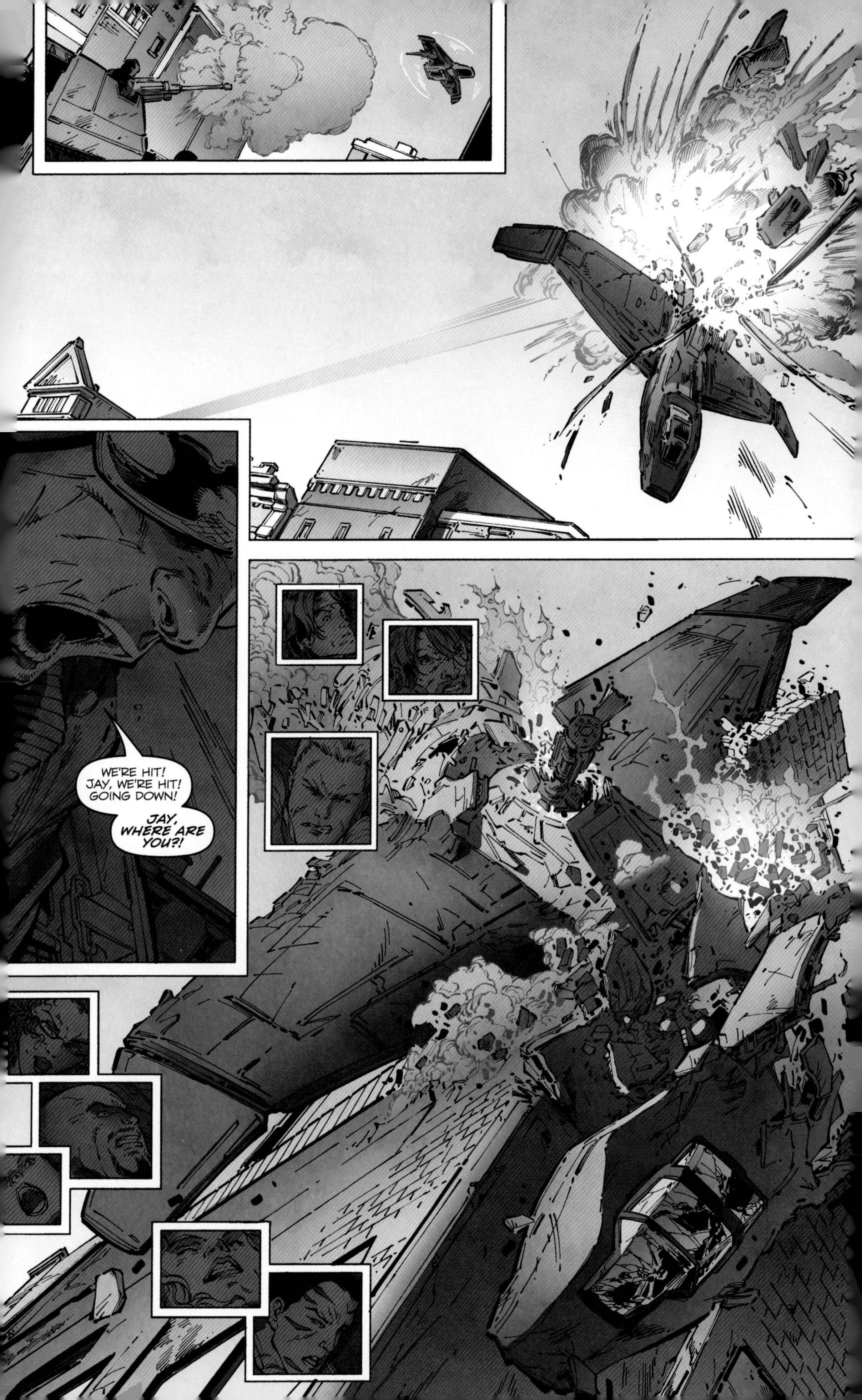
WE'RE HIT!
JAY, WE'RE HIT!
GOING DOWN!
JAY, WHERE ARE YOU?!

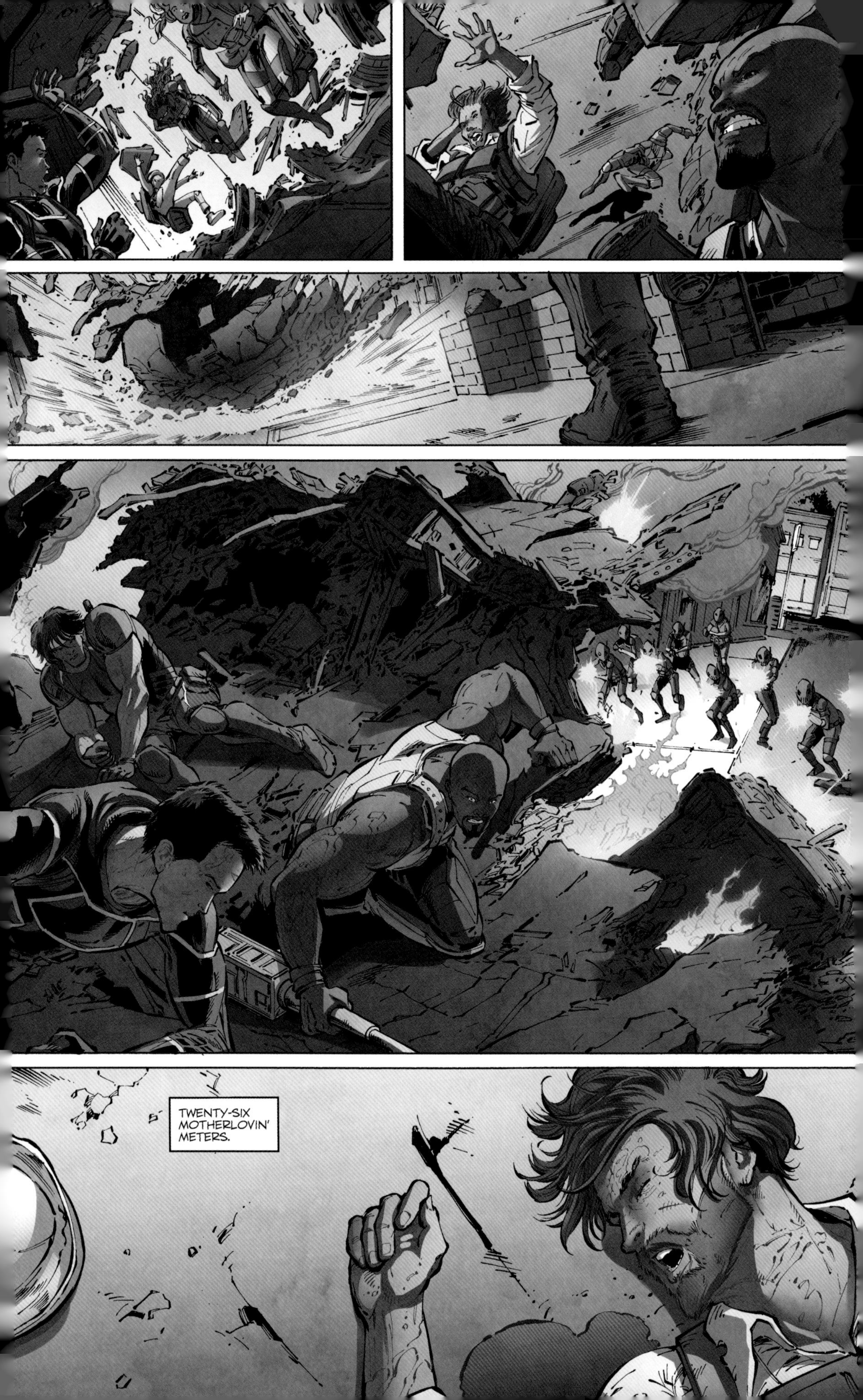
TWENTY-SIX MOTHERLOVIN' METERS.

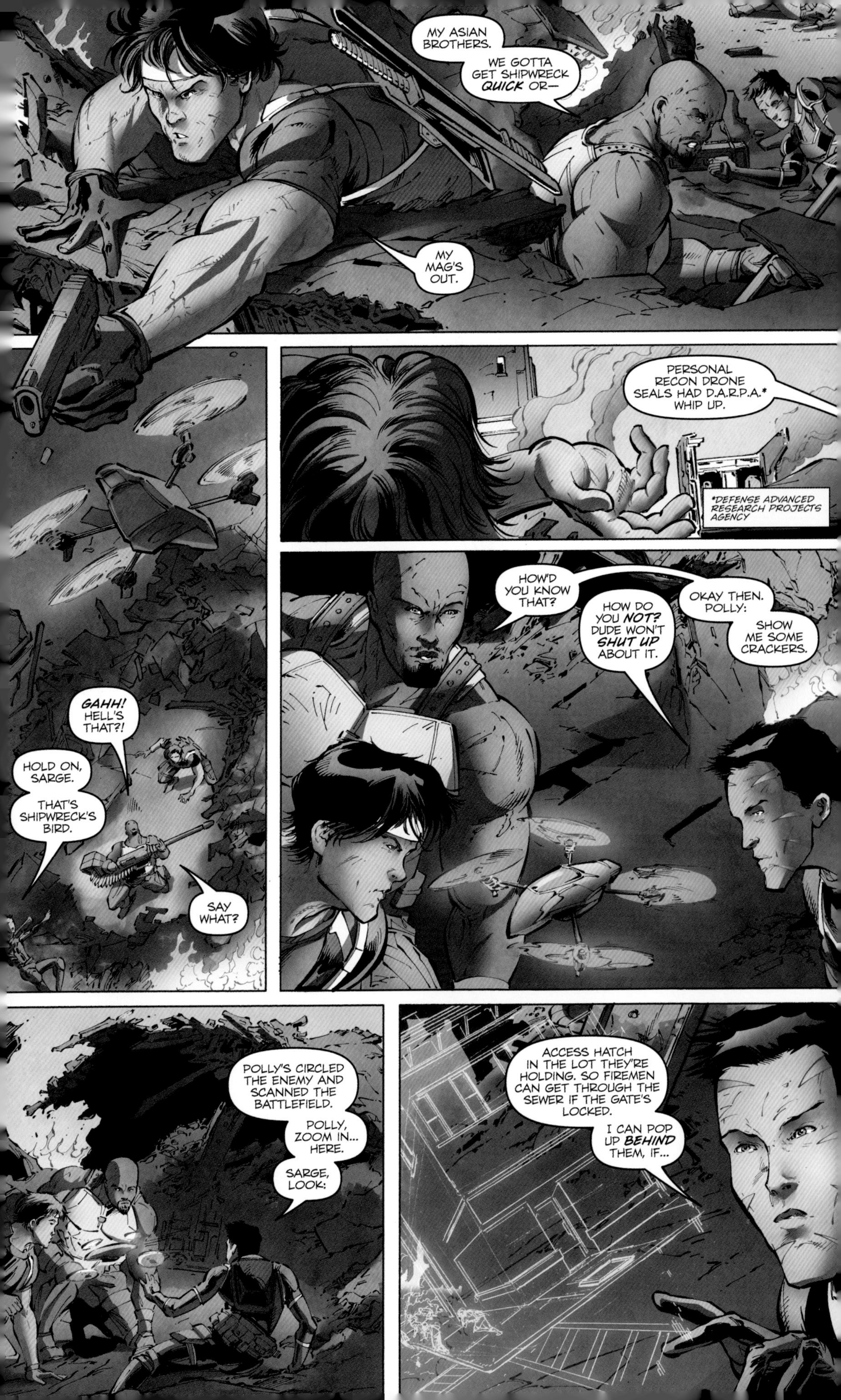

MY ASIAN BROTHERS.
WE GOTTA GET SHIPWRECK *QUICK* OR—
MY MAG'S OUT.
PERSONAL RECON DRONE SEALS HAD D.A.R.P.A.* WHIP UP.
*DEFENSE ADVANCED RESEARCH PROJECTS AGENCY
GAHH! HELL'S THAT?!
HOLD ON, SARGE.
THAT'S SHIPWRECK'S BIRD.
SAY WHAT?
HOW'D YOU KNOW THAT?
HOW DO YOU *NOT?* DUDE WON'T *SHUT UP* ABOUT IT.
OKAY THEN. POLLY:
SHOW ME SOME CRACKERS.
POLLY'S CIRCLED THE ENEMY AND SCANNED THE BATTLEFIELD.
POLLY, ZOOM IN... HERE.
SARGE, LOOK:
ACCESS HATCH IN THE LOT THEY'RE HOLDING. SO FIREMEN CAN GET THROUGH THE SEWER IF THE GATE'S LOCKED.
I CAN POP UP *BEHIND* THEM, IF...

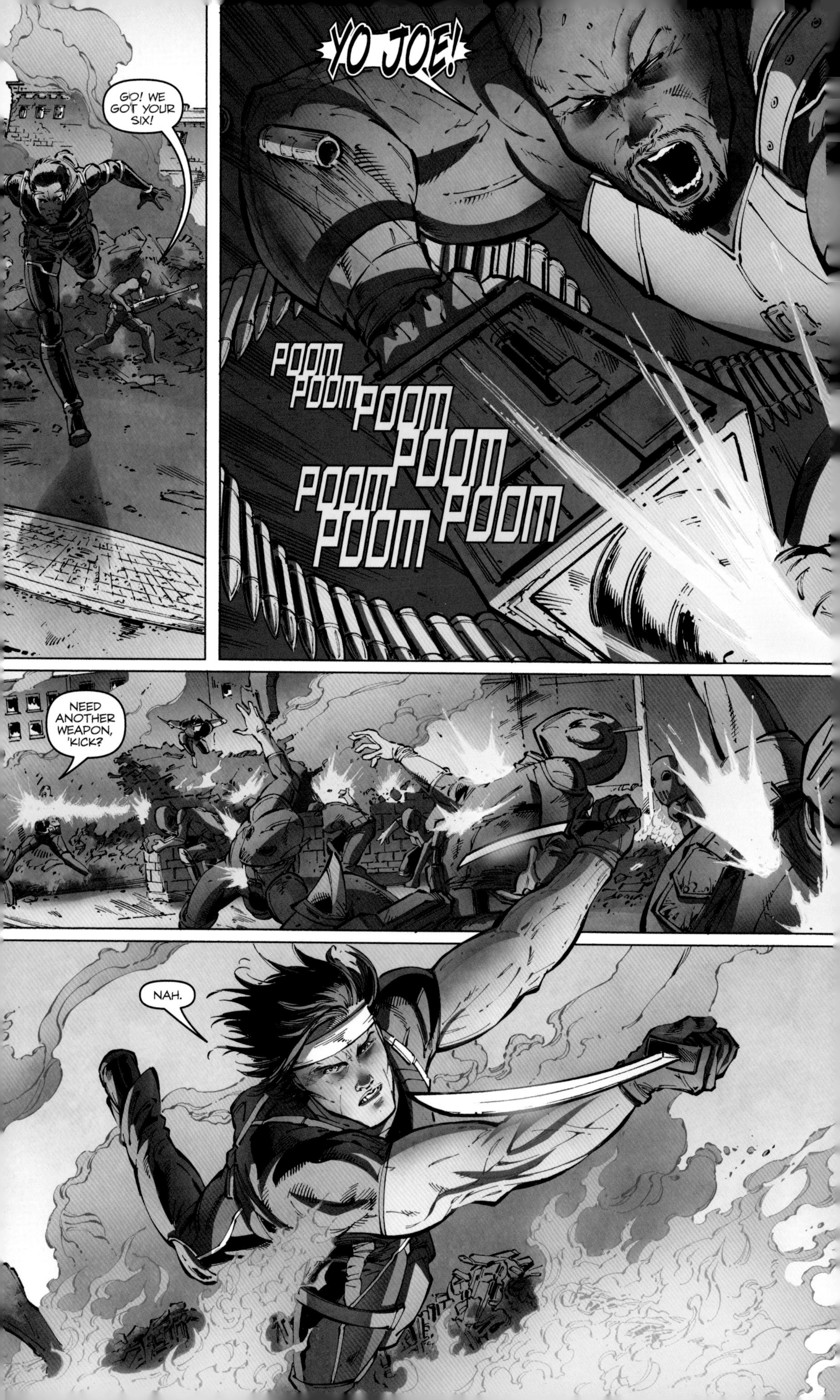
GO! WE GOT YOUR SIX!
YO JOE!
POOM POOM POOM POOM POOM POOM POOM
NEED ANOTHER WEAPON, 'KICK?
NAH.

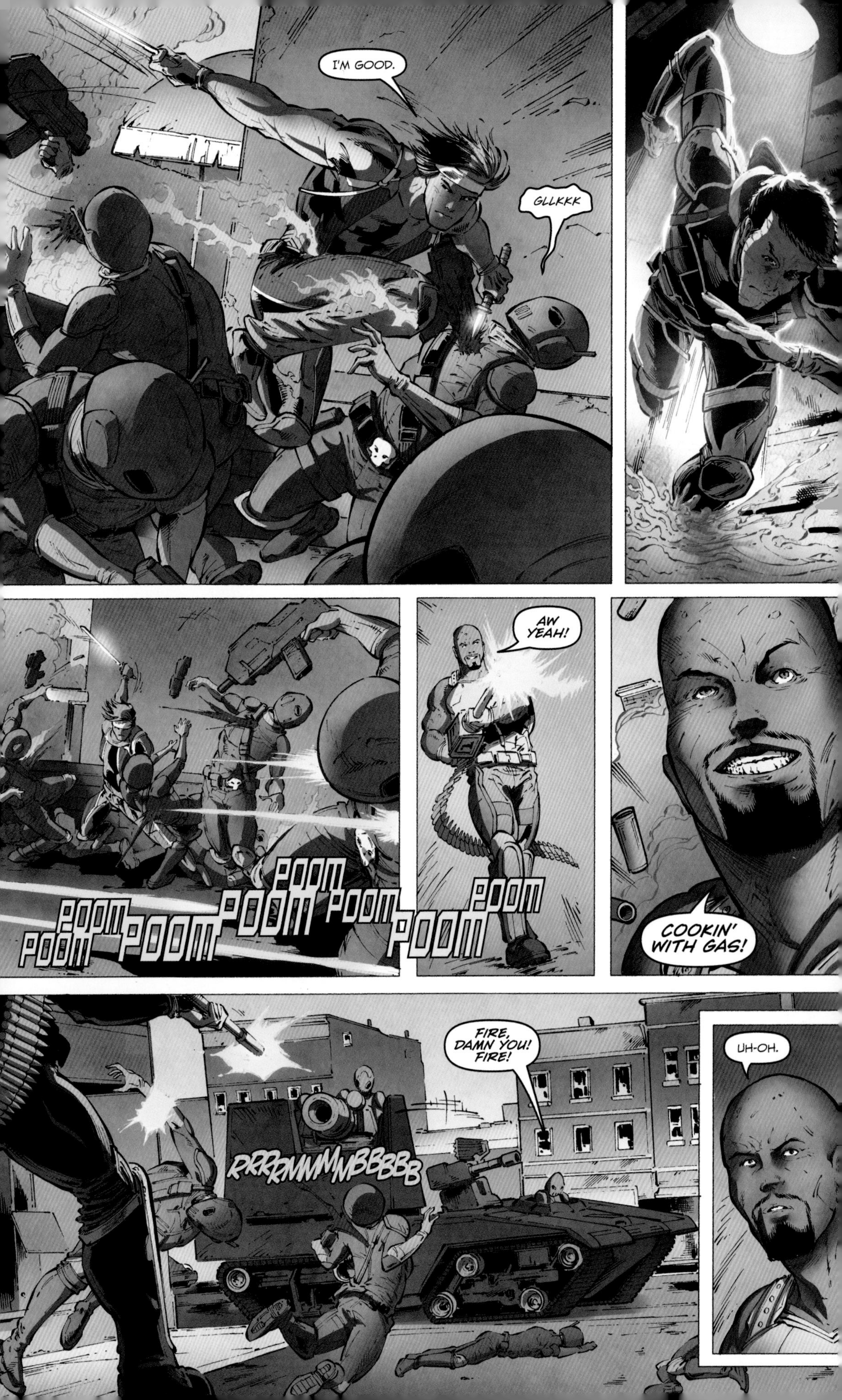
I'M GOOD.
GLLKKK
POOM POOM POOM POOM POOM POOM POOM POOM POOM
AW YEAH!
COOKIN' WITH GAS!
RRRRMMMMBBBBB
FIRE, DAMN YOU! FIRE!
UH-OH.

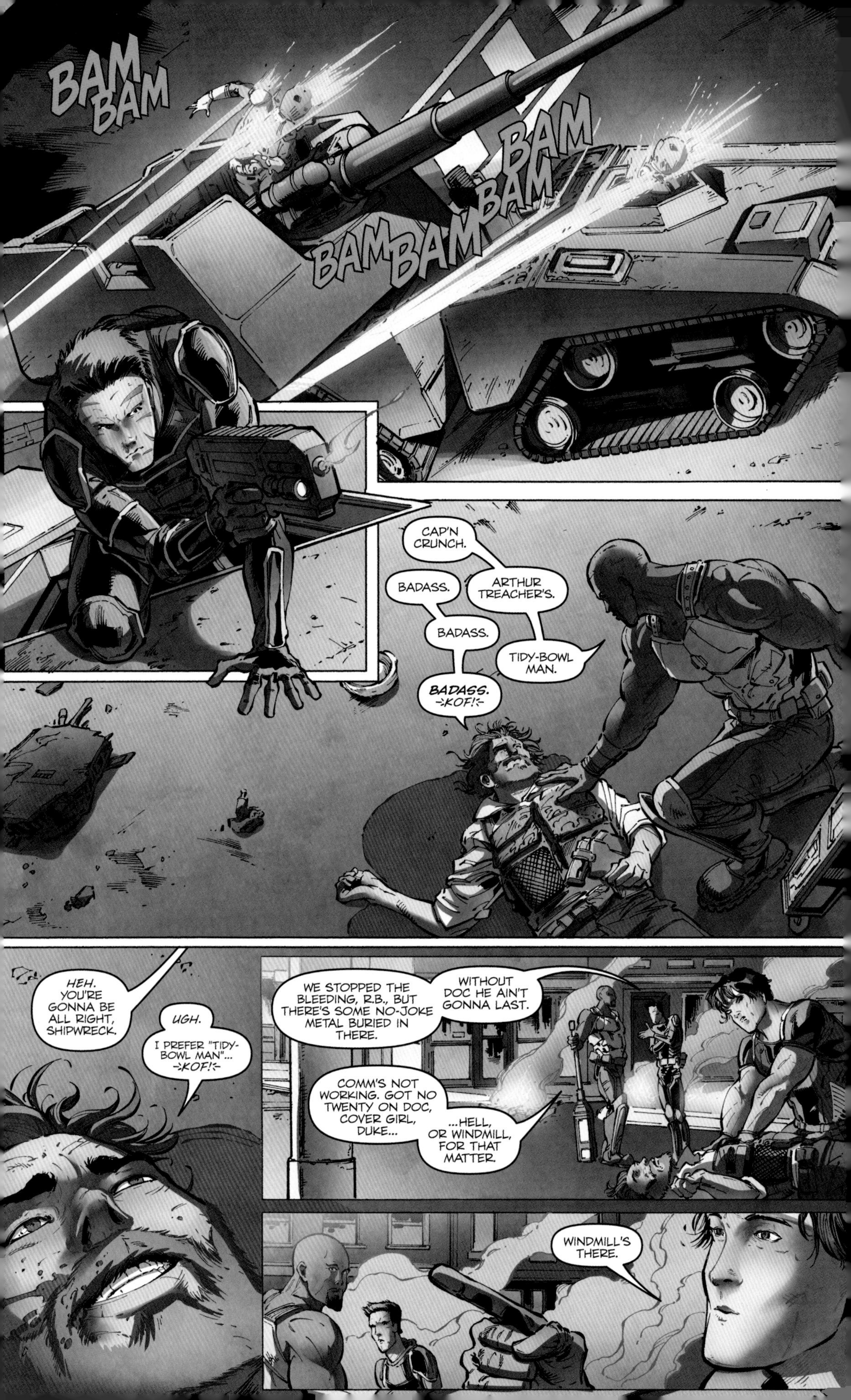
BAM BAM
BAM BAM BAM BAM
CAP'N CRUNCH.
ARTHUR TREACHER'S.
BADASS.
BADASS.
TIDY-BOWL MAN.
BADASS. -KOF!-
HEH. YOU'RE GONNA BE ALL RIGHT, SHIPWRECK.
UGH.
I PREFER "TIDY-BOWL MAN"... -KOF!-
WE STOPPED THE BLEEDING, R.B., BUT THERE'S SOME NO-JOKE METAL BURIED IN THERE.
WITHOUT DOC HE AIN'T GONNA LAST.
COMM'S NOT WORKING. GOT NO TWENTY ON DOC, COVER GIRL, DUKE...
...HELL, OR WINDMILL, FOR THAT MATTER.
WINDMILL'S THERE.

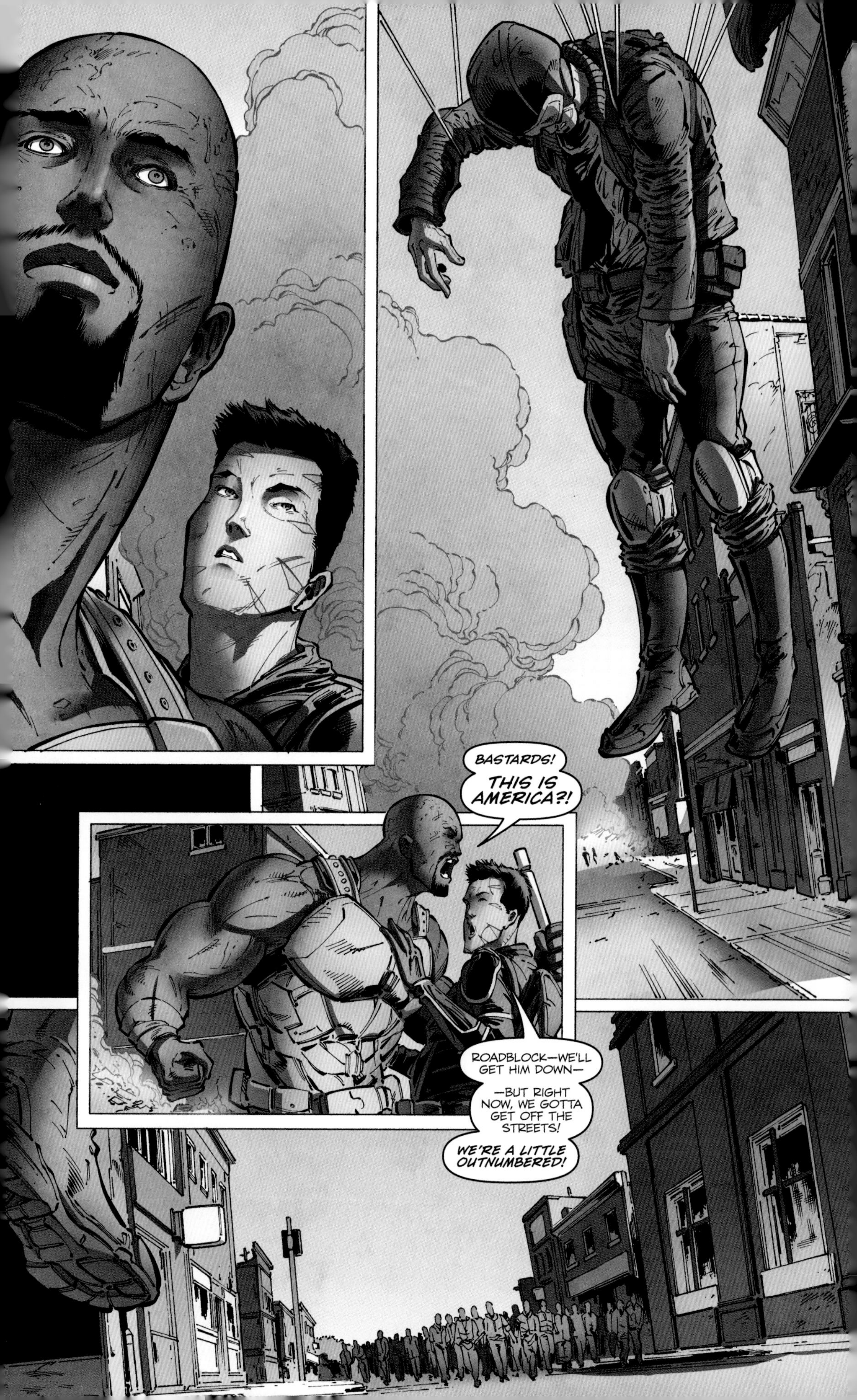
BASTARDS!
THIS IS AMERICA?!
ROADBLOCK—WE'LL GET HIM DOWN—
—BUT RIGHT NOW, WE GOTTA GET OFF THE STREETS!
WE'RE A LITTLE OUTNUMBERED!

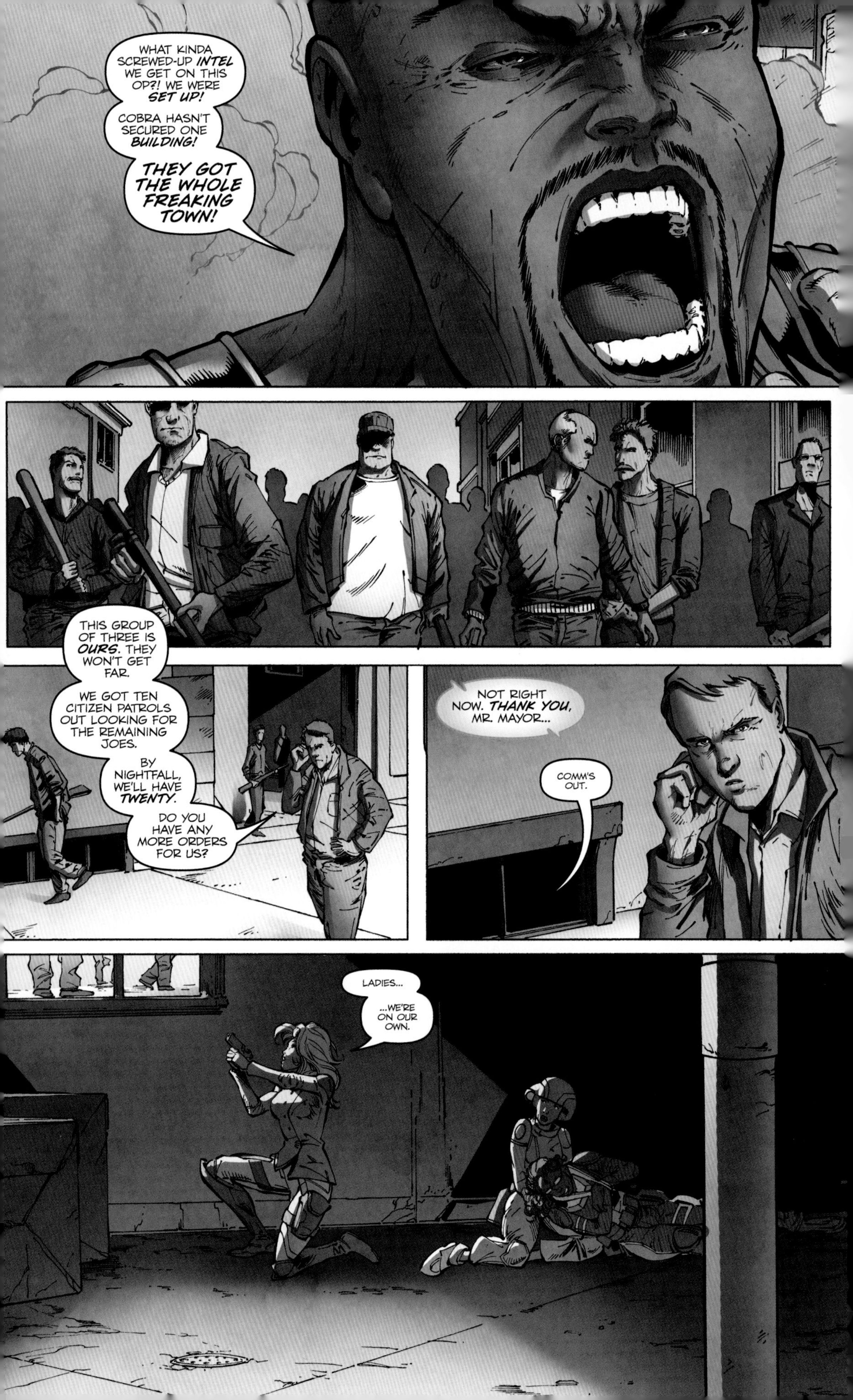
WHAT KINDA SCREWED-UP *INTEL* WE GET ON THIS OP?! WE WERE *SET UP!*
COBRA HASN'T SECURED ONE *BUILDING!*
THEY GOT THE WHOLE FREAKING TOWN!
THIS GROUP OF THREE IS *OURS*. THEY WON'T GET FAR.
WE GOT TEN CITIZEN PATROLS OUT LOOKING FOR THE REMAINING JOES.
BY NIGHTFALL, WE'LL HAVE *TWENTY*.
DO YOU HAVE ANY MORE ORDERS FOR US?
NOT RIGHT NOW. *THANK YOU*, MR. MAYOR...
COMM'S OUT.
LADIES...
...WE'RE ON OUR OWN.

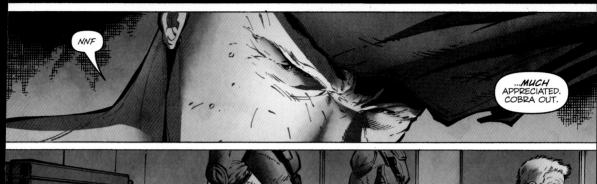

...YOU AND YOUR NEIGHBORS' COOPERATION, AS ALWAYS, MR. MAYOR...

NNF

...MUCH APPRECIATED. COBRA OUT.

SO. "DUKE."

IF THAT IS YOUR REAL NAME.

GENERAL JOE MADE YOU FAMOUS.

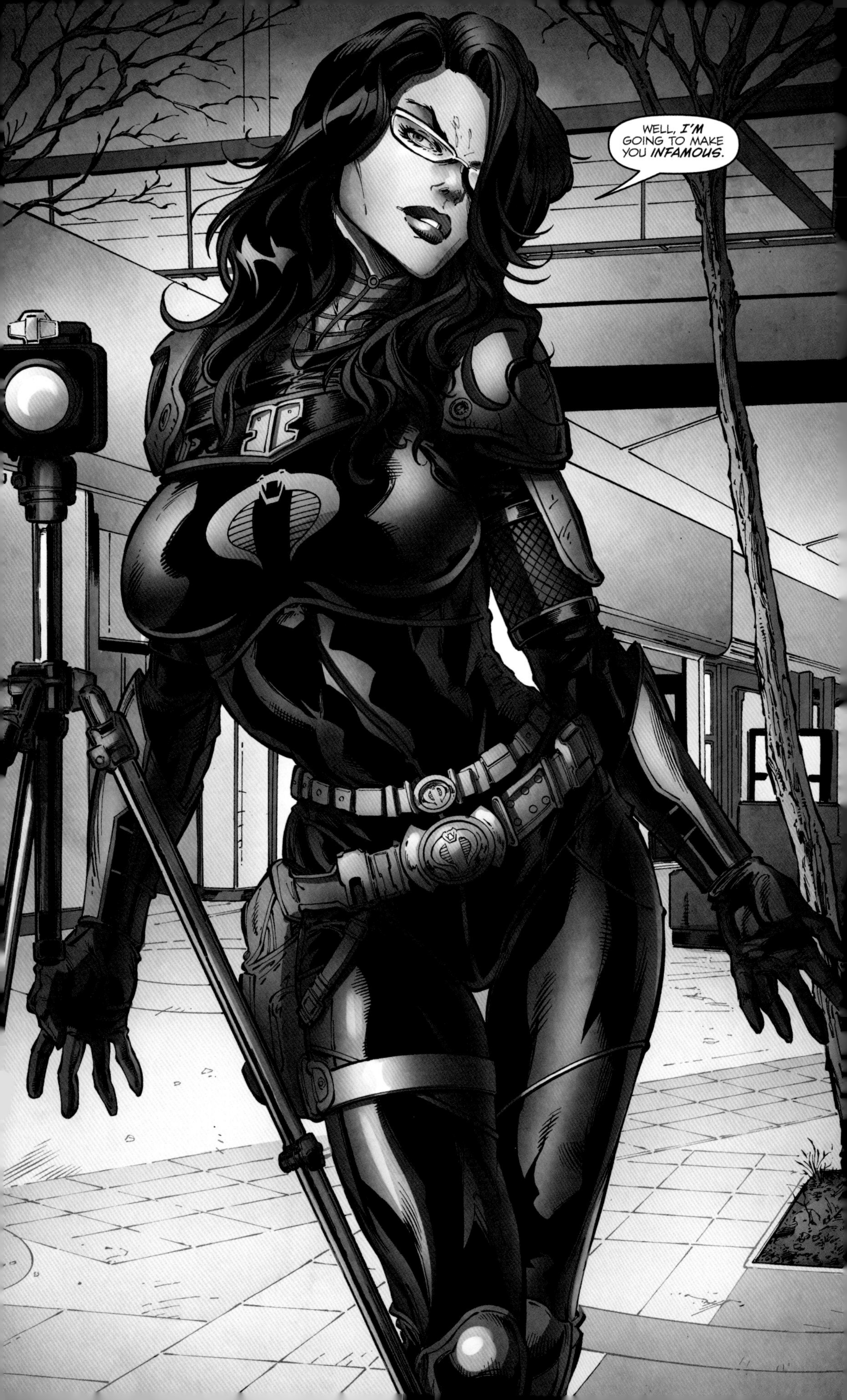
WELL, *I'M* GOING TO MAKE YOU *INFAMOUS*.

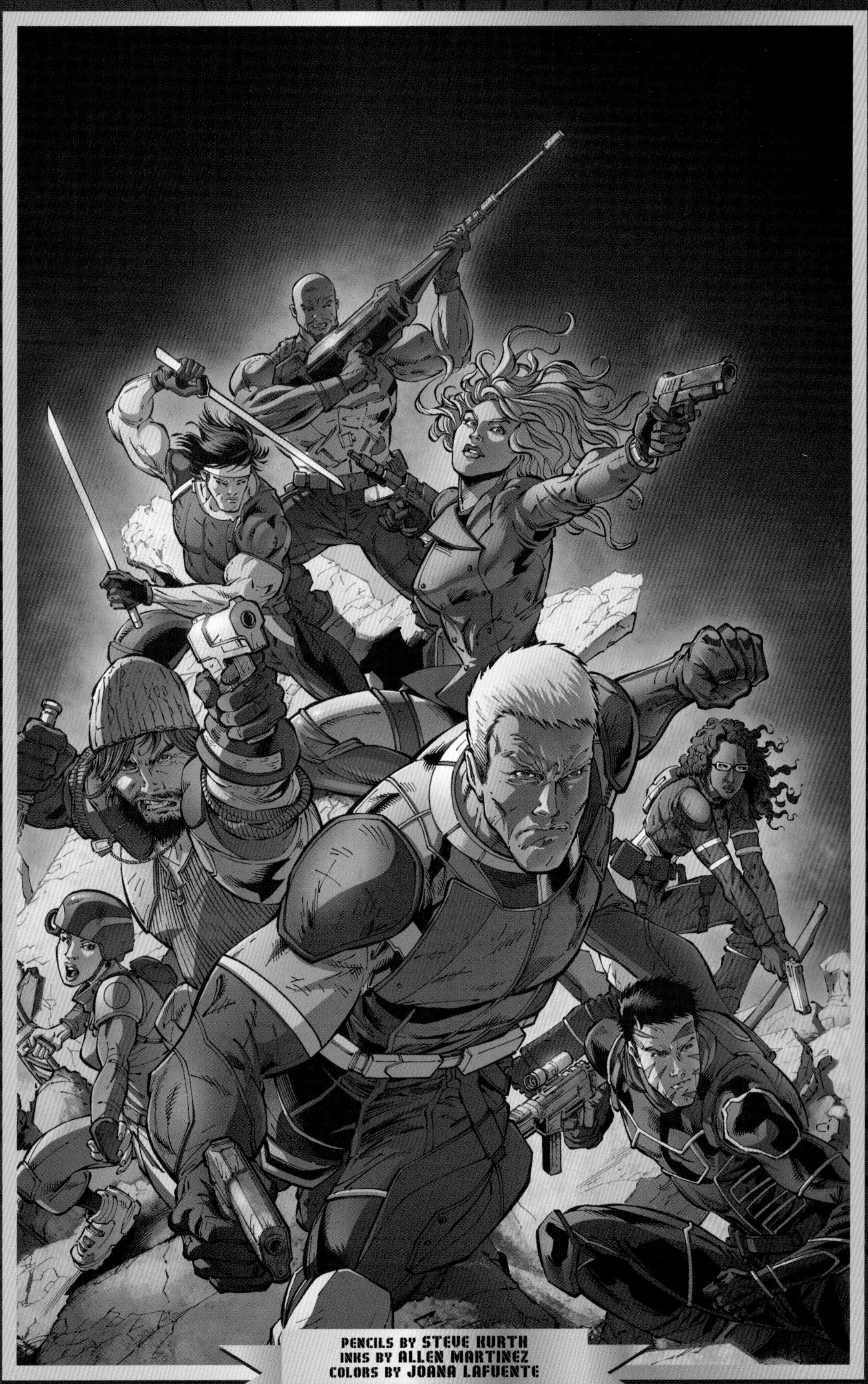
PENCILS BY STEVE KURTH
INKS BY ALLEN MARTINEZ
COLORS BY JOANA LAFUENTE

CHAPTER TWO

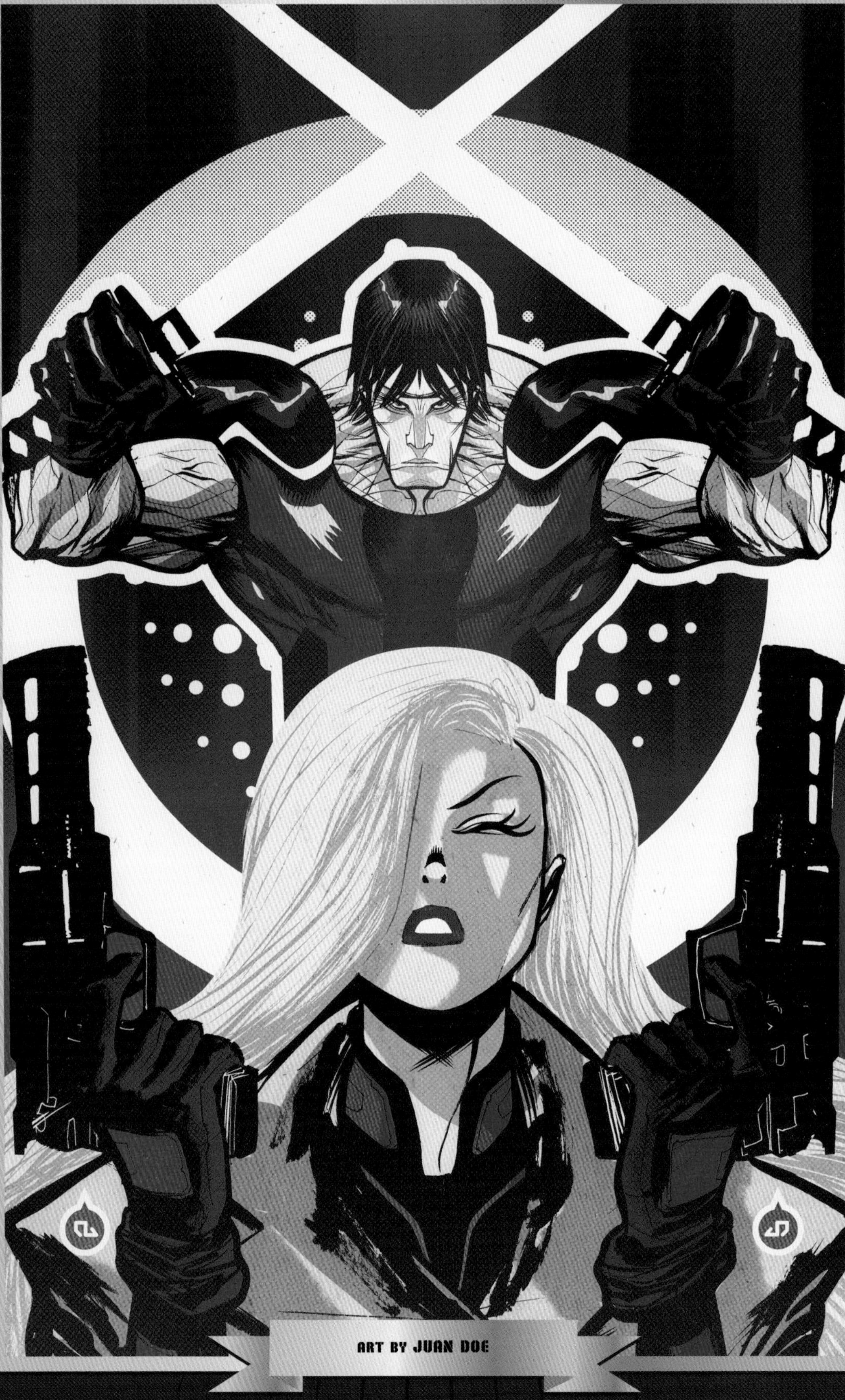

ART BY JUAN DOE

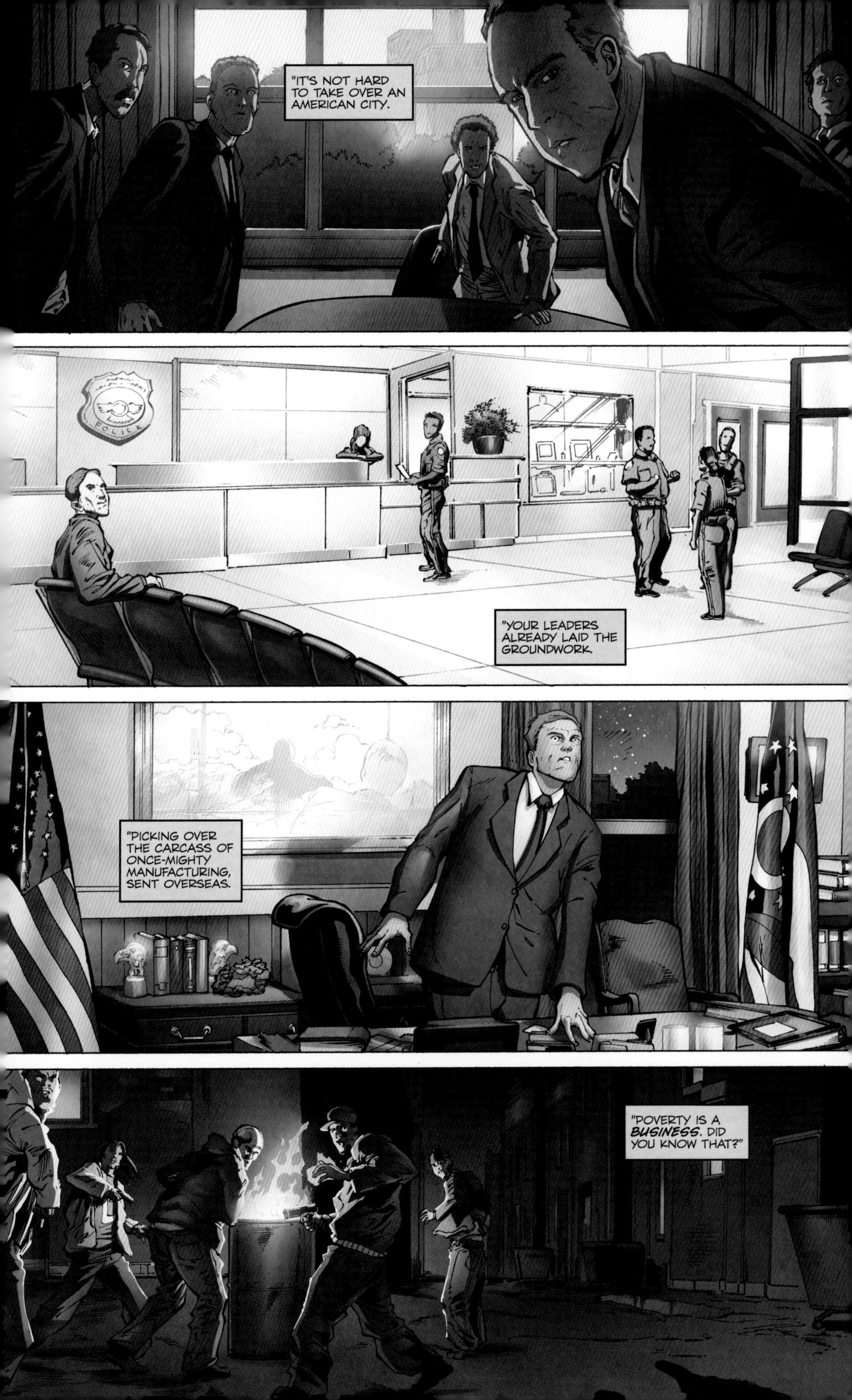
"IT'S NOT HARD TO TAKE OVER AN AMERICAN CITY.
"YOUR LEADERS ALREADY LAID THE GROUNDWORK.
"PICKING OVER THE CARCASS OF ONCE-MIGHTY MANUFACTURING, SENT OVERSEAS.
"POVERTY IS A *BUSINESS*. DID YOU KNOW THAT?"
POLICE

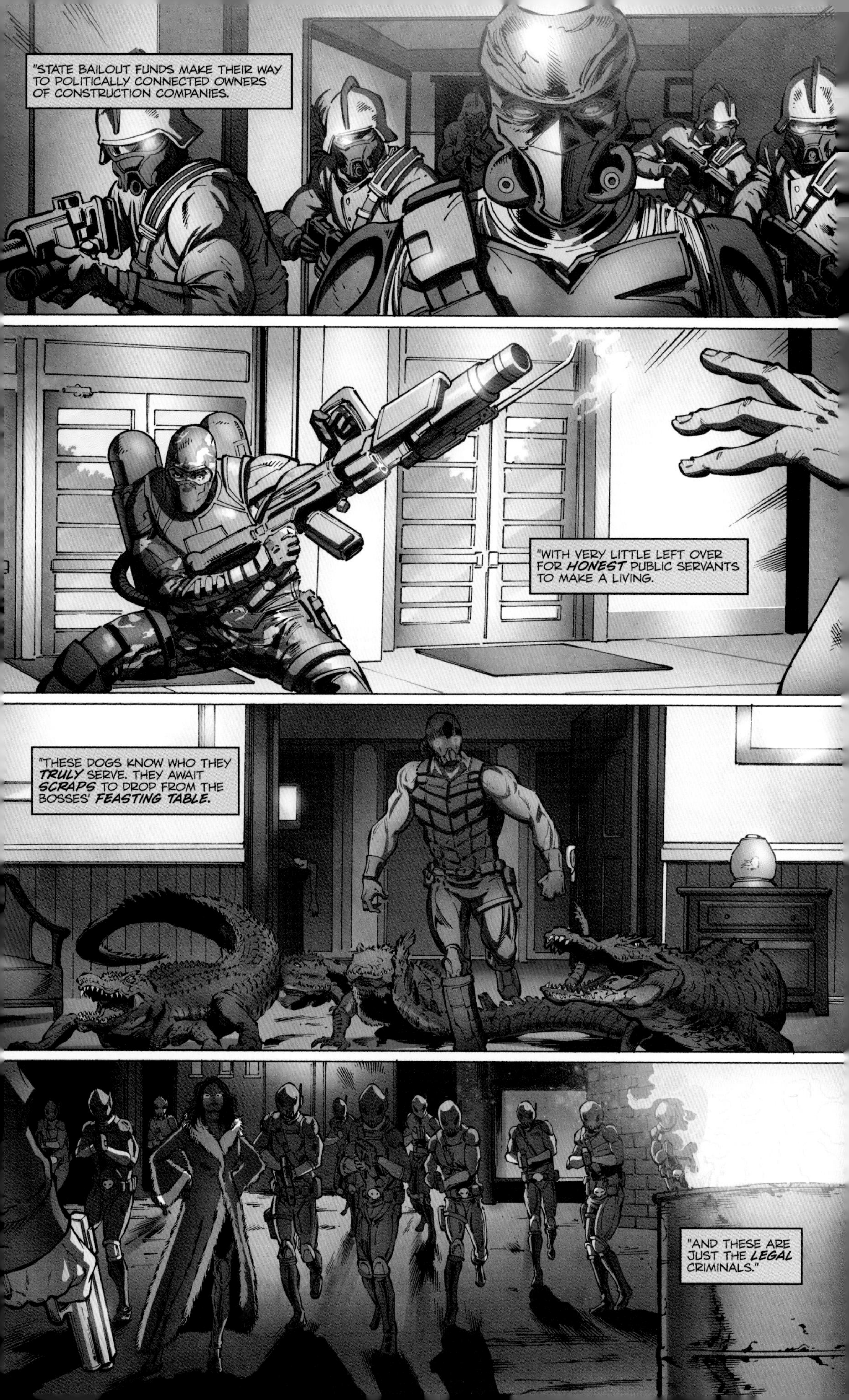
"STATE BAILOUT FUNDS MAKE THEIR WAY TO POLITICALLY CONNECTED OWNERS OF CONSTRUCTION COMPANIES.
"WITH VERY LITTLE LEFT OVER FOR HONEST PUBLIC SERVANTS TO MAKE A LIVING.
"THESE DOGS KNOW WHO THEY TRULY SERVE. THEY AWAIT SCRAPS TO DROP FROM THE BOSSES' FEASTING TABLE.
"AND THESE ARE JUST THE LEGAL CRIMINALS."

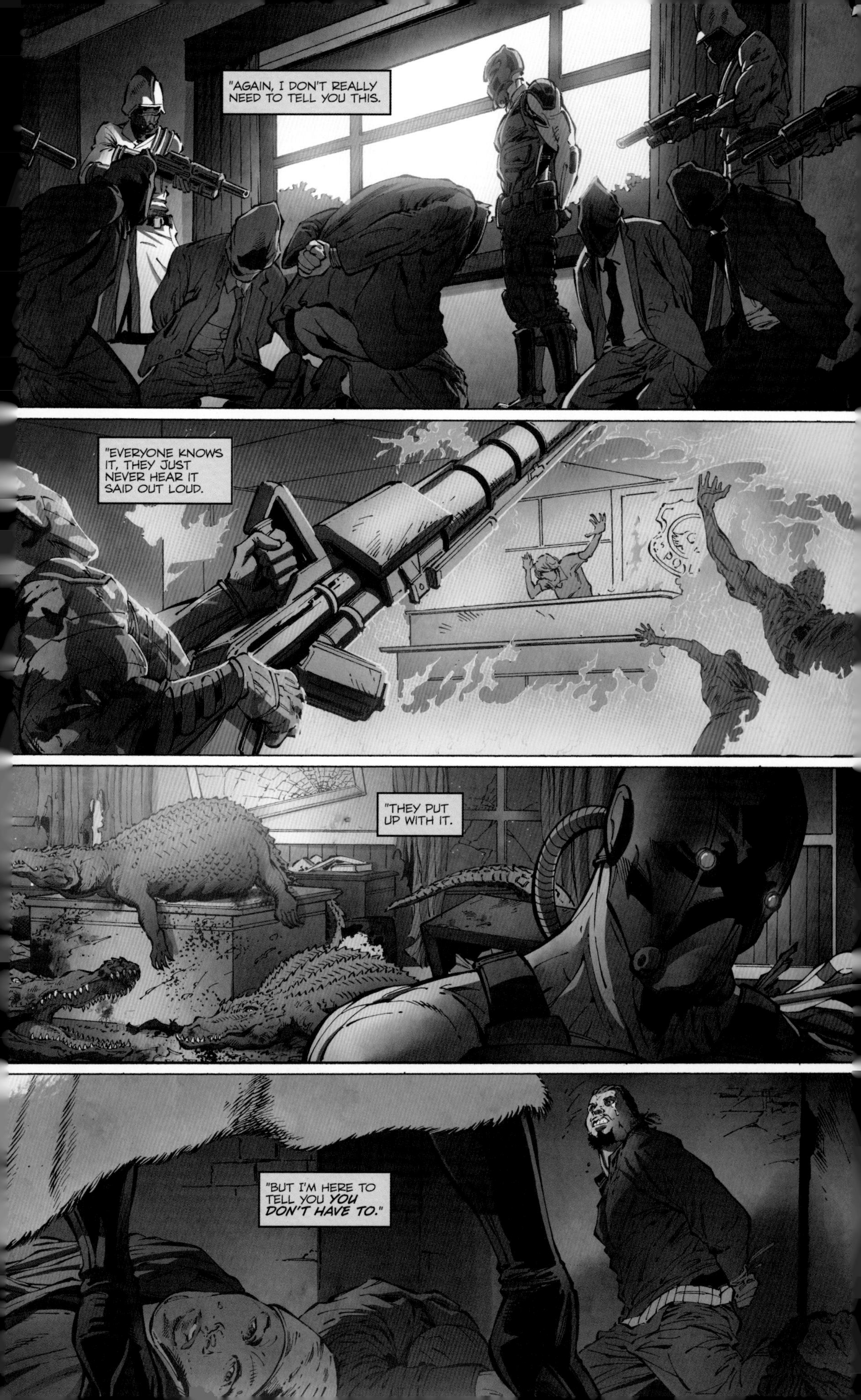
"AGAIN, I DON'T REALLY NEED TO TELL YOU THIS.
"EVERYONE KNOWS IT, THEY JUST NEVER HEAR IT SAID OUT LOUD.
"THEY PUT UP WITH IT.
"BUT I'M HERE TO TELL YOU *YOU DON'T HAVE TO.*"

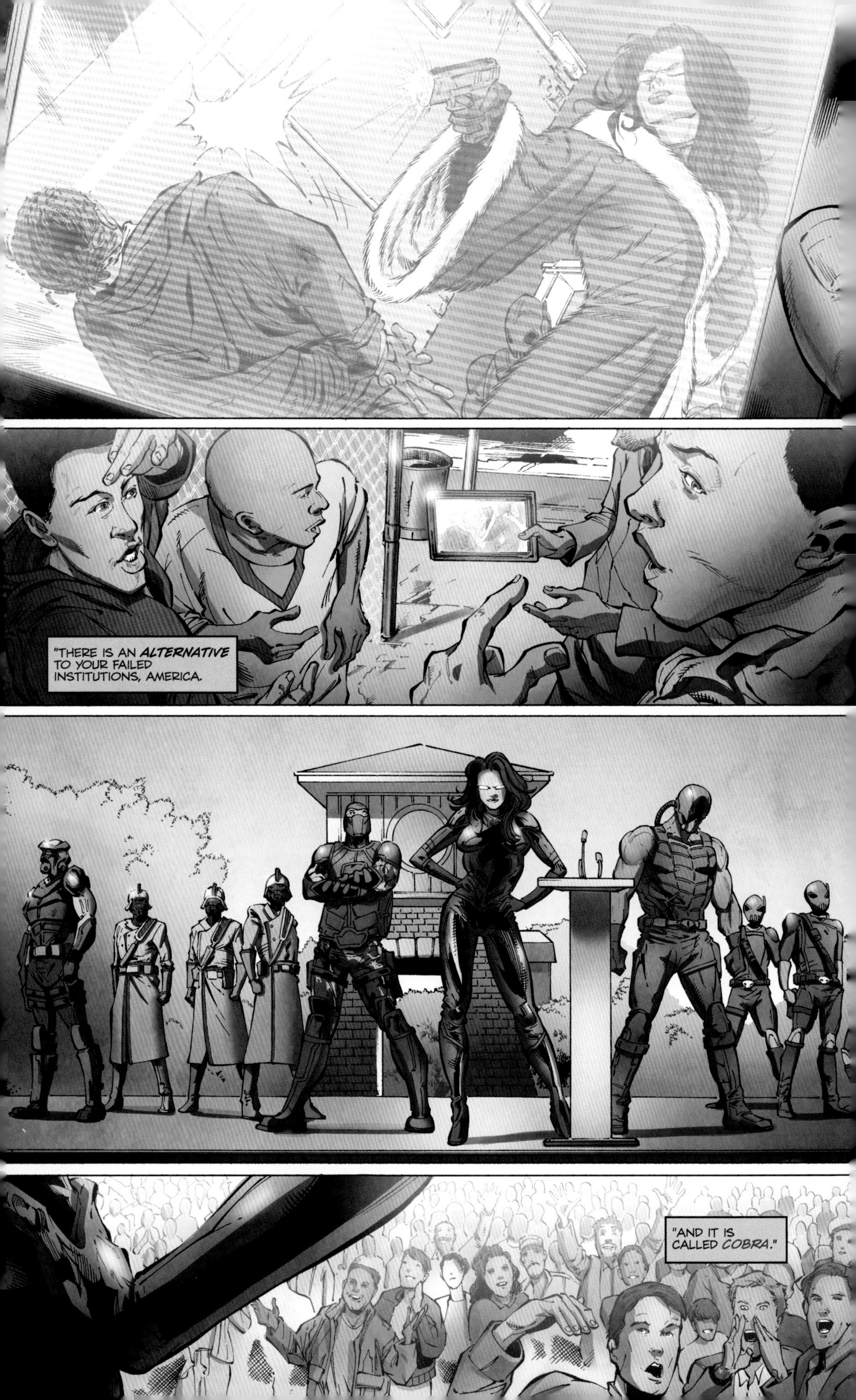
"THERE IS AN ALTERNATIVE TO YOUR FAILED INSTITUTIONS, AMERICA.
"AND IT IS CALLED COBRA."

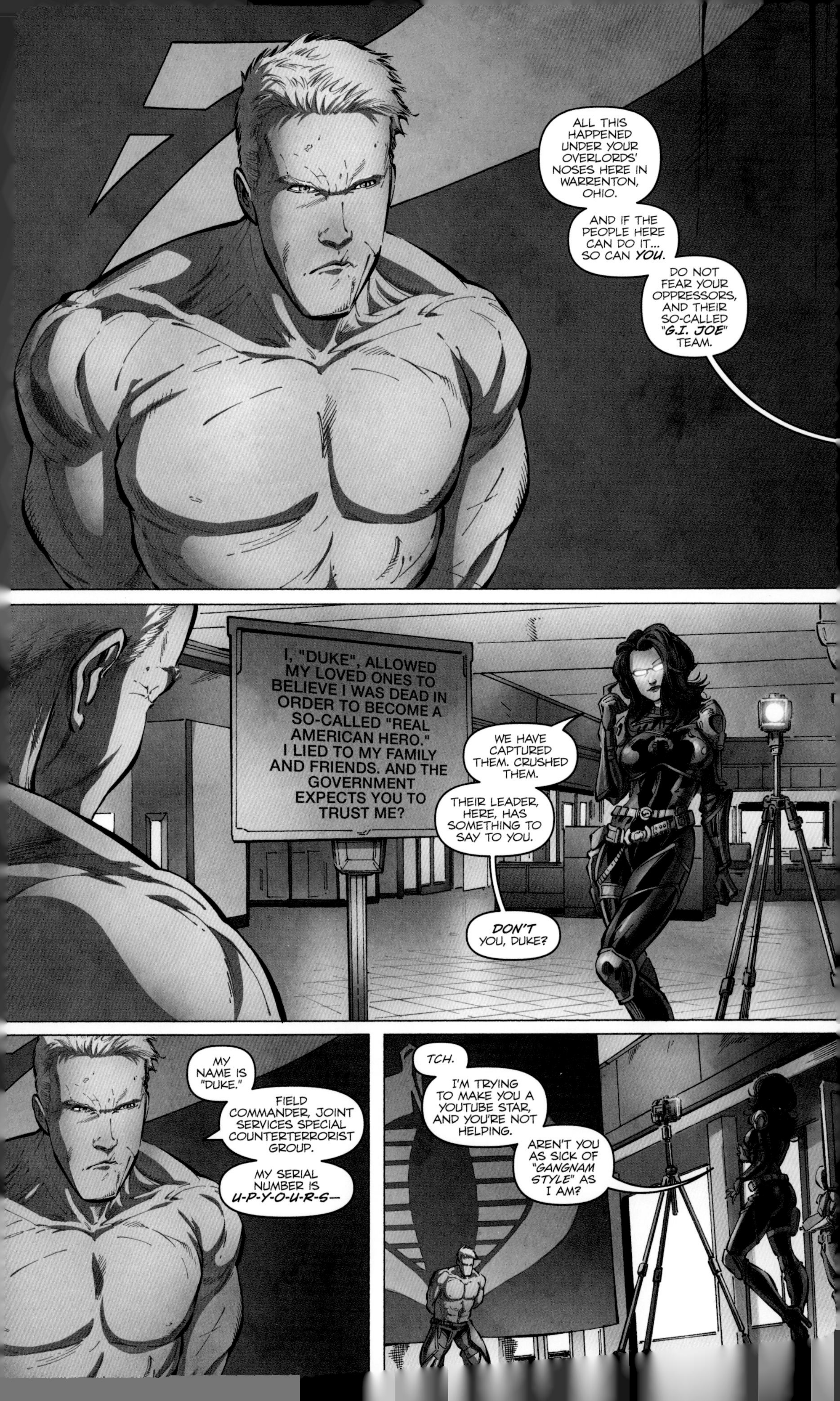
ALL THIS HAPPENED UNDER YOUR OVERLORDS' NOSES HERE IN WARRENTON, OHIO.
AND IF THE PEOPLE HERE CAN DO IT... SO CAN YOU.
DO NOT FEAR YOUR OPPRESSORS, AND THEIR SO-CALLED "G.I. JOE" TEAM.
I, "DUKE", ALLOWED MY LOVED ONES TO BELIEVE I WAS DEAD IN ORDER TO BECOME A SO-CALLED "REAL AMERICAN HERO." I LIED TO MY FAMILY AND FRIENDS. AND THE GOVERNMENT EXPECTS YOU TO TRUST ME?
WE HAVE CAPTURED THEM. CRUSHED THEM.
THEIR LEADER, HERE, HAS SOMETHING TO SAY TO YOU.
DON'T YOU, DUKE?
MY NAME IS "DUKE."
FIELD COMMANDER, JOINT SERVICES SPECIAL COUNTERTERRORIST GROUP.
MY SERIAL NUMBER IS U-P-Y-O-U-R-S—
TCH.
I'M TRYING TO MAKE YOU A YOUTUBE STAR, AND YOU'RE NOT HELPING.
AREN'T YOU AS SICK OF "GANGNAM STYLE" AS I AM?

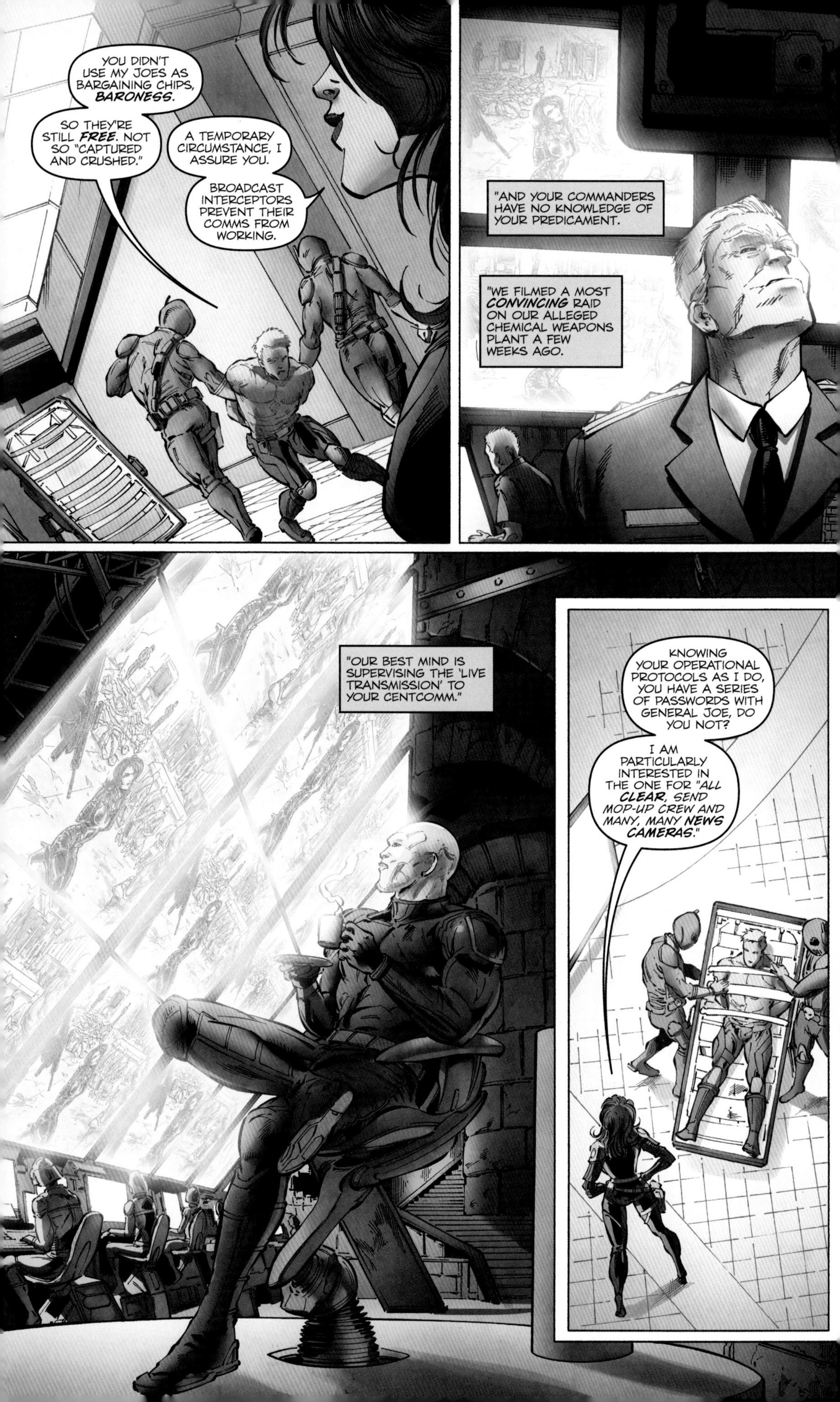

YOU DIDN'T USE MY JOES AS BARGAINING CHIPS, BARONESS.
SO THEY'RE STILL FREE. NOT SO "CAPTURED AND CRUSHED."
A TEMPORARY CIRCUMSTANCE, I ASSURE YOU.
BROADCAST INTERCEPTORS PREVENT THEIR COMMS FROM WORKING.
"AND YOUR COMMANDERS HAVE NO KNOWLEDGE OF YOUR PREDICAMENT.
"WE FILMED A MOST CONVINCING RAID ON OUR ALLEGED CHEMICAL WEAPONS PLANT A FEW WEEKS AGO.
"OUR BEST MIND IS SUPERVISING THE 'LIVE TRANSMISSION' TO YOUR CENTCOMM."
KNOWING YOUR OPERATIONAL PROTOCOLS AS I DO, YOU HAVE A SERIES OF PASSWORDS WITH GENERAL JOE, DO YOU NOT?
I AM PARTICULARLY INTERESTED IN THE ONE FOR "ALL CLEAR, SEND MOP-UP CREW AND MANY, MANY NEWS CAMERAS."

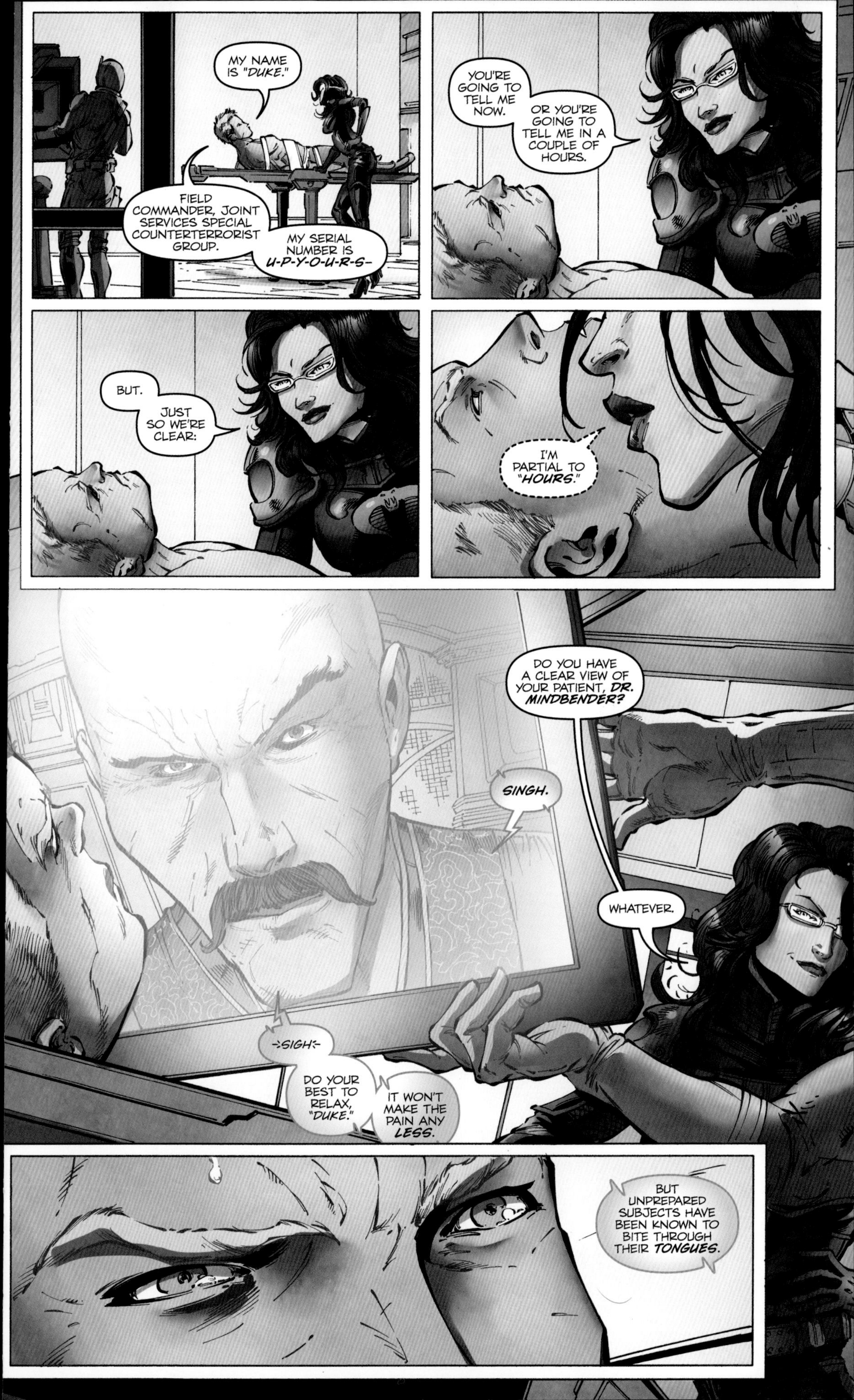

MY NAME IS "DUKE."
FIELD COMMANDER, JOINT SERVICES SPECIAL COUNTERTERRORIST GROUP.
MY SERIAL NUMBER IS U-P-Y-O-U-R-S-
YOU'RE GOING TO TELL ME NOW.
OR YOU'RE GOING TO TELL ME IN A COUPLE OF HOURS.
BUT.
JUST SO WE'RE CLEAR:
I'M PARTIAL TO "HOURS."
DO YOU HAVE A CLEAR VIEW OF YOUR PATIENT, DR. MINDBENDER?
SINGH.
WHATEVER.
-SIGH-
DO YOUR BEST TO RELAX, "DUKE."
IT WON'T MAKE THE PAIN ANY LESS.
BUT UNPREPARED SUBJECTS HAVE BEEN KNOWN TO BITE THROUGH THEIR TONGUES.

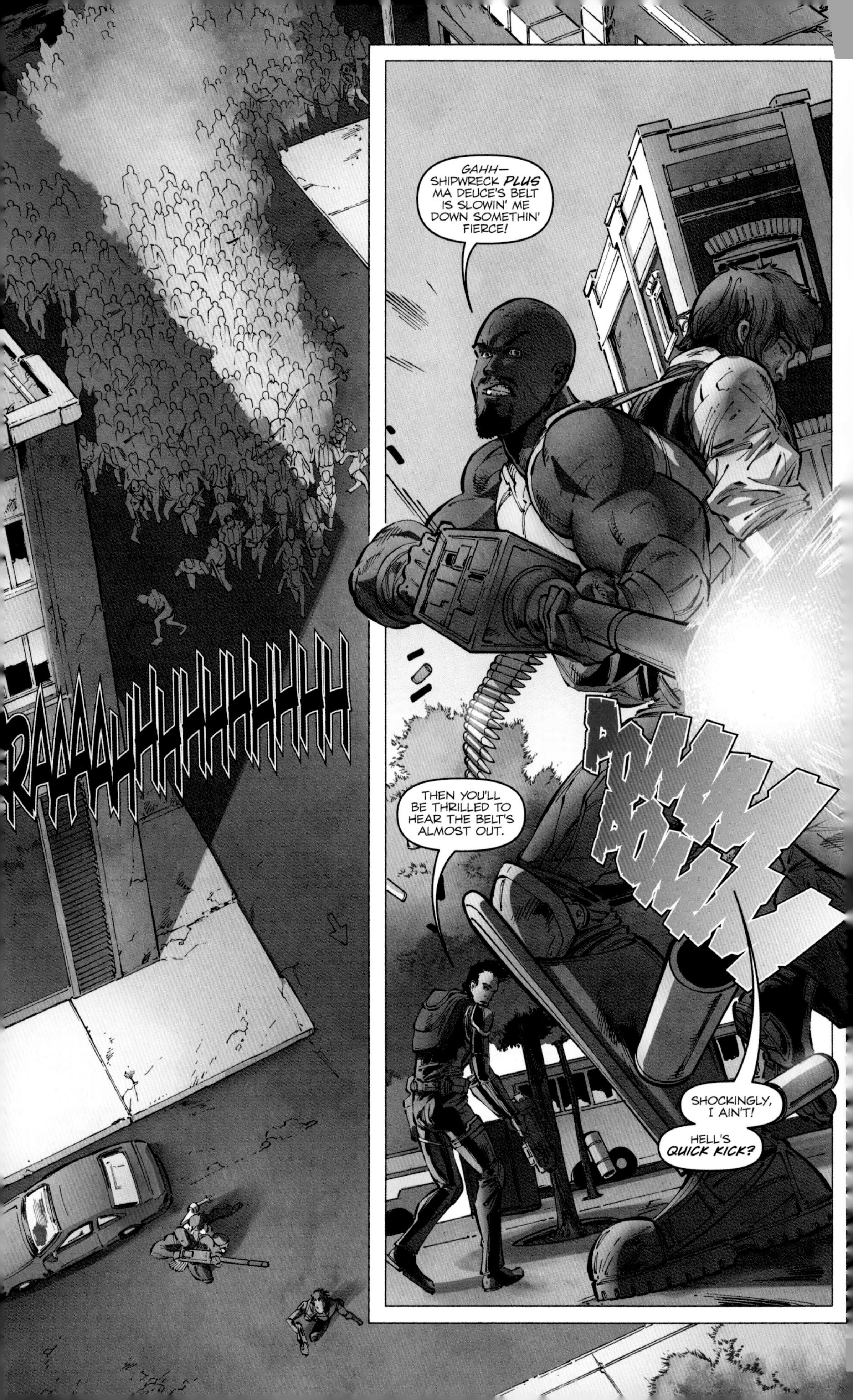
RAAAAUHHHHHHHHHH
GAHH— SHIPWRECK PLUS MA DEUCE'S BELT IS SLOWIN' ME DOWN SOMETHIN' FIERCE!
POW POW POW
THEN YOU'LL BE THRILLED TO HEAR THE BELT'S ALMOST OUT.
SHOCKINGLY, I AIN'T!
HELL'S QUICK KICK?

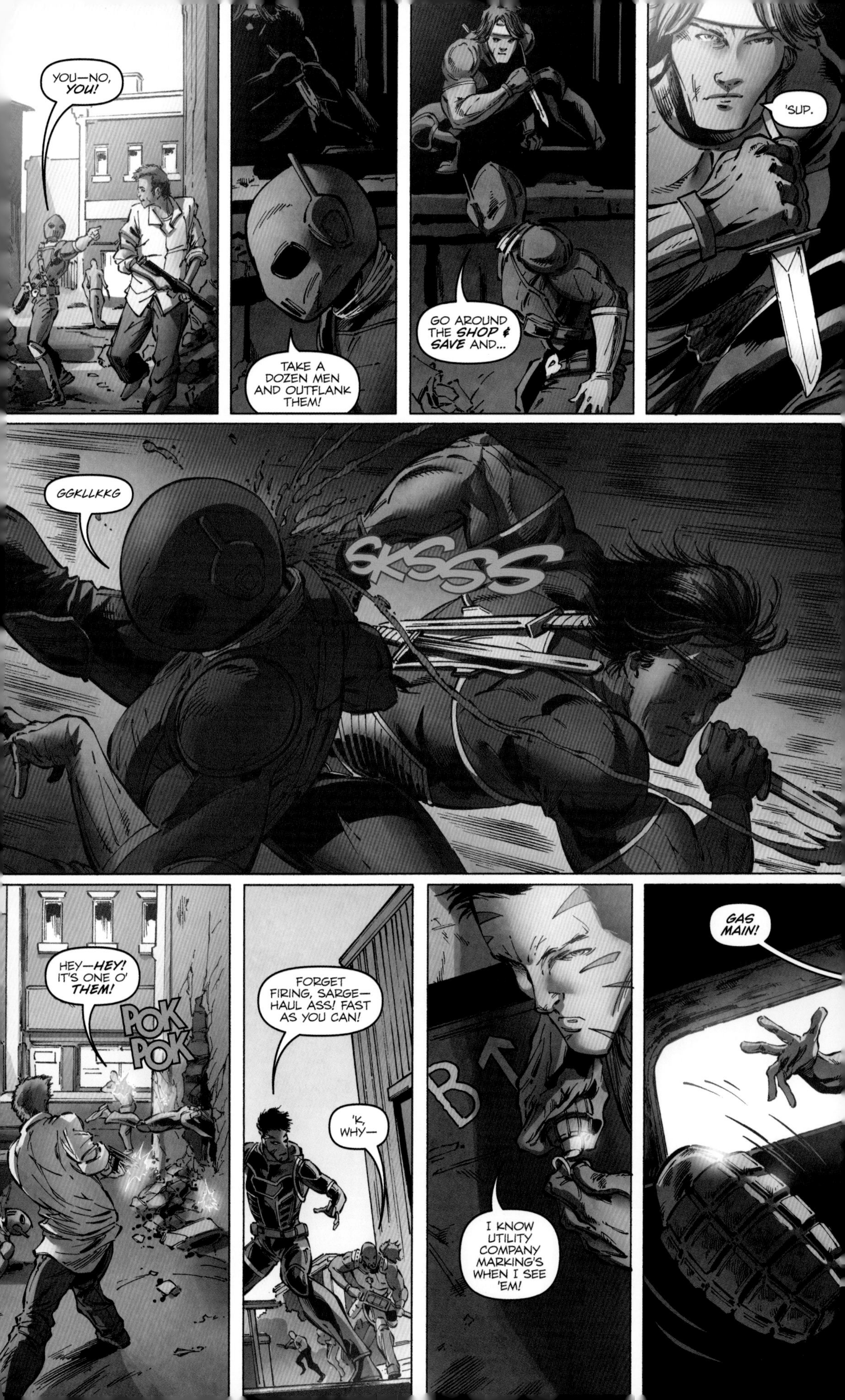
YOU—NO, YOU!
TAKE A DOZEN MEN AND OUTFLANK THEM!
GO AROUND THE SHOP & SAVE AND...
'SUP.
GGKLLKKG
SKSSS
HEY—HEY! IT'S ONE O' THEM!
POK POK
FORGET FIRING, SARGE—HAUL ASS! FAST AS YOU CAN!
'K, WHY—
I KNOW UTILITY COMPANY MARKING'S WHEN I SEE 'EM!
GAS MAIN!

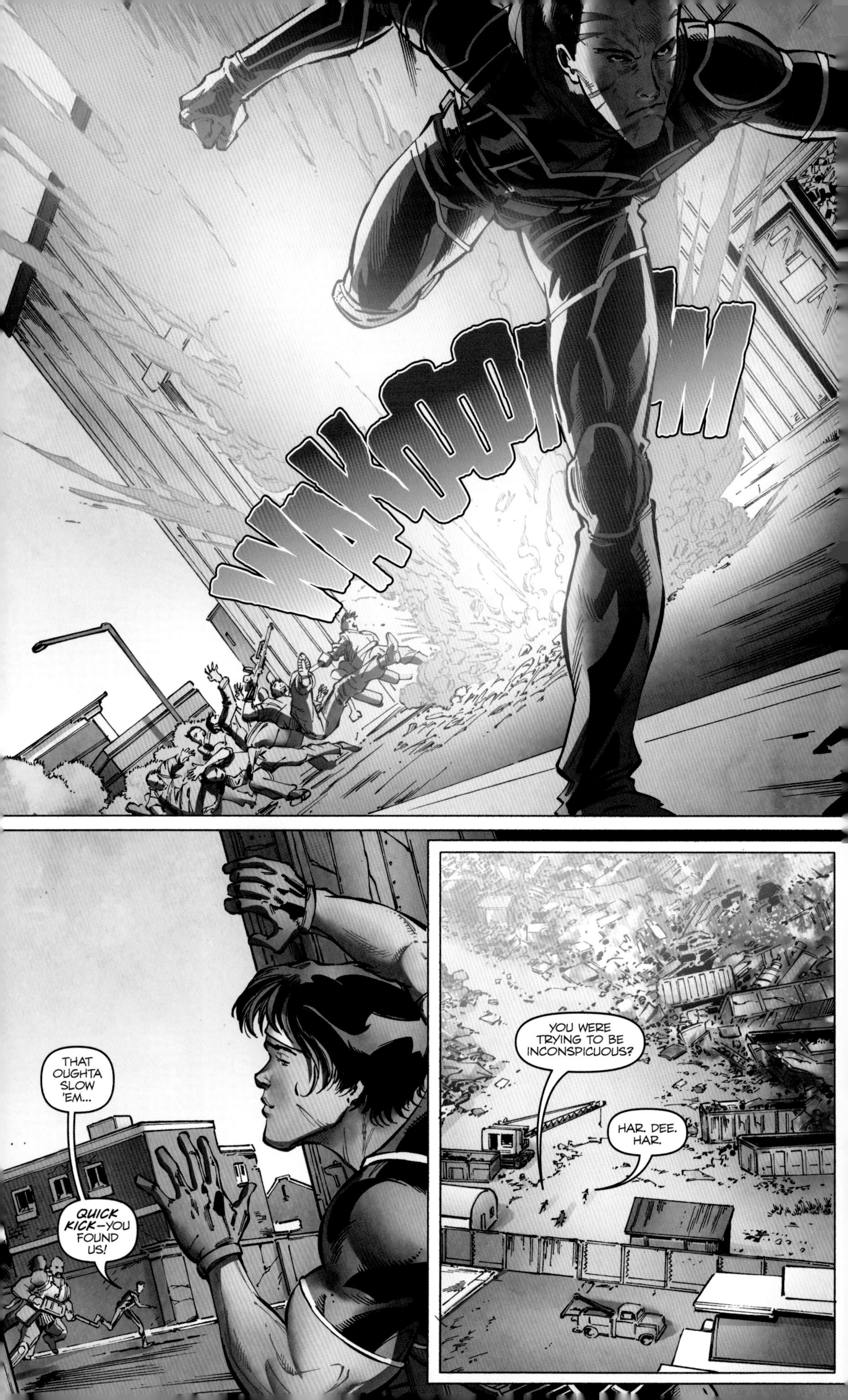
THAT OUGHTA SLOW 'EM...
QUICK KICK—YOU FOUND US!
YOU WERE TRYING TO BE INCONSPICUOUS?
HAR. DEE. HAR.

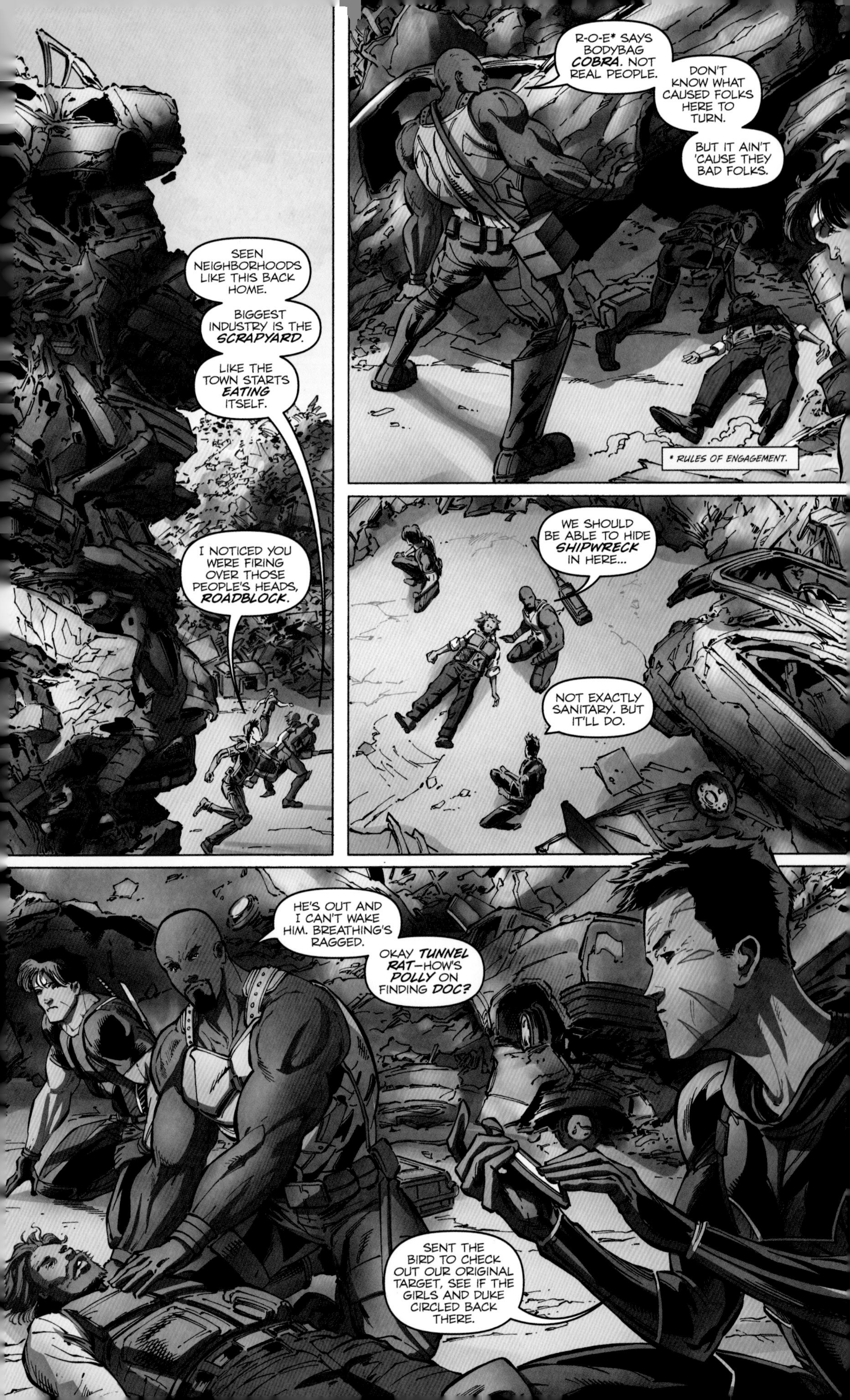
SEEN NEIGHBORHOODS LIKE THIS BACK HOME.
BIGGEST INDUSTRY IS THE SCRAPYARD.
LIKE THE TOWN STARTS EATING ITSELF.
I NOTICED YOU WERE FIRING OVER THOSE PEOPLE'S HEADS, ROADBLOCK.
R-O-E* SAYS BODYBAG COBRA. NOT REAL PEOPLE.
DON'T KNOW WHAT CAUSED FOLKS HERE TO TURN.
BUT IT AIN'T 'CAUSE THEY BAD FOLKS.
* RULES OF ENGAGEMENT.
WE SHOULD BE ABLE TO HIDE SHIPWRECK IN HERE...
NOT EXACTLY SANITARY. BUT IT'LL DO.
HE'S OUT AND I CAN'T WAKE HIM. BREATHING'S RAGGED.
OKAY TUNNEL RAT—HOW'S POLLY ON FINDING DOC?
SENT THE BIRD TO CHECK OUT OUR ORIGINAL TARGET, SEE IF THE GIRLS AND DUKE CIRCLED BACK THERE.

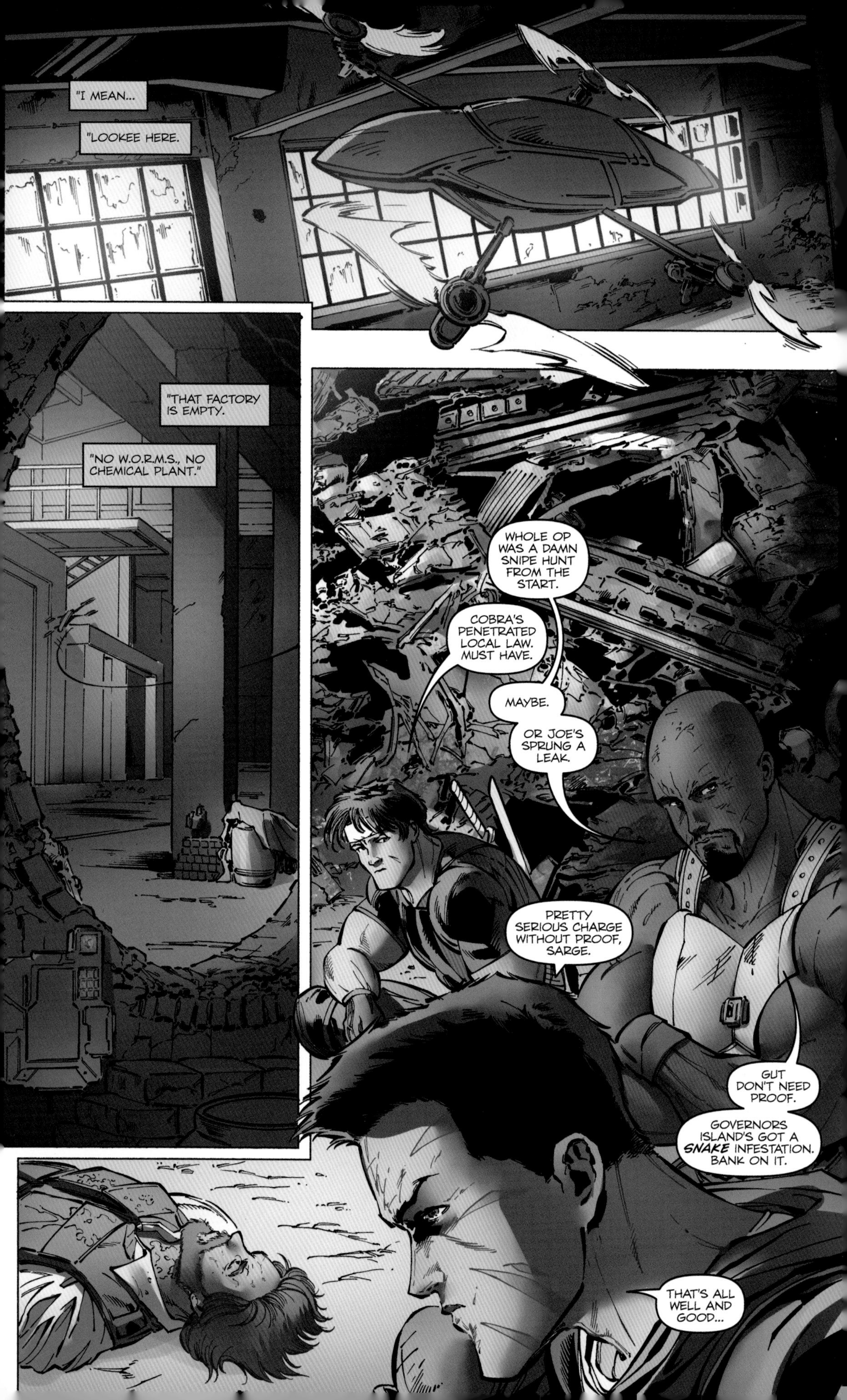

"I MEAN...
"LOOKEE HERE.
"THAT FACTORY IS EMPTY.
"NO W.O.R.M.S., NO CHEMICAL PLANT."
WHOLE OP WAS A DAMN SNIPE HUNT FROM THE START.
COBRA'S PENETRATED LOCAL LAW. MUST HAVE.
MAYBE.
OR JOE'S SPRUNG A LEAK.
PRETTY SERIOUS CHARGE WITHOUT PROOF, SARGE.
GUT DON'T NEED PROOF.
GOVERNORS ISLAND'S GOT A *SNAKE* INFESTATION. BANK ON IT.
THAT'S ALL WELL AND GOOD...

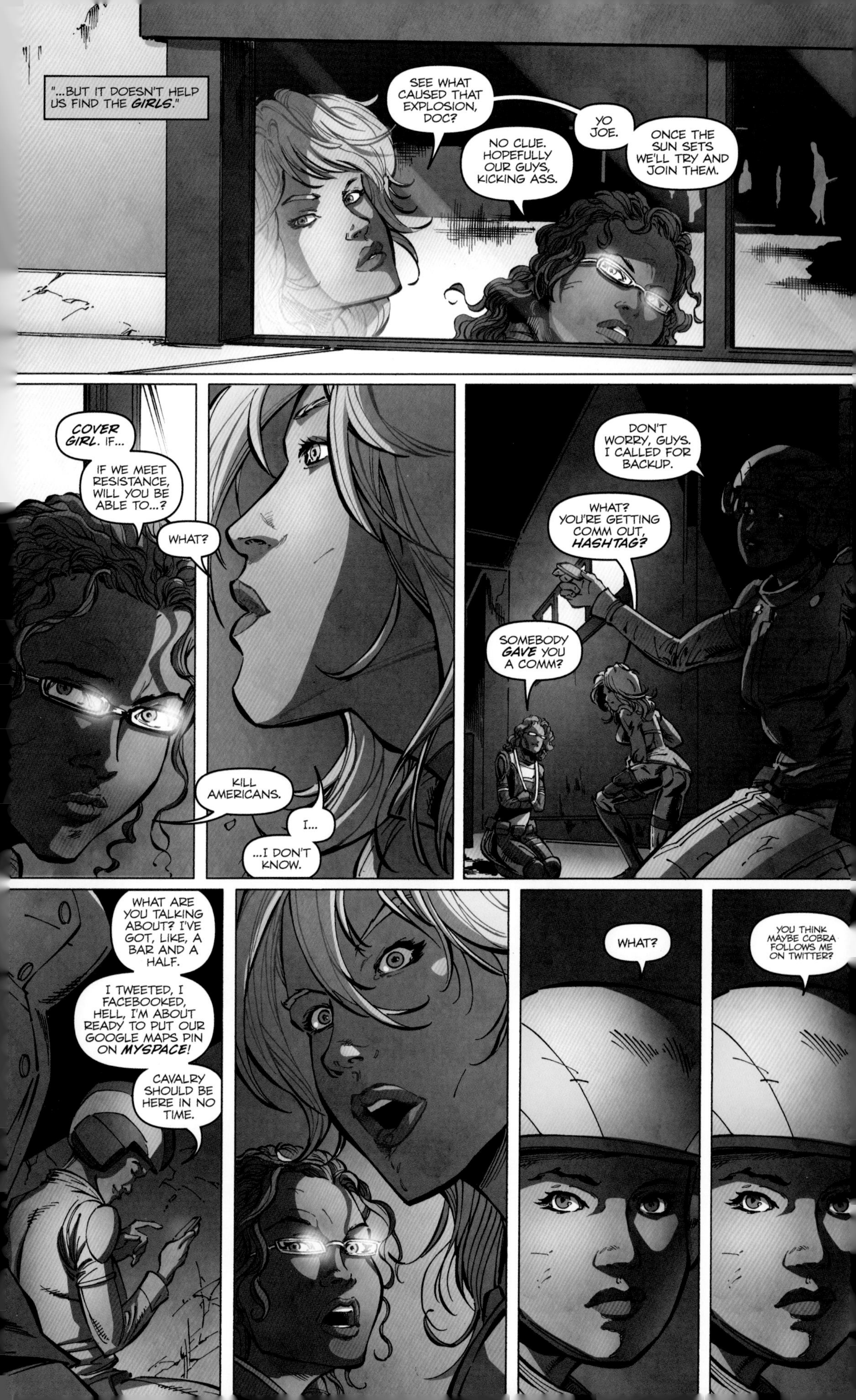
"...BUT IT DOESN'T HELP US FIND THE GIRLS."
SEE WHAT CAUSED THAT EXPLOSION, DOC?
NO CLUE. HOPEFULLY OUR GUYS, KICKING ASS.
YO JOE.
ONCE THE SUN SETS WE'LL TRY AND JOIN THEM.
COVER GIRL. IF...
IF WE MEET RESISTANCE, WILL YOU BE ABLE TO...?
WHAT?
KILL AMERICANS.
I...
...I DON'T KNOW.
DON'T WORRY, GUYS. I CALLED FOR BACKUP.
WHAT? YOU'RE GETTING COMM OUT, HASHTAG?
SOMEBODY GAVE YOU A COMM?
WHAT ARE YOU TALKING ABOUT? I'VE GOT, LIKE, A BAR AND A HALF.
I TWEETED, I FACEBOOKED, HELL, I'M ABOUT READY TO PUT OUR GOOGLE MAPS PIN ON MYSPACE!
CAVALRY SHOULD BE HERE IN NO TIME.
WHAT?
YOU THINK MAYBE COBRA FOLLOWS ME ON TWITTER?

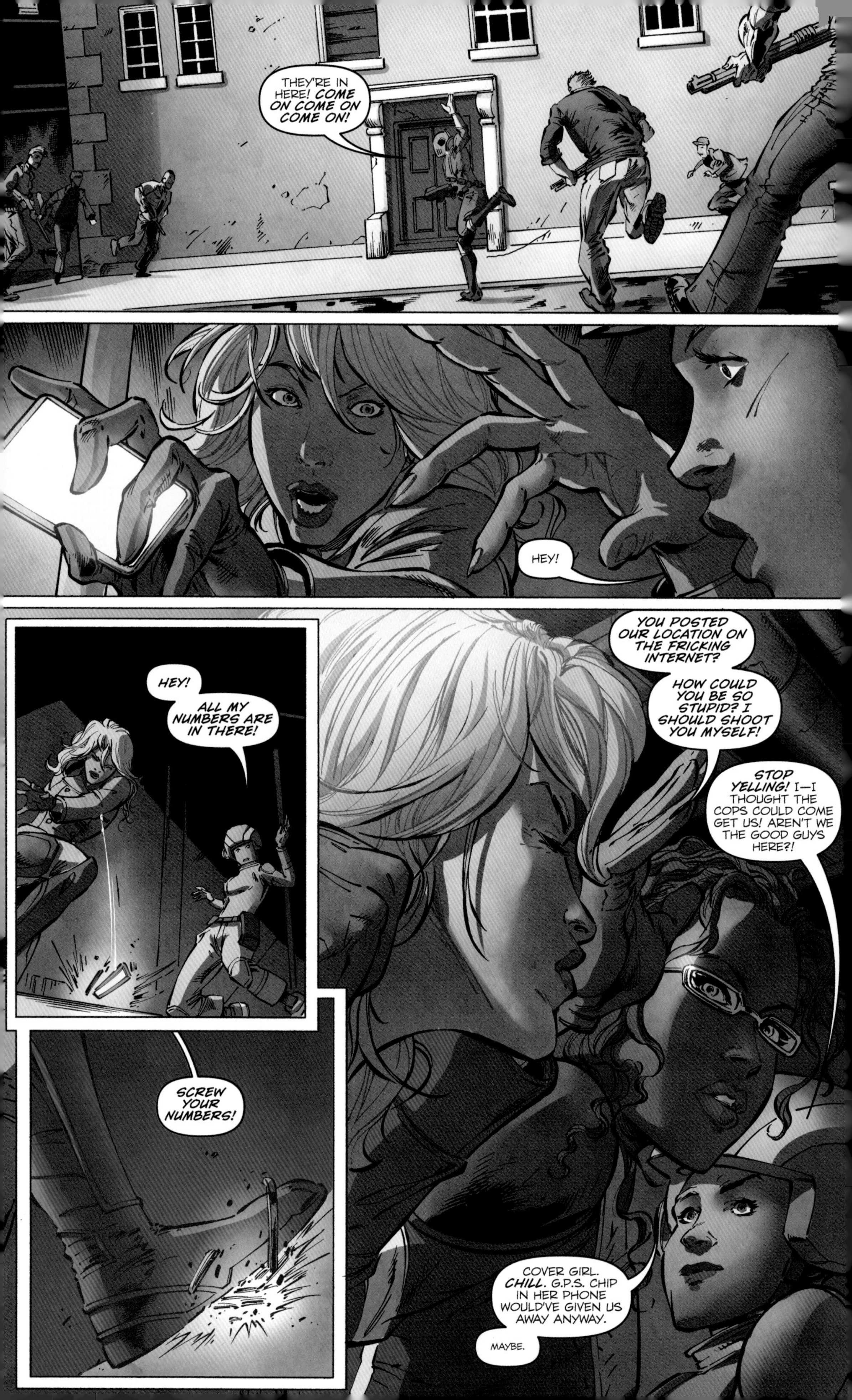
THEY'RE IN HERE! COME ON COME ON COME ON!
HEY!
HEY! ALL MY NUMBERS ARE IN THERE!
SCREW YOUR NUMBERS!
YOU POSTED OUR LOCATION ON THE FRICKING INTERNET?
HOW COULD YOU BE SO STUPID? I SHOULD SHOOT YOU MYSELF!
STOP YELLING! I—I THOUGHT THE COPS COULD COME GET US! AREN'T WE THE GOOD GUYS HERE?!
COVER GIRL. CHILL. G.P.S. CHIP IN HER PHONE WOULD'VE GIVEN US AWAY ANYWAY.
MAYBE.

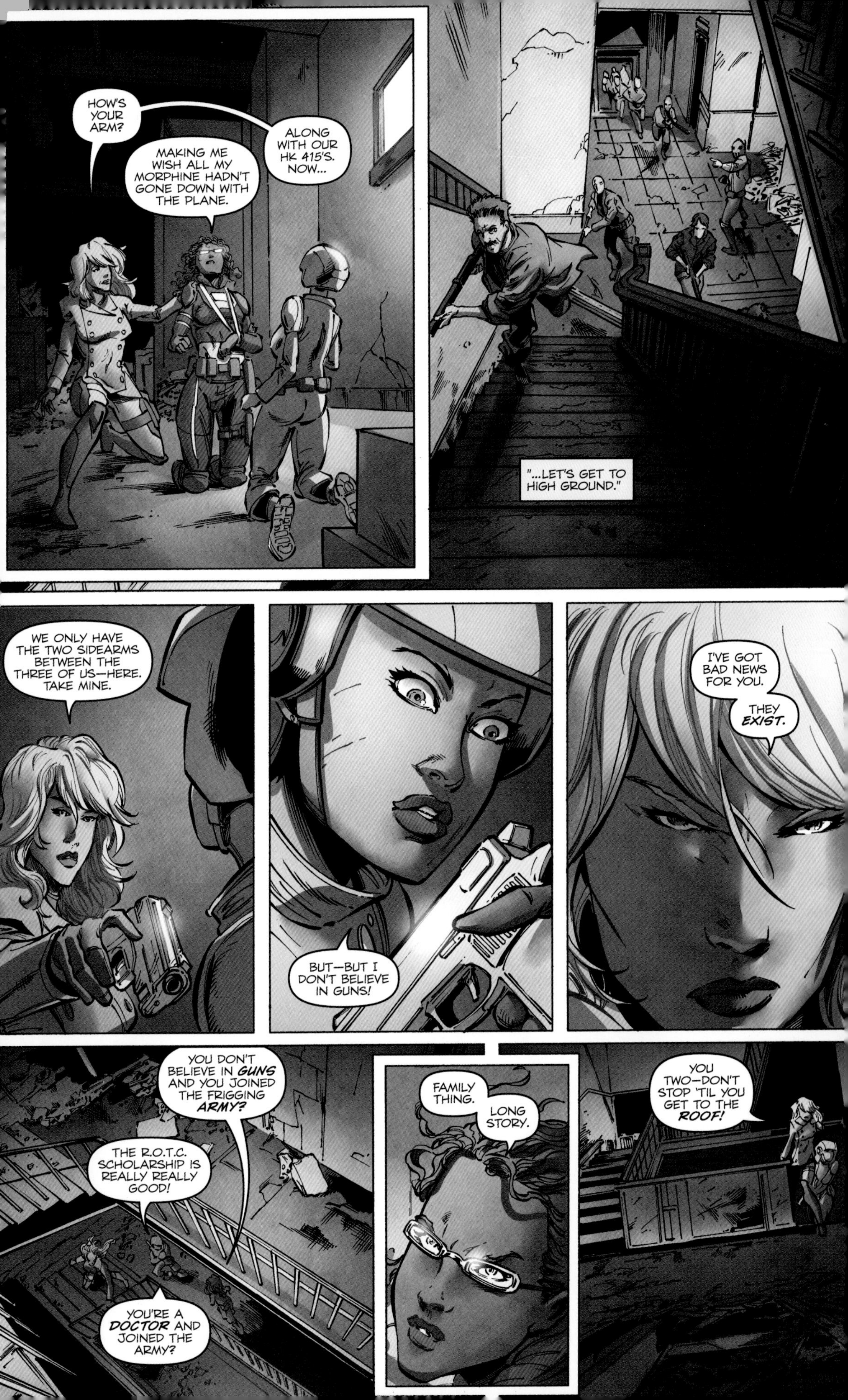
HOW'S YOUR ARM?
MAKING ME WISH ALL MY MORPHINE HADN'T GONE DOWN WITH THE PLANE.
ALONG WITH OUR HK 415'S. NOW...
"...LET'S GET TO HIGH GROUND."
WE ONLY HAVE THE TWO SIDEARMS BETWEEN THE THREE OF US—HERE. TAKE MINE.
BUT—BUT I DON'T BELIEVE IN GUNS!
I'VE GOT BAD NEWS FOR YOU.
THEY EXIST.
YOU DON'T BELIEVE IN GUNS AND YOU JOINED THE FRIGGING ARMY?
THE R.O.T.C. SCHOLARSHIP IS REALLY REALLY GOOD!
YOU'RE A DOCTOR AND JOINED THE ARMY?
FAMILY THING.
LONG STORY.
YOU TWO—DON'T STOP 'TIL YOU GET TO THE ROOF!

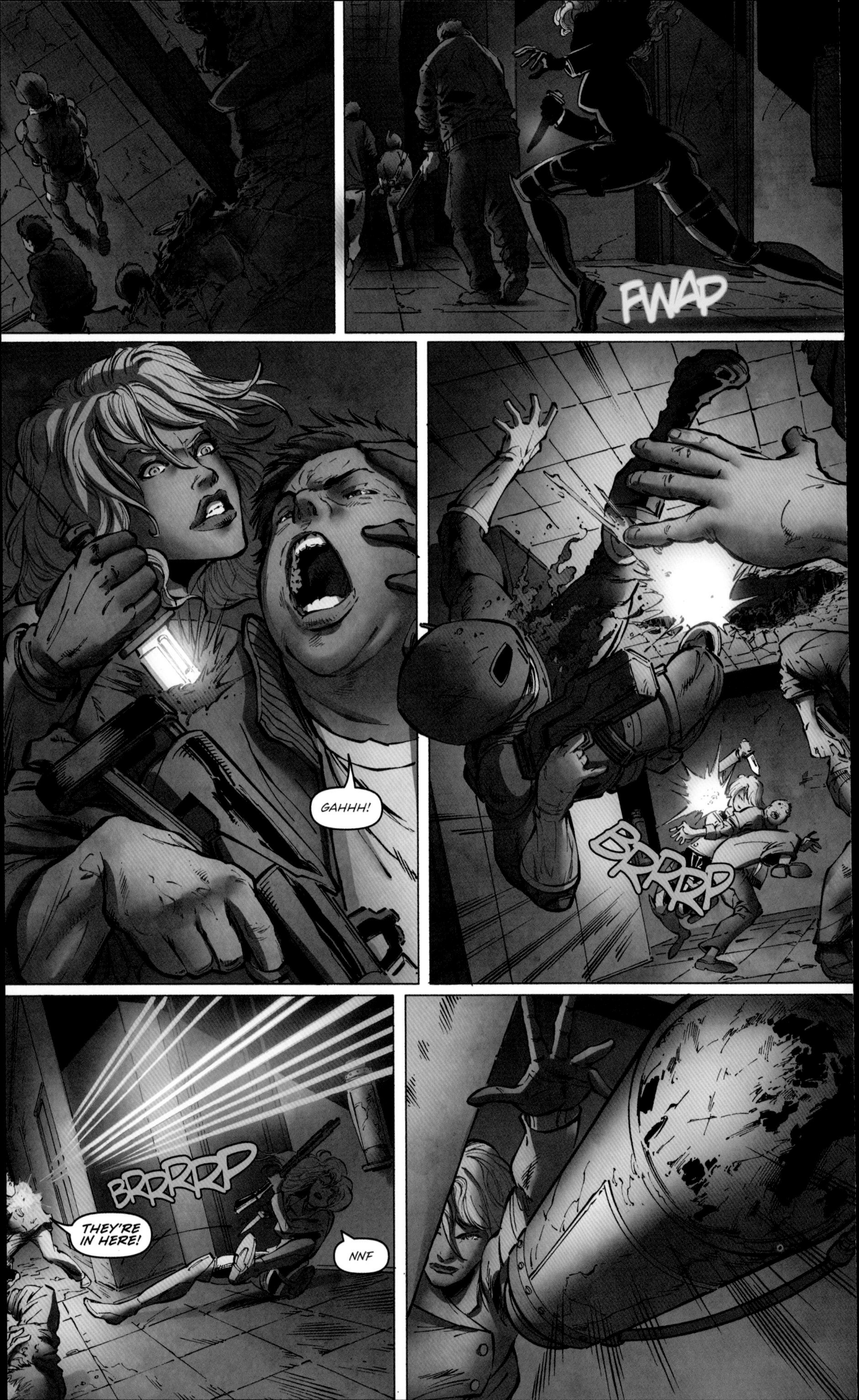
FWAP
GAHHH!
BRRRRP
BRRRRP
THEY'RE IN HERE!
NNF

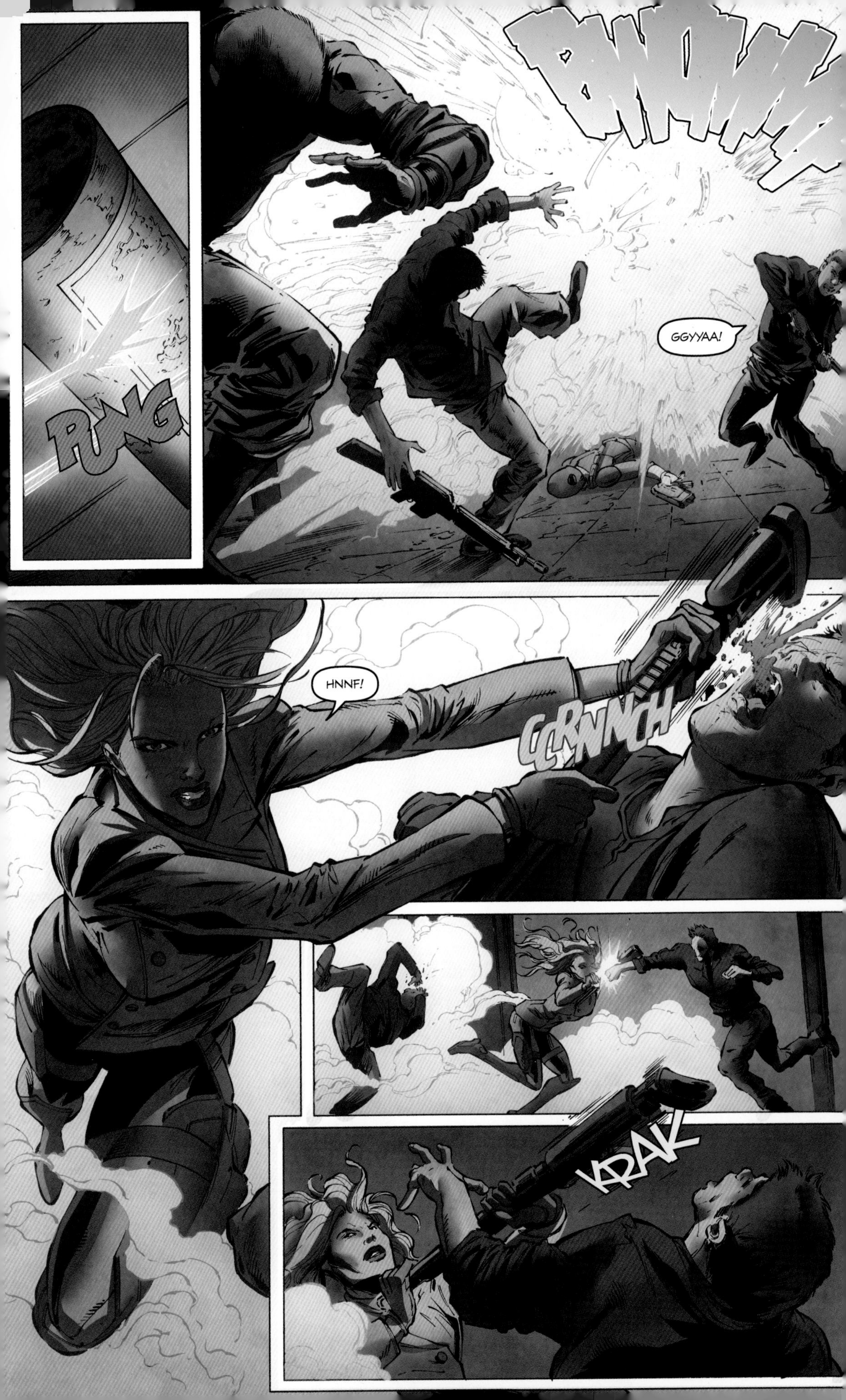
PUNG
BWOMM
GGYYAA!
HNNF!
CCRNNCH
KRAK

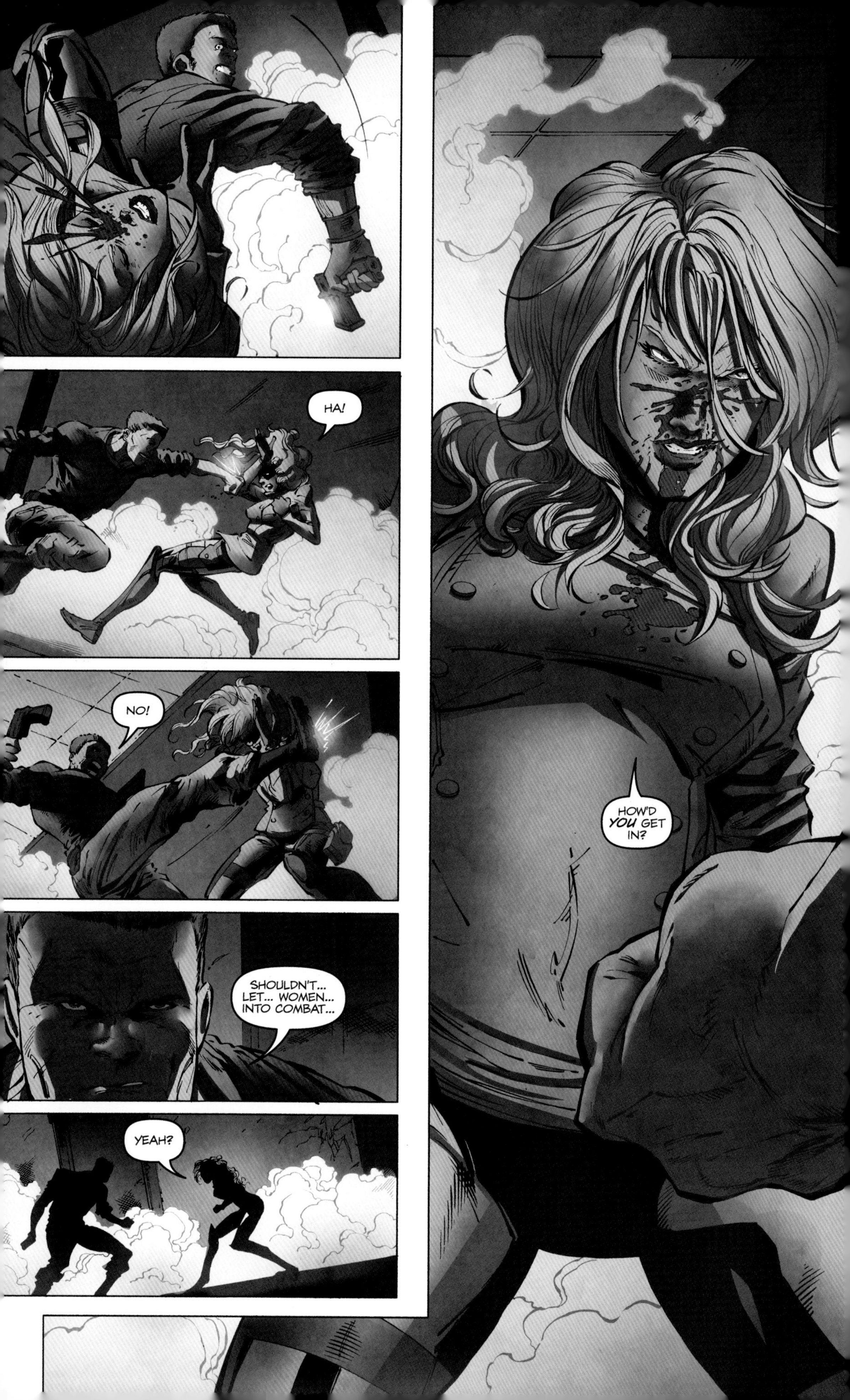
HA!
NO!
SHOULDN'T... LET... WOMEN... INTO COMBAT...
YEAH?
HOW'D *YOU* GET IN?

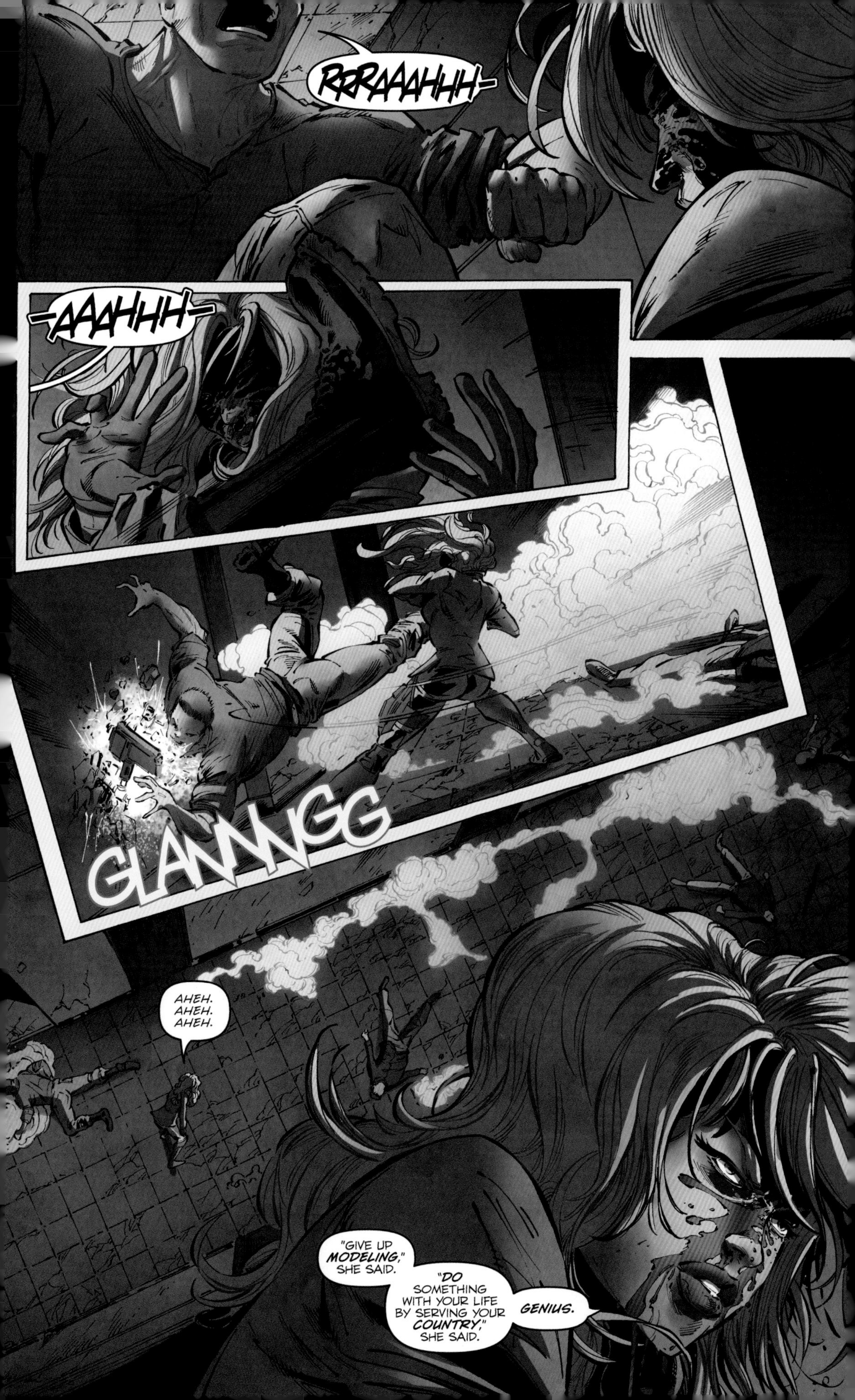
RRRAAAHHH—
—AAAHHH—
GLANNGG
AHEH. AHEH. AHEH.
"GIVE UP *MODELING*," SHE SAID.
"*DO* SOMETHING WITH YOUR LIFE BY SERVING YOUR *COUNTRY*," SHE SAID.
GENIUS.

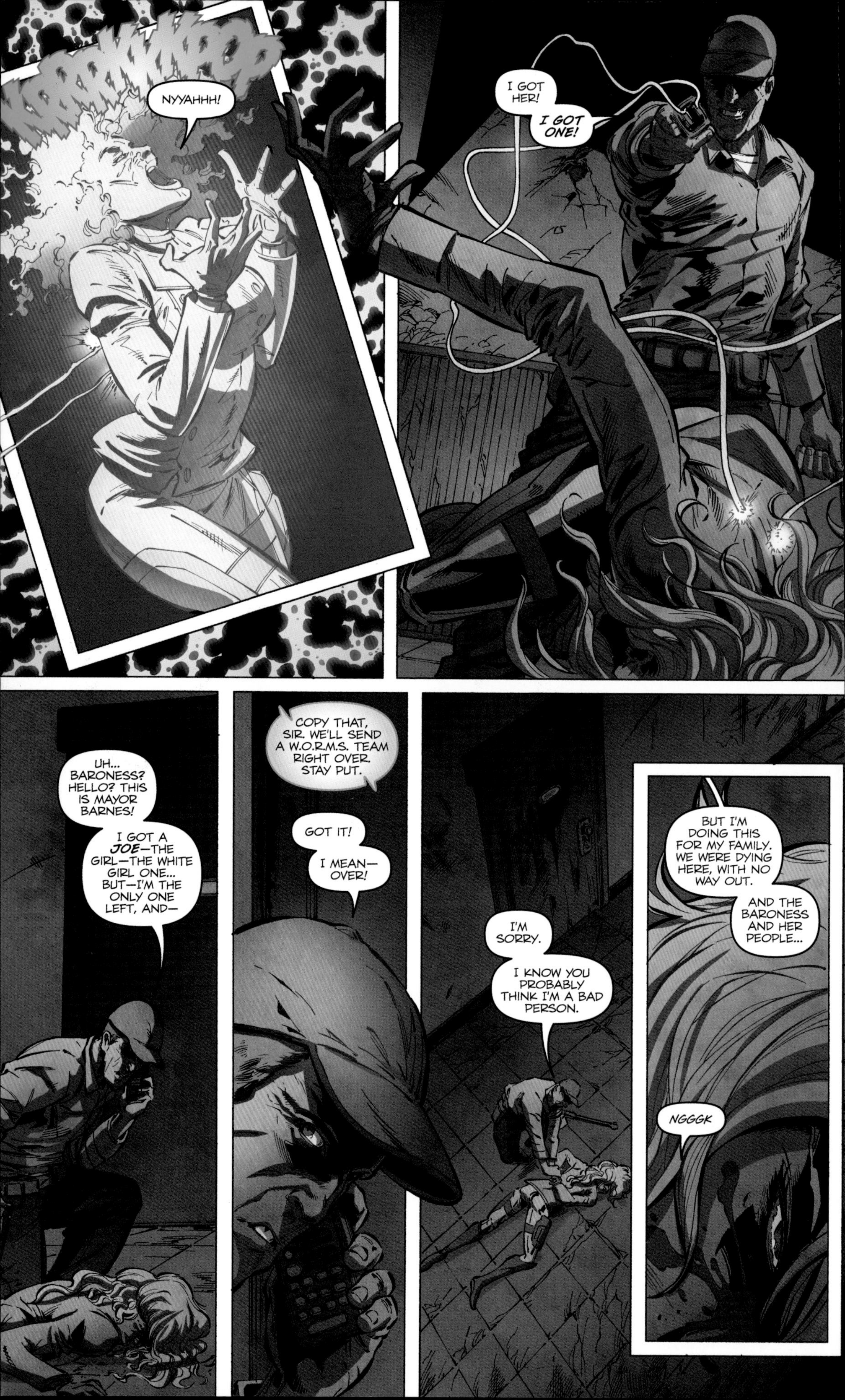
NYYAHHH!
I GOT HER!
I GOT ONE!
UH... BARONESS? HELLO? THIS IS MAYOR BARNES!
I GOT A JOE—THE GIRL—THE WHITE GIRL ONE... BUT—I'M THE ONLY ONE LEFT, AND—
COPY THAT, SIR. WE'LL SEND A W.O.R.M.S. TEAM RIGHT OVER. STAY PUT.
GOT IT!
I MEAN—OVER!
I'M SORRY.
I KNOW YOU PROBABLY THINK I'M A BAD PERSON.
BUT I'M DOING THIS FOR MY FAMILY. WE WERE DYING HERE, WITH NO WAY OUT.
AND THE BARONESS AND HER PEOPLE...
NGGGK

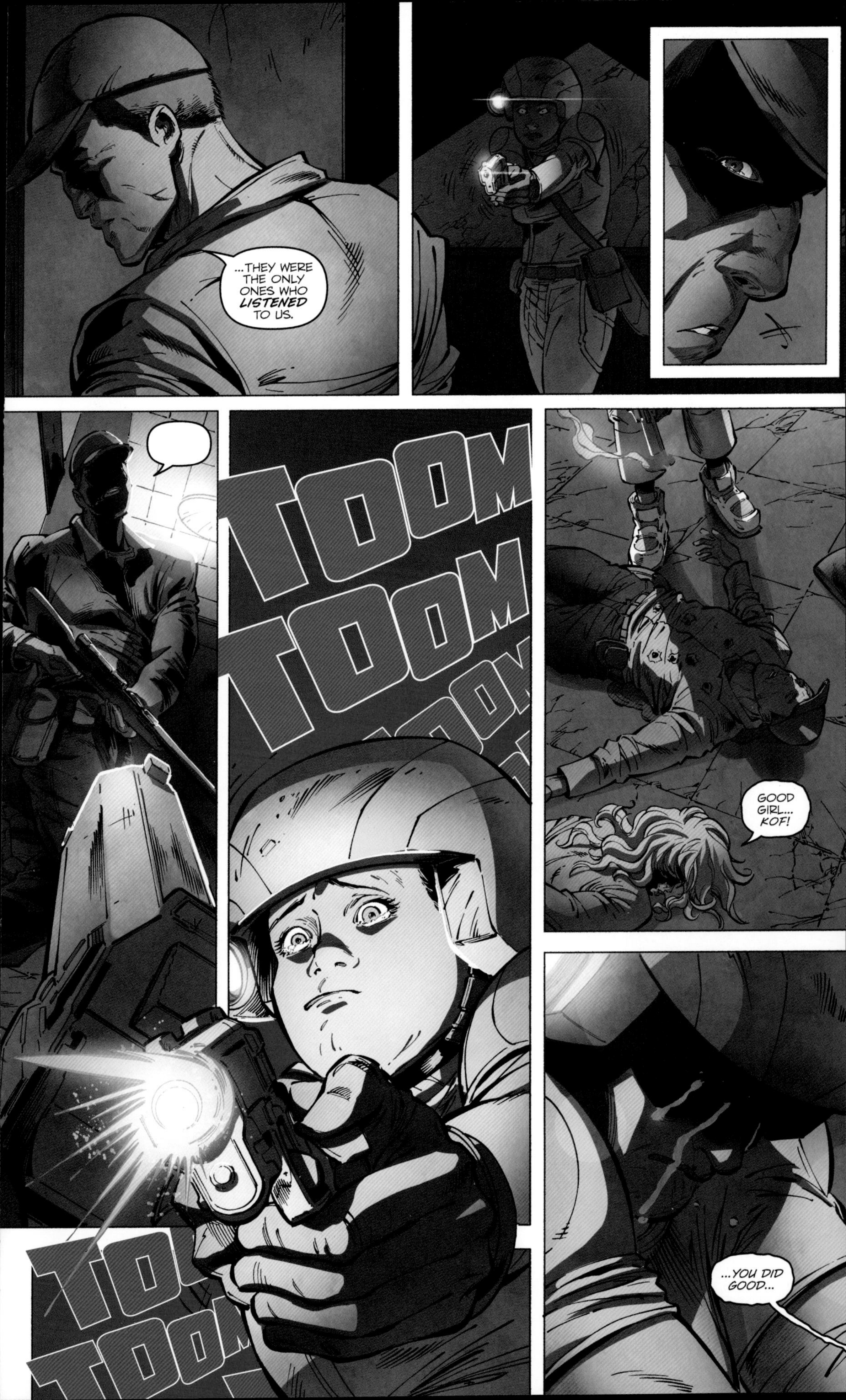
...THEY WERE THE ONLY ONES WHO *LISTENED* TO US.
TOOM
TOOM
GOOD GIRL... KOF!
...YOU DID GOOD...

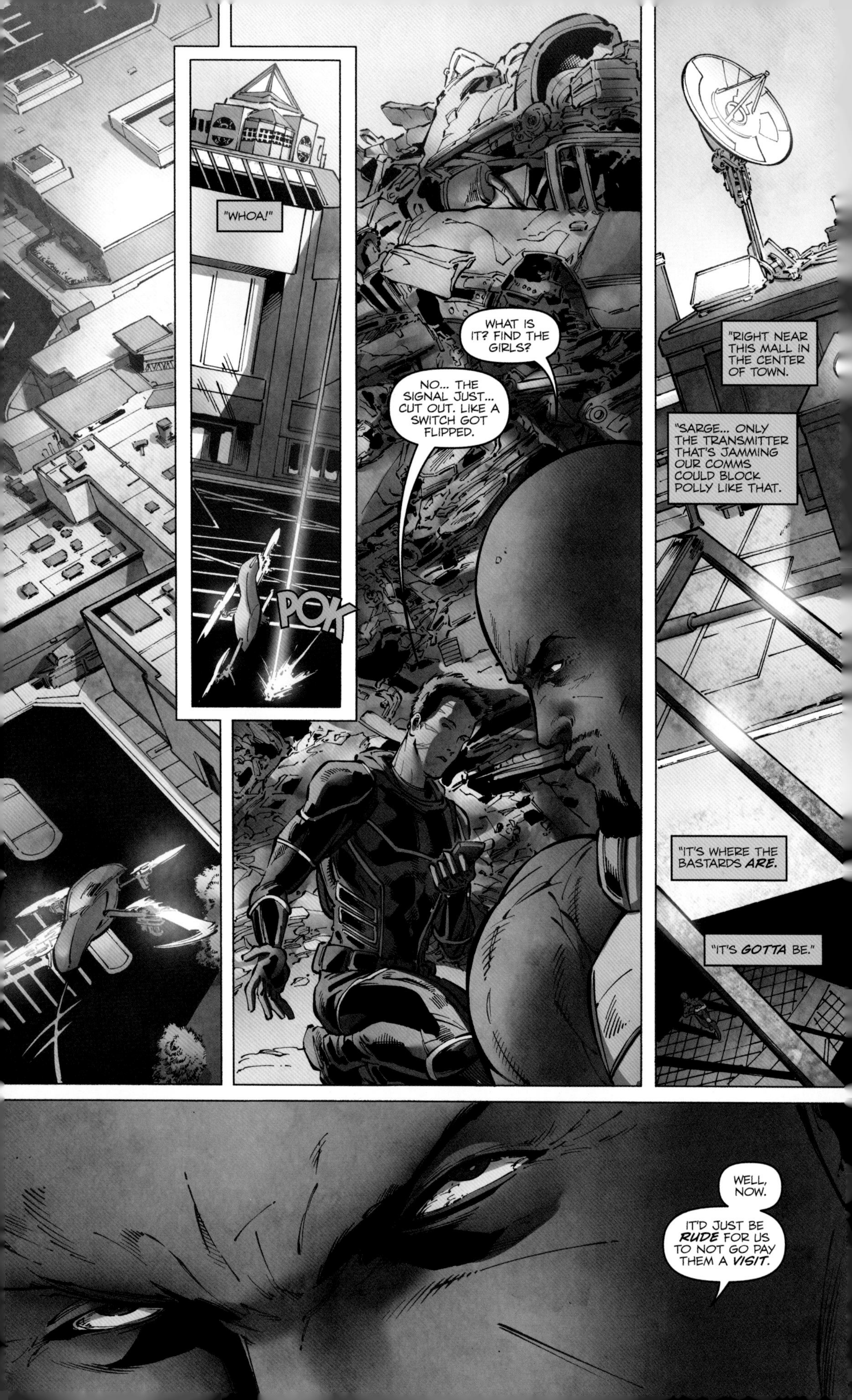
"WHOA!"
POK
WHAT IS IT? FIND THE GIRLS?
NO... THE SIGNAL JUST... CUT OUT. LIKE A SWITCH GOT FLIPPED.
"RIGHT NEAR THIS MALL IN THE CENTER OF TOWN.
"SARGE... ONLY THE TRANSMITTER THAT'S JAMMING OUR COMMS COULD BLOCK POLLY LIKE THAT.
"IT'S WHERE THE BASTARDS *ARE.*
"IT'S *GOTTA* BE."
WELL, NOW.
IT'D JUST BE *RUDE* FOR US TO NOT GO PAY THEM A *VISIT.*

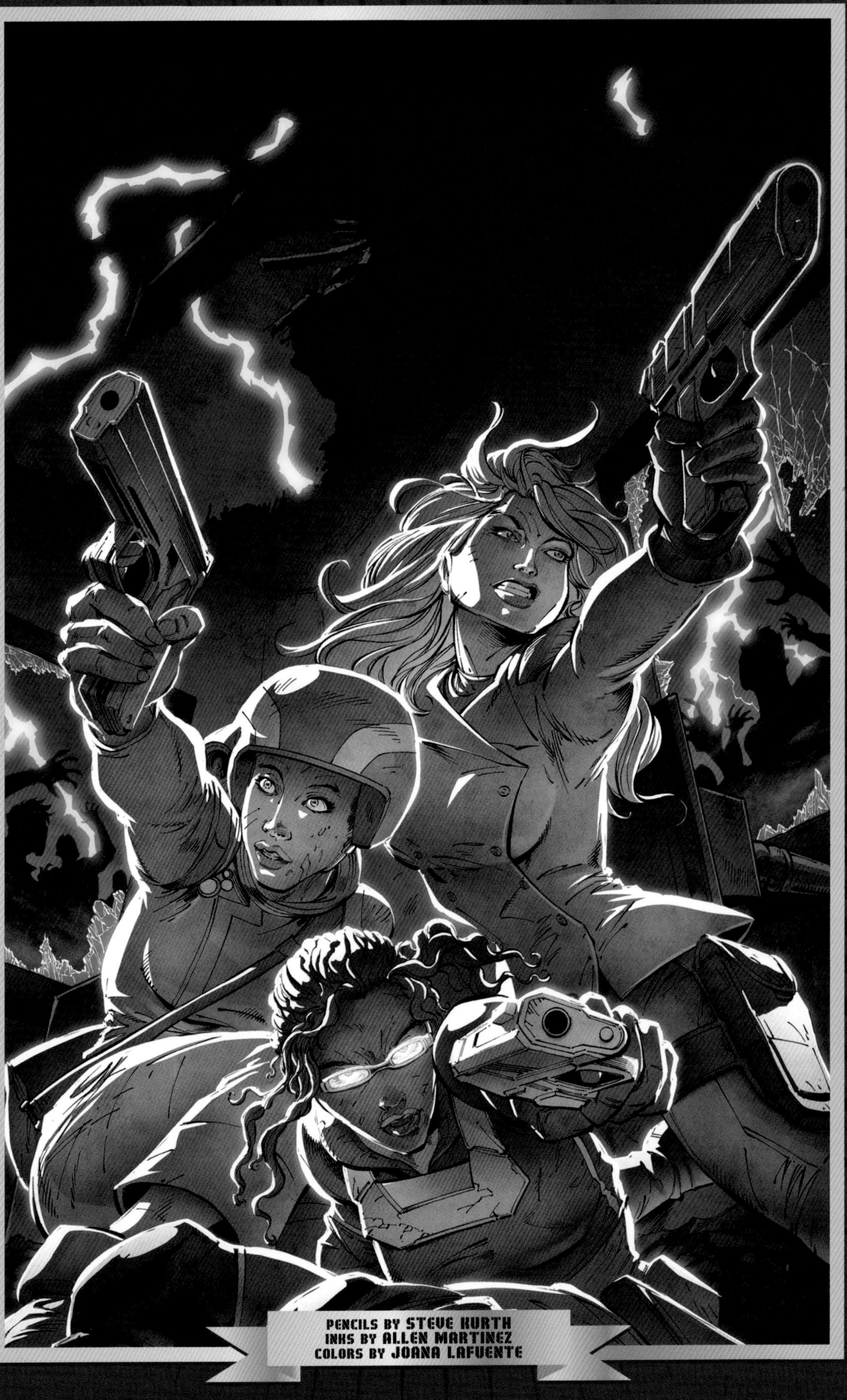
PENCILS BY STEVE KURTH
INKS BY ALLEN MARTINEZ
COLORS BY JOANA LAFUENTE

CHAPTER THREE

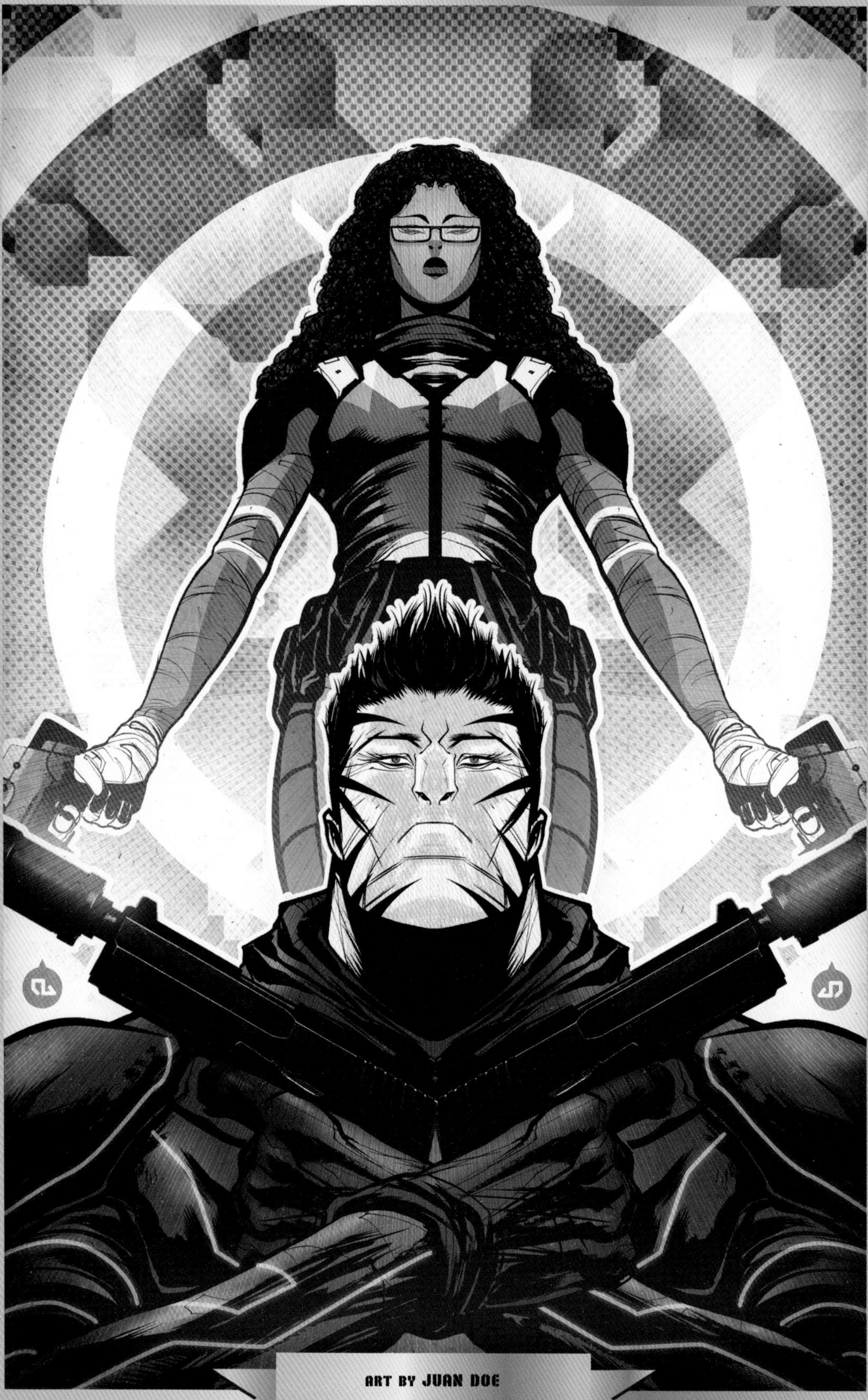
ART BY JUAN DOE

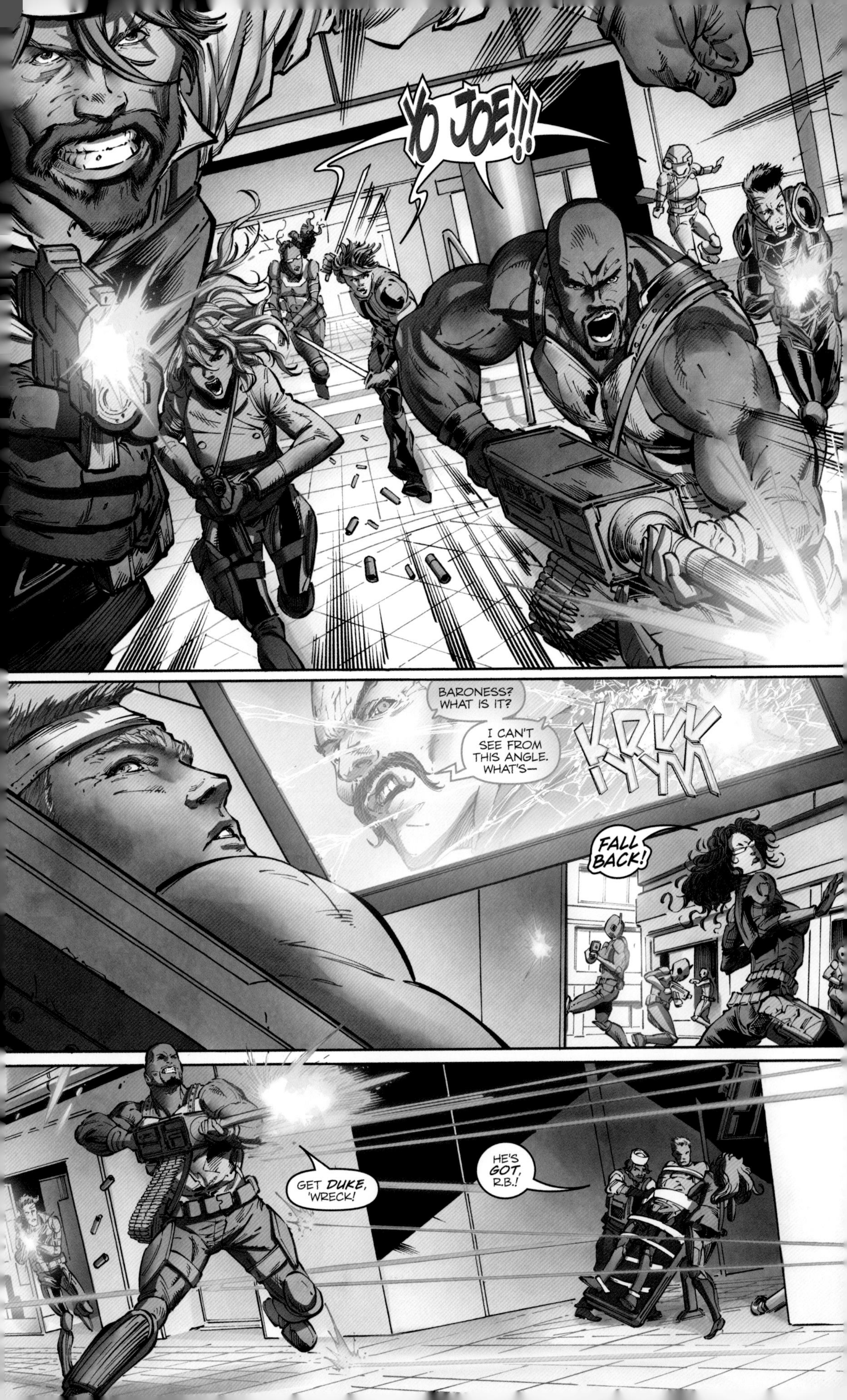
YO JOE!!!
BARONESS? WHAT IS IT?
I CAN'T SEE FROM THIS ANGLE. WHAT'S—
KRKK
FALL BACK!
GET **DUKE**, 'WRECK!
HE'S **GOT**, R.B.!

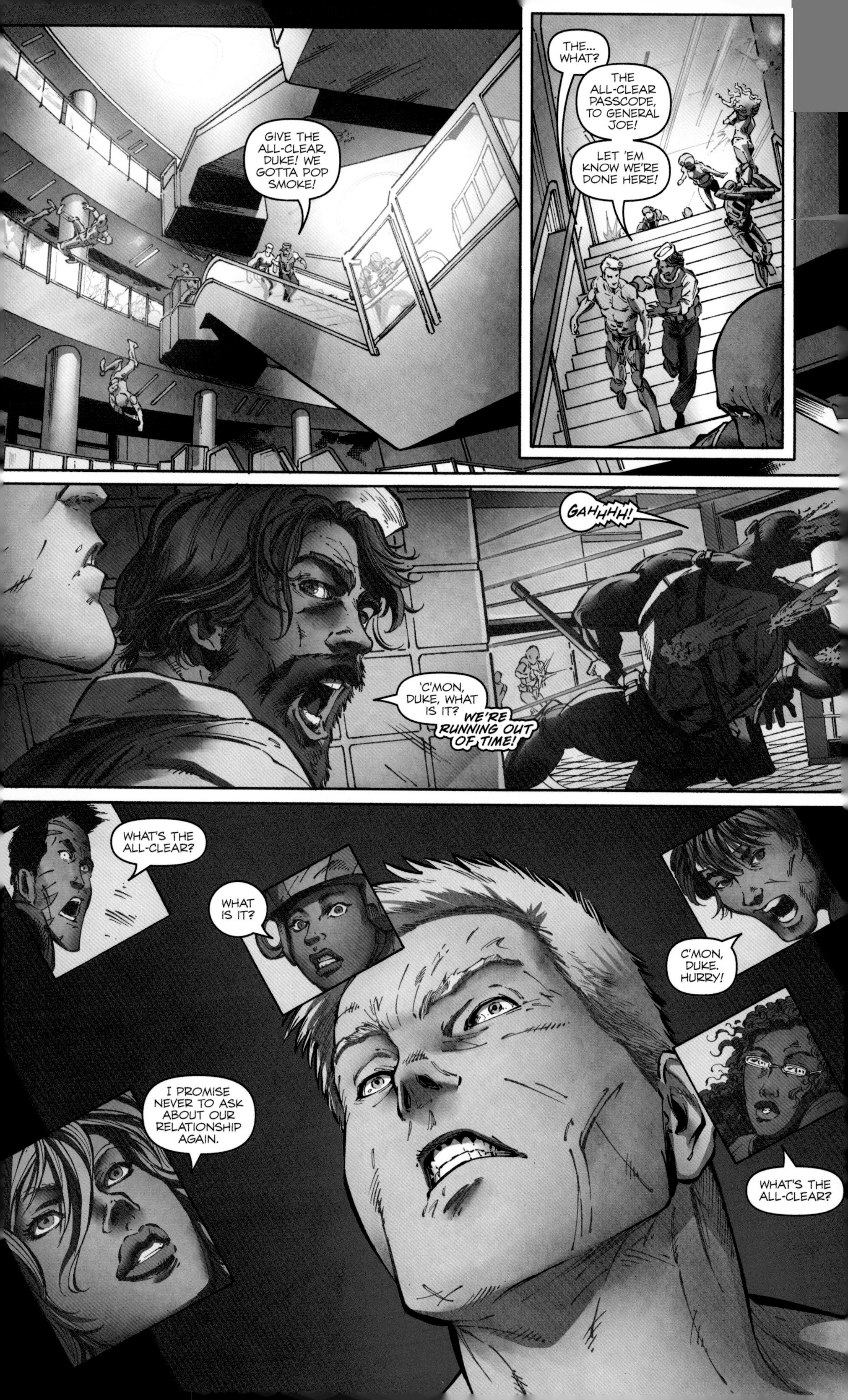
GIVE THE ALL-CLEAR, DUKE! WE GOTTA POP SMOKE!
THE... WHAT?
THE ALL-CLEAR PASSCODE, TO GENERAL JOE!
LET 'EM KNOW WE'RE DONE HERE!
GAHHHH!
'C'MON, DUKE, WHAT IS IT? WE'RE RUNNING OUT OF TIME!
WHAT'S THE ALL-CLEAR?
WHAT IS IT?
C'MON, DUKE. HURRY!
I PROMISE NEVER TO ASK ABOUT OUR RELATIONSHIP AGAIN.
WHAT'S THE ALL-CLEAR?

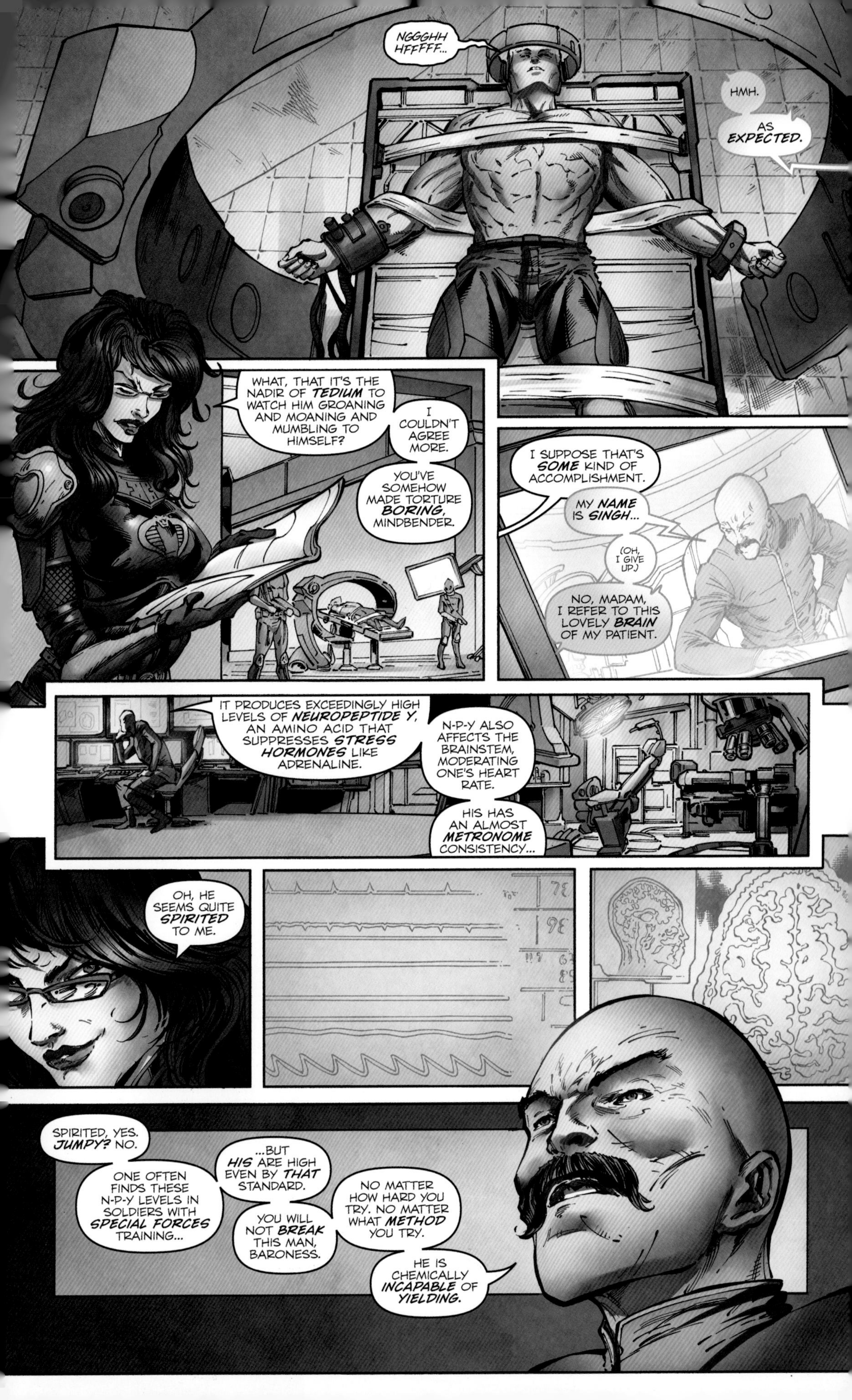
NGGGHH HFFFFF...
HMH.
AS EXPECTED.
WHAT, THAT IT'S THE NADIR OF TEDIUM TO WATCH HIM GROANING AND MOANING AND MUMBLING TO HIMSELF?
I COULDN'T AGREE MORE.
YOU'VE SOMEHOW MADE TORTURE BORING, MINDBENDER.
I SUPPOSE THAT'S SOME KIND OF ACCOMPLISHMENT.
MY NAME IS SINGH...
(OH, I GIVE UP.)
NO, MADAM, I REFER TO THIS LOVELY BRAIN OF MY PATIENT.
IT PRODUCES EXCEEDINGLY HIGH LEVELS OF NEUROPEPTIDE Y, AN AMINO ACID THAT SUPPRESSES STRESS HORMONES LIKE ADRENALINE.
N-P-Y ALSO AFFECTS THE BRAINSTEM, MODERATING ONE'S HEART RATE.
HIS HAS AN ALMOST METRONOME CONSISTENCY...
OH, HE SEEMS QUITE SPIRITED TO ME.
SPIRITED, YES. JUMPY? NO.
ONE OFTEN FINDS THESE N-P-Y LEVELS IN SOLDIERS WITH SPECIAL FORCES TRAINING...
...BUT HIS ARE HIGH EVEN BY THAT STANDARD.
YOU WILL NOT BREAK THIS MAN, BARONESS.
NO MATTER HOW HARD YOU TRY. NO MATTER WHAT METHOD YOU TRY.
HE IS CHEMICALLY INCAPABLE OF YIELDING.

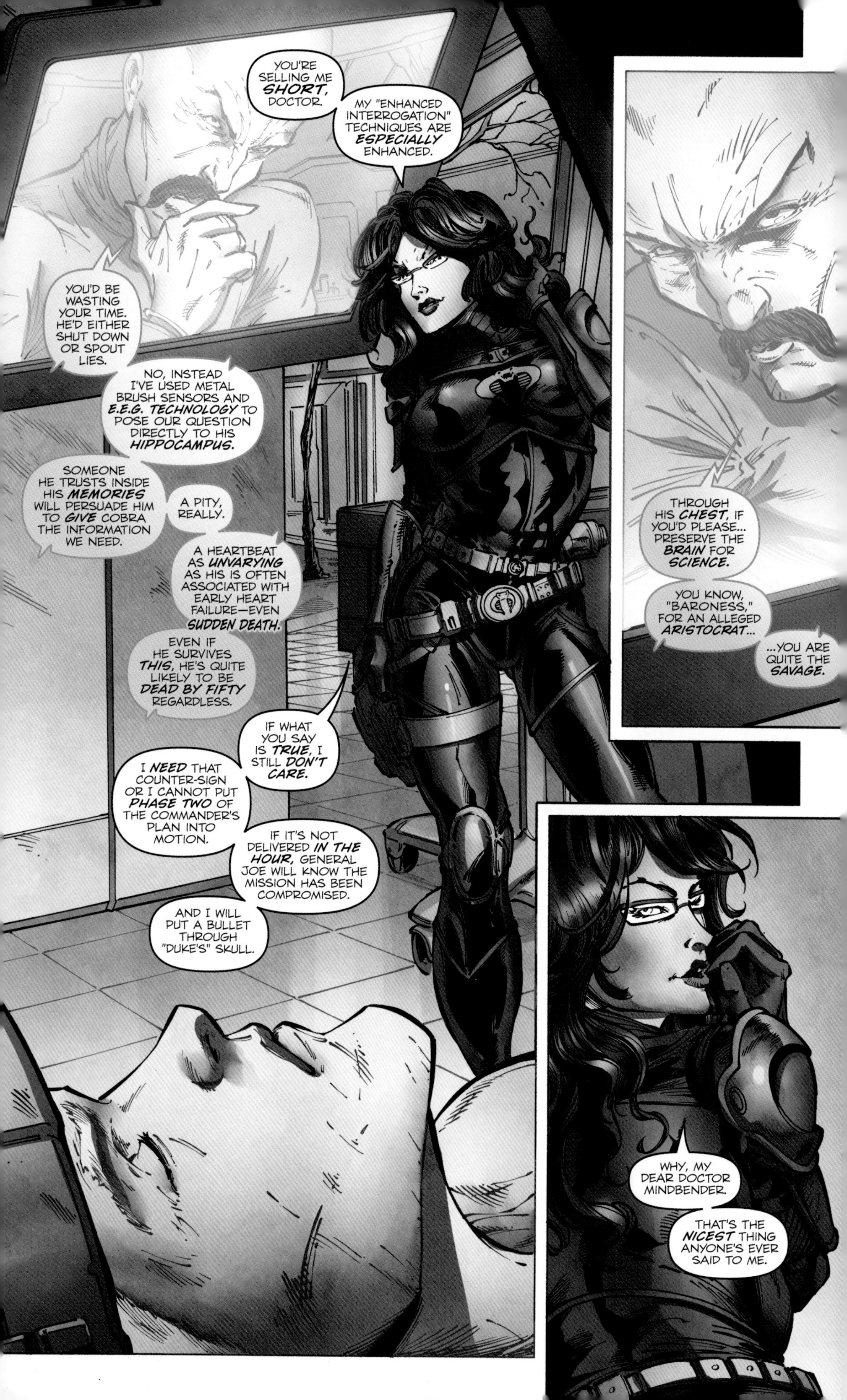
YOU'RE SELLING ME SHORT, DOCTOR.
MY "ENHANCED INTERROGATION" TECHNIQUES ARE ESPECIALLY ENHANCED.
YOU'D BE WASTING YOUR TIME. HE'D EITHER SHUT DOWN OR SPOUT LIES.
NO, INSTEAD I'VE USED METAL BRUSH SENSORS AND E.E.G. TECHNOLOGY TO POSE OUR QUESTION DIRECTLY TO HIS HIPPOCAMPUS.
SOMEONE HE TRUSTS INSIDE HIS MEMORIES WILL PERSUADE HIM TO GIVE COBRA THE INFORMATION WE NEED.
A PITY, REALLY.
A HEARTBEAT AS UNVARYING AS HIS IS OFTEN ASSOCIATED WITH EARLY HEART FAILURE—EVEN SUDDEN DEATH.
EVEN IF HE SURVIVES THIS, HE'S QUITE LIKELY TO BE DEAD BY FIFTY REGARDLESS.
IF WHAT YOU SAY IS TRUE, I STILL DON'T CARE.
I NEED THAT COUNTER-SIGN OR I CANNOT PUT PHASE TWO OF THE COMMANDER'S PLAN INTO MOTION.
IF IT'S NOT DELIVERED IN THE HOUR, GENERAL JOE WILL KNOW THE MISSION HAS BEEN COMPROMISED.
AND I WILL PUT A BULLET THROUGH "DUKE'S" SKULL.
THROUGH HIS CHEST, IF YOU'D PLEASE... PRESERVE THE BRAIN FOR SCIENCE.
YOU KNOW, "BARONESS," FOR AN ALLEGED ARISTOCRAT...
...YOU ARE QUITE THE SAVAGE.
WHY, MY DEAR DOCTOR MINDBENDER.
THAT'S THE NICEST THING ANYONE'S EVER SAID TO ME.

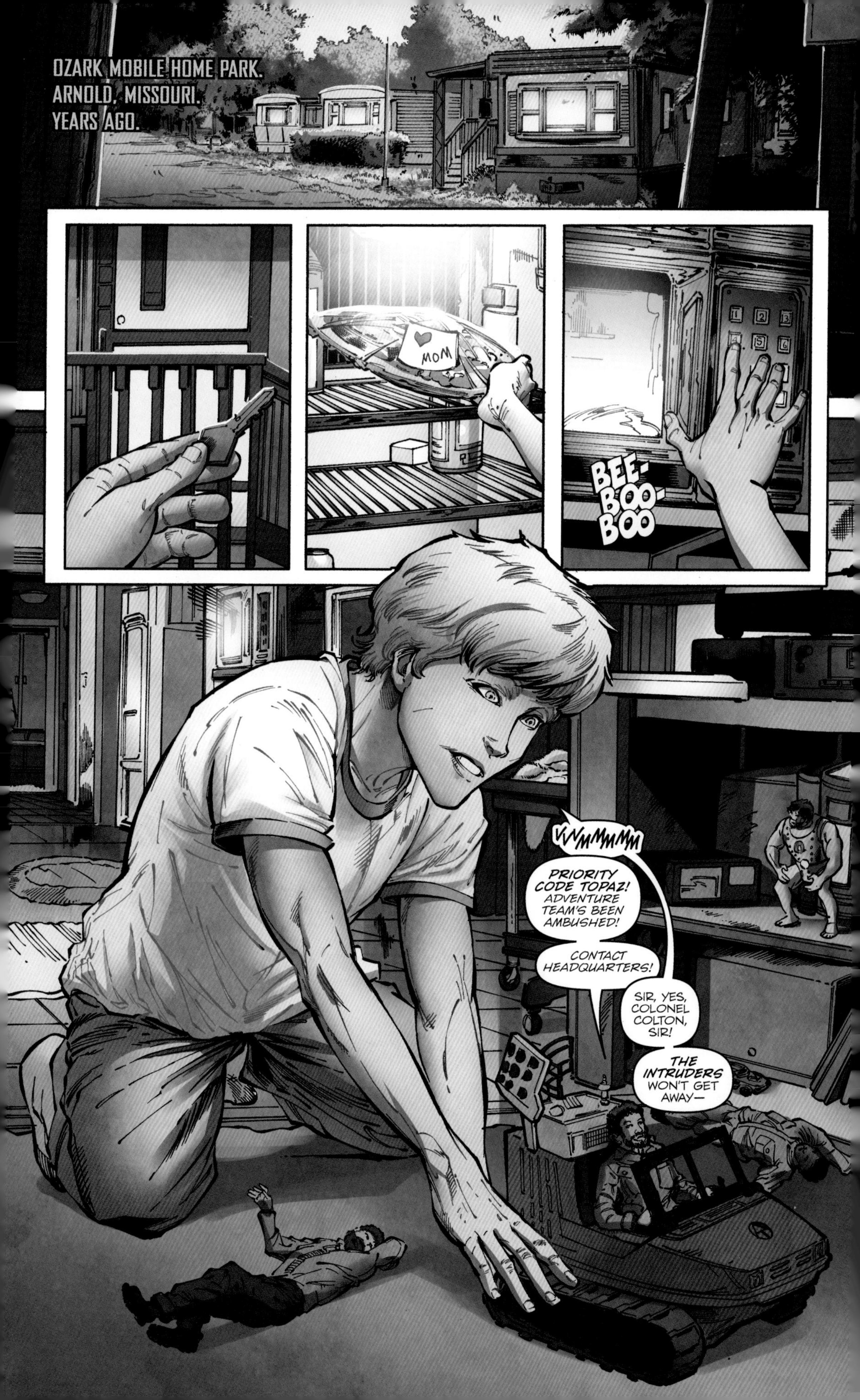

OZARK MOBILE HOME PARK.
ARNOLD, MISSOURI.
YEARS AGO.
MOM
BEE-BOO-BOO
VVVMMMMMM
PRIORITY CODE TOPAZ! ADVENTURE TEAM'S BEEN AMBUSHED!
CONTACT HEADQUARTERS!
SIR, YES, COLONEL COLTON, SIR!
THE INTRUDERS WON'T GET AWAY—

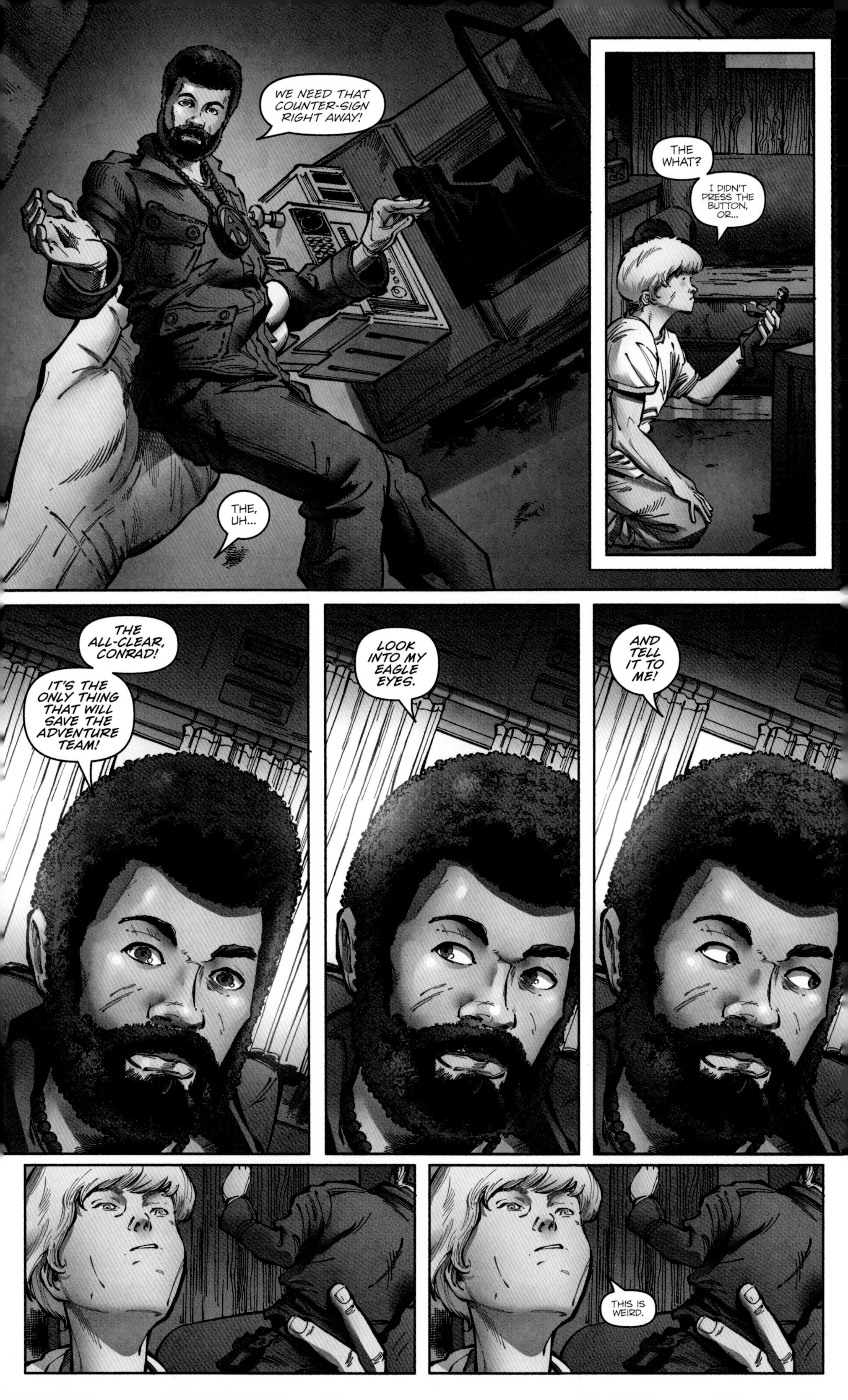
WE NEED THAT COUNTER-SIGN RIGHT AWAY!
THE, UH...
THE WHAT?
I DIDN'T PRESS THE BUTTON, OR...
THE ALL-CLEAR, CONRAD!
IT'S THE ONLY THING THAT WILL SAVE THE ADVENTURE TEAM!
LOOK INTO MY EAGLE EYES.
AND TELL IT TO ME!
THIS IS WEIRD.

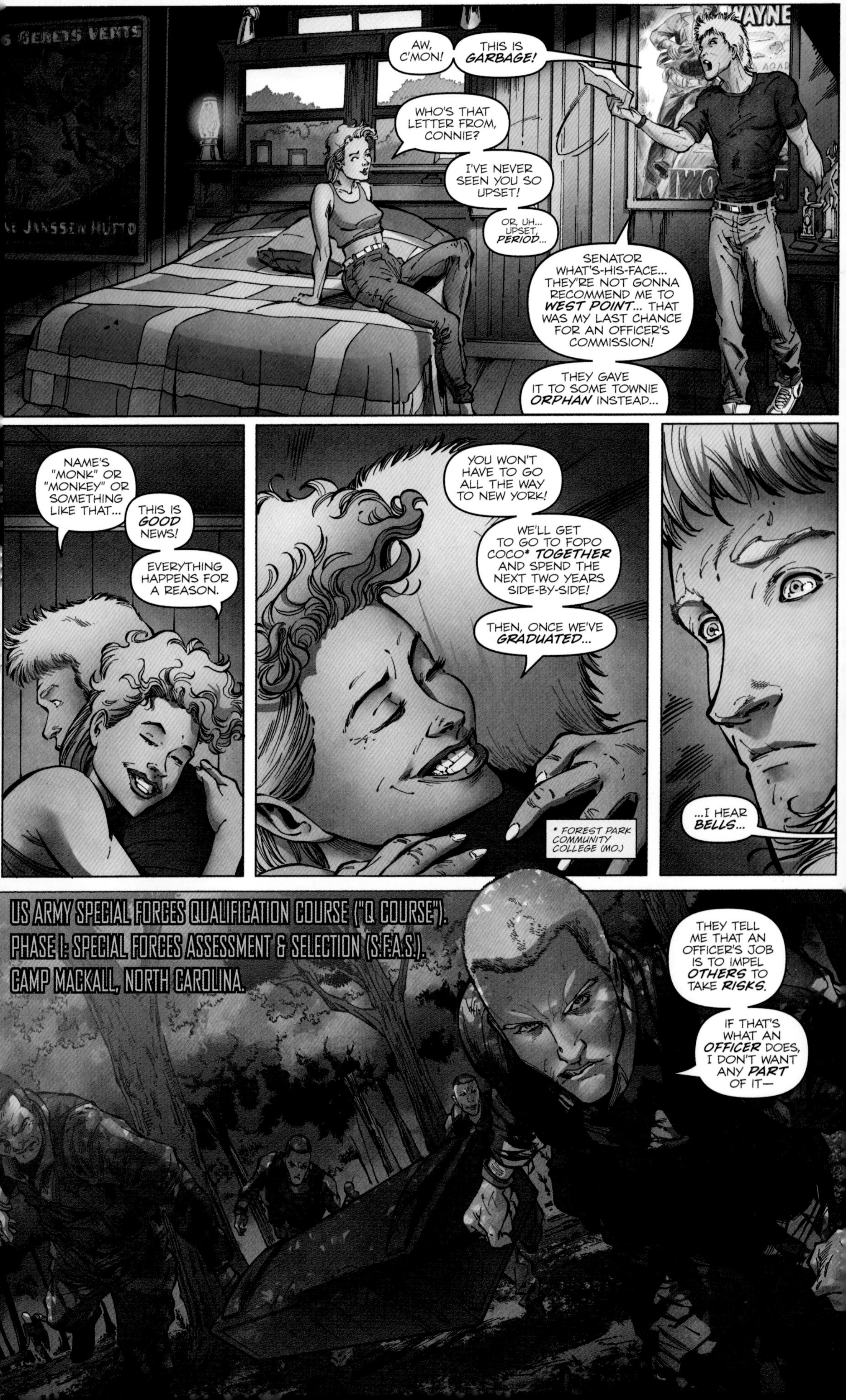
AW, C'MON!
THIS IS GARBAGE!
WHO'S THAT LETTER FROM, CONNIE?
I'VE NEVER SEEN YOU SO UPSET!
OR, UH... UPSET, PERIOD...
SENATOR WHAT'S-HIS-FACE... THEY'RE NOT GONNA RECOMMEND ME TO WEST POINT... THAT WAS MY LAST CHANCE FOR AN OFFICER'S COMMISSION!
THEY GAVE IT TO SOME TOWNIE ORPHAN INSTEAD...
NAME'S "MONK" OR "MONKEY" OR SOMETHING LIKE THAT...
THIS IS GOOD NEWS!
EVERYTHING HAPPENS FOR A REASON.
YOU WON'T HAVE TO GO ALL THE WAY TO NEW YORK!
WE'LL GET TO GO TO FOPO COCO* TOGETHER AND SPEND THE NEXT TWO YEARS SIDE-BY-SIDE!
THEN, ONCE WE'VE GRADUATED...
* FOREST PARK COMMUNITY COLLEGE (MO.)
...I HEAR BELLS...
US ARMY SPECIAL FORCES QUALIFICATION COURSE ("Q COURSE").
PHASE I: SPECIAL FORCES ASSESSMENT & SELECTION (S.F.A.S.).
CAMP MACKALL, NORTH CAROLINA.
THEY TELL ME THAT AN OFFICER'S JOB IS TO IMPEL OTHERS TO TAKE RISKS.
IF THAT'S WHAT AN OFFICER DOES, I DON'T WANT ANY PART OF IT—

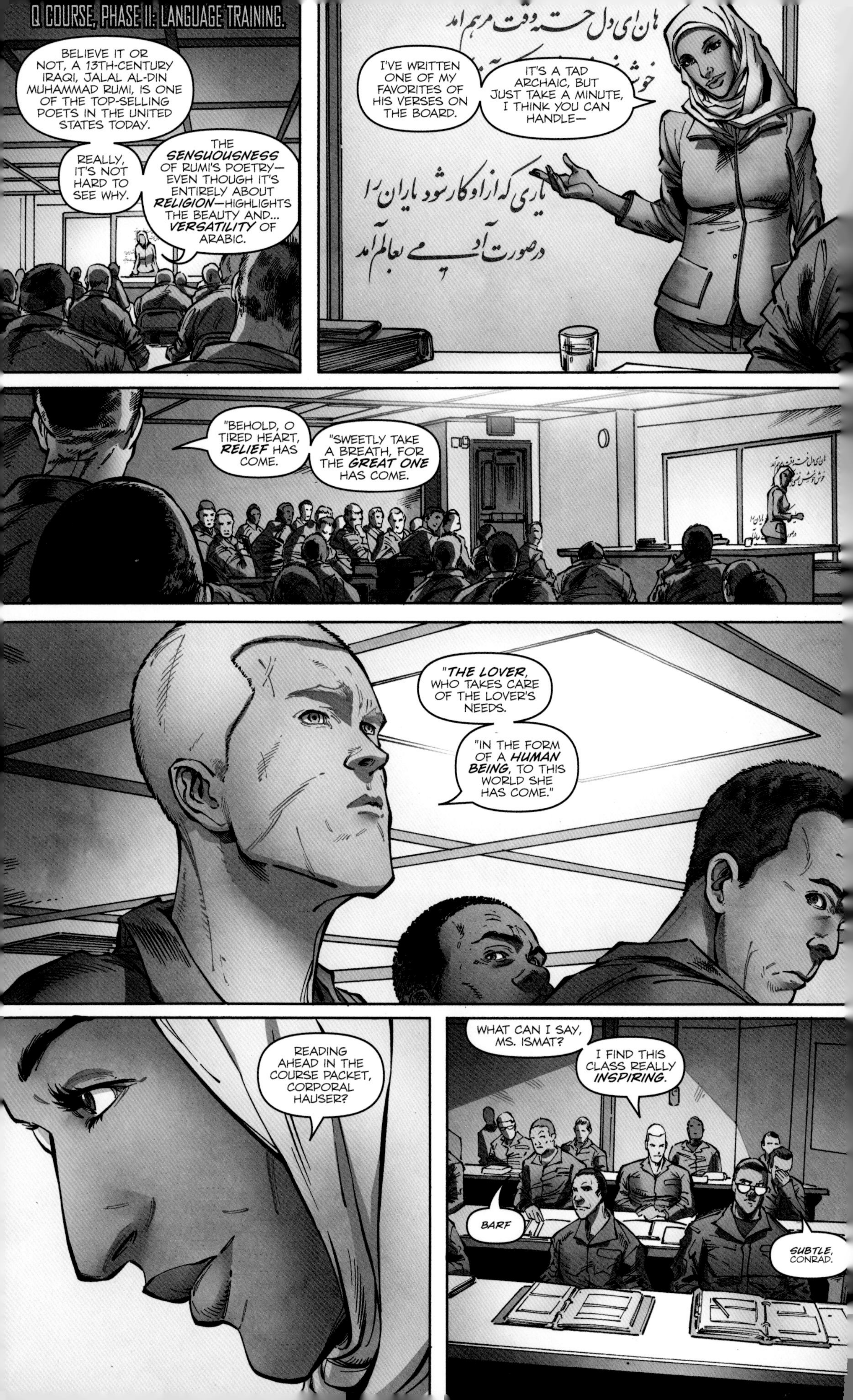
Q COURSE, PHASE II: LANGUAGE TRAINING.
BELIEVE IT OR NOT, A 13TH-CENTURY IRAQI, JALAL AL-DIN MUHAMMAD RUMI, IS ONE OF THE TOP-SELLING POETS IN THE UNITED STATES TODAY.
REALLY, IT'S NOT HARD TO SEE WHY.
THE SENSUOUSNESS OF RUMI'S POETRY—EVEN THOUGH IT'S ENTIRELY ABOUT RELIGION—HIGHLIGHTS THE BEAUTY AND... VERSATILITY OF ARABIC.
هان ای دل خسته وقت مرهم آمد
I'VE WRITTEN ONE OF MY FAVORITES OF HIS VERSES ON THE BOARD.
IT'S A TAD ARCHAIC, BUT JUST TAKE A MINUTE, I THINK YOU CAN HANDLE—
یاری که از او کار شود یاران را
در صورت آدمی به عالم آمد
"BEHOLD, O TIRED HEART, RELIEF HAS COME.
"SWEETLY TAKE A BREATH, FOR THE GREAT ONE HAS COME.
"THE LOVER, WHO TAKES CARE OF THE LOVER'S NEEDS.
"IN THE FORM OF A HUMAN BEING, TO THIS WORLD SHE HAS COME."
READING AHEAD IN THE COURSE PACKET, CORPORAL HAUSER?
WHAT CAN I SAY, MS. ISMAT?
I FIND THIS CLASS REALLY INSPIRING.
BARF
SUBTLE, CONRAD.

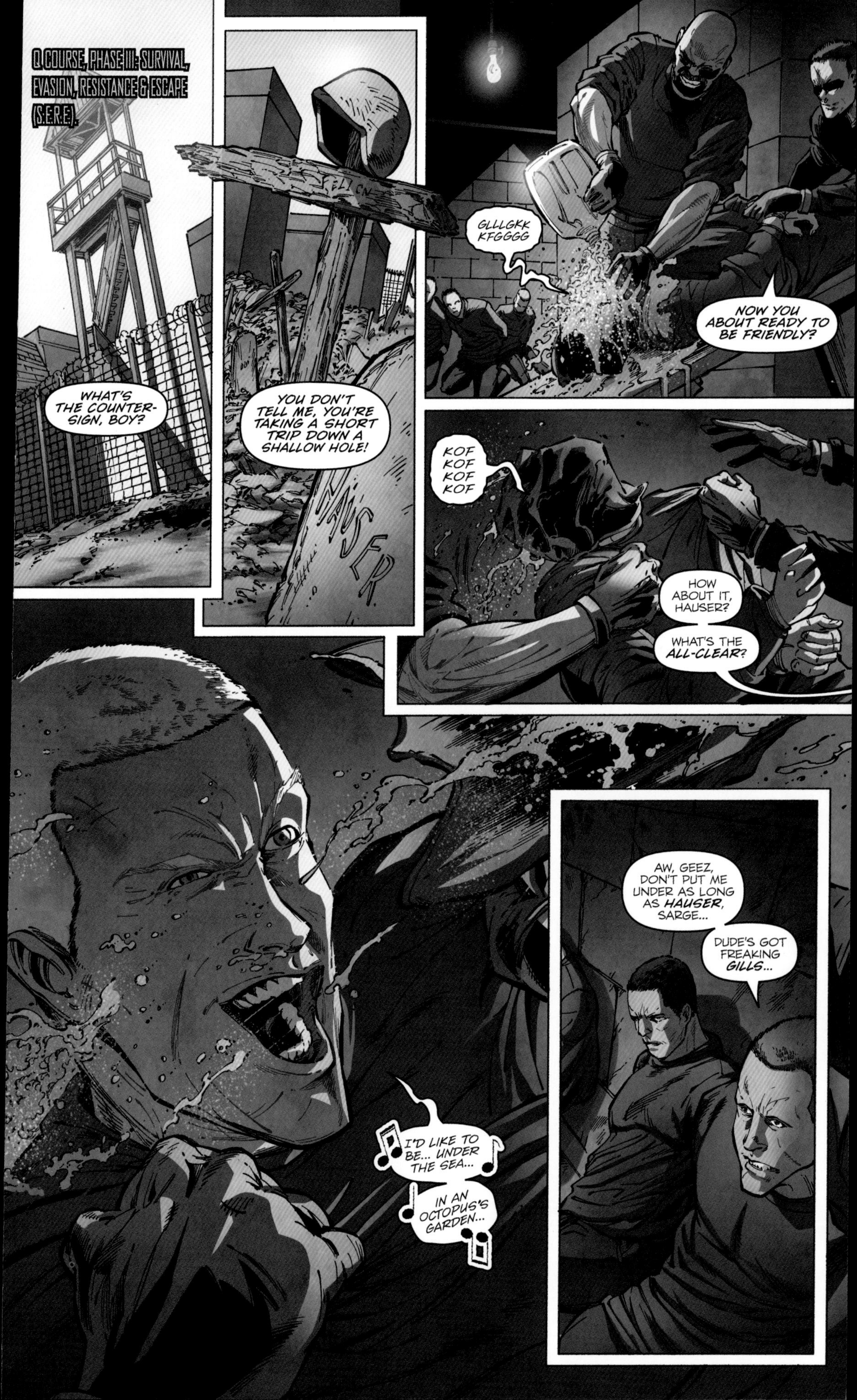
Q COURSE, PHASE III: SURVIVAL, EVASION, RESISTANCE & ESCAPE (S.E.R.E).
WHAT'S THE COUNTER-SIGN, BOY?
YOU DON'T TELL ME, YOU'RE TAKING A SHORT TRIP DOWN A SHALLOW HOLE!
HAUSER
GLLLGKK KFGGGG
NOW YOU ABOUT READY TO BE FRIENDLY?
KOF KOF KOF KOF
HOW ABOUT IT, HAUSER?
WHAT'S THE ALL-CLEAR?
I'D LIKE TO BE... UNDER THE SEA...
IN AN OCTOPUS'S GARDEN...
AW, GEEZ, DON'T PUT ME UNDER AS LONG AS HAUSER, SARGE...
DUDE'S GOT FREAKING GILLS...

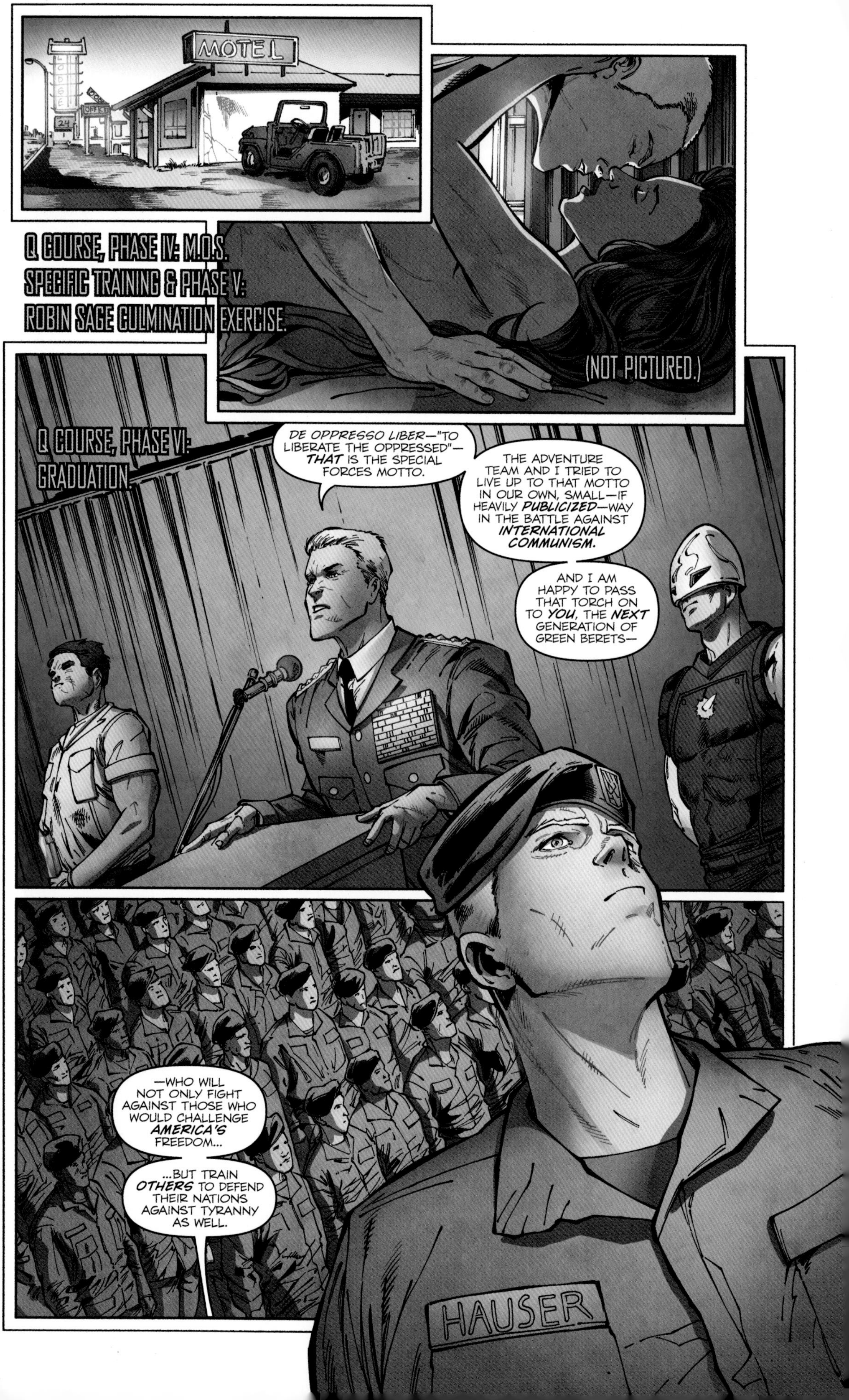
MOTEL
LODGE
24
OFFICE
Q COURSE, PHASE IV: M.O.S. SPECIFIC TRAINING & PHASE V: ROBIN SAGE CULMINATION EXERCISE.
(NOT PICTURED.)
Q COURSE, PHASE VI: GRADUATION.
DE OPPRESSO LIBER—"TO LIBERATE THE OPPRESSED"—THAT IS THE SPECIAL FORCES MOTTO.
THE ADVENTURE TEAM AND I TRIED TO LIVE UP TO THAT MOTTO IN OUR OWN, SMALL—IF HEAVILY PUBLICIZED—WAY IN THE BATTLE AGAINST INTERNATIONAL COMMUNISM.
AND I AM HAPPY TO PASS THAT TORCH ON TO YOU, THE NEXT GENERATION OF GREEN BERETS—
—WHO WILL NOT ONLY FIGHT AGAINST THOSE WHO WOULD CHALLENGE AMERICA'S FREEDOM...
...BUT TRAIN OTHERS TO DEFEND THEIR NATIONS AGAINST TYRANNY AS WELL.
HAUSER

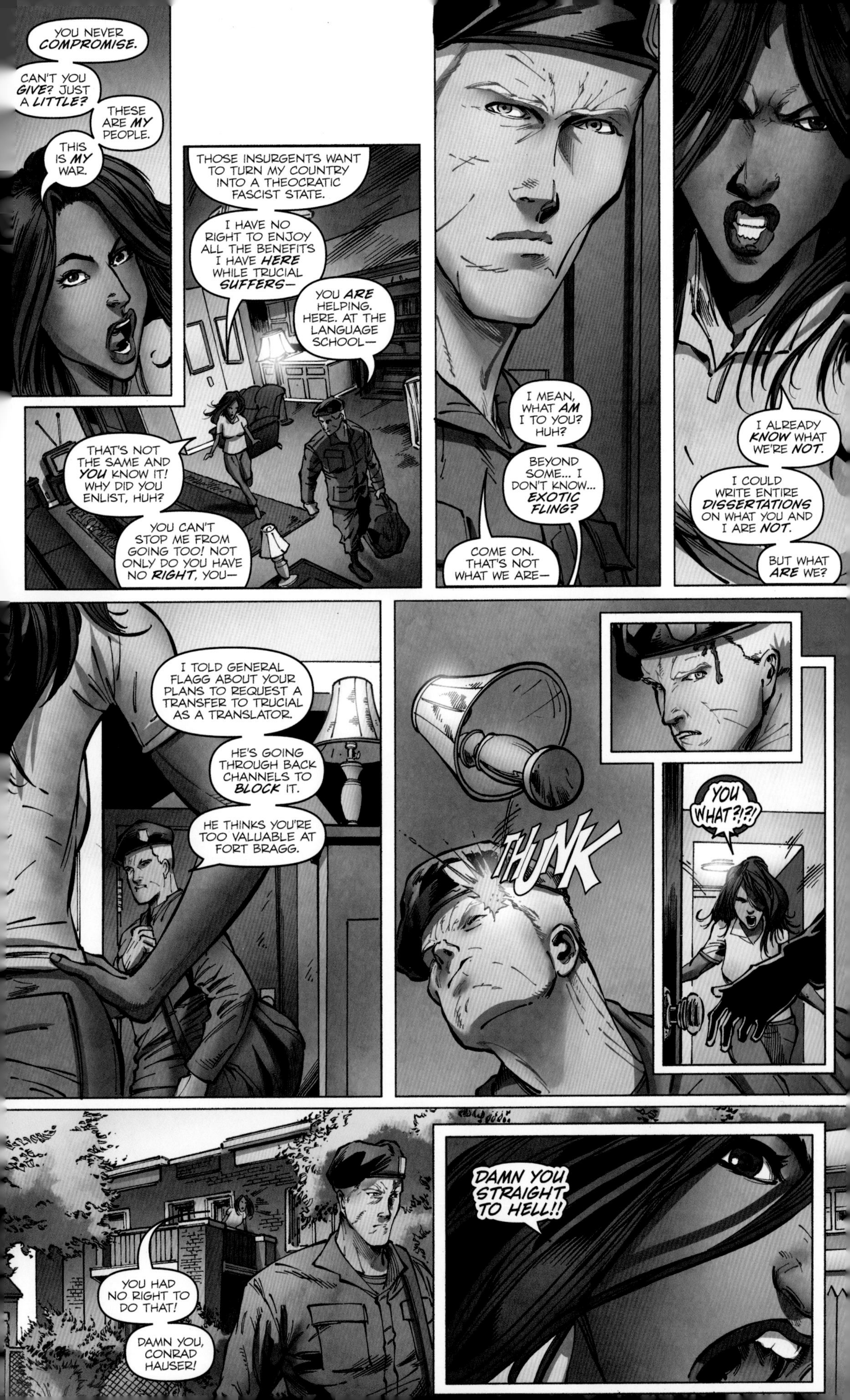
YOU NEVER COMPROMISE.
CAN'T YOU GIVE? JUST A LITTLE?
THESE ARE MY PEOPLE.
THIS IS MY WAR.
THOSE INSURGENTS WANT TO TURN MY COUNTRY INTO A THEOCRATIC FASCIST STATE.
I HAVE NO RIGHT TO ENJOY ALL THE BENEFITS I HAVE HERE WHILE TRUCIAL SUFFERS—
YOU ARE HELPING. HERE. AT THE LANGUAGE SCHOOL—
THAT'S NOT THE SAME AND YOU KNOW IT! WHY DID YOU ENLIST, HUH?
YOU CAN'T STOP ME FROM GOING TOO! NOT ONLY DO YOU HAVE NO RIGHT, YOU—
I MEAN, WHAT AM I TO YOU? HUH?
BEYOND SOME... I DON'T KNOW... EXOTIC FLING?
COME ON. THAT'S NOT WHAT WE ARE—
I ALREADY KNOW WHAT WE'RE NOT.
I COULD WRITE ENTIRE DISSERTATIONS ON WHAT YOU AND I ARE NOT.
BUT WHAT ARE WE?
I TOLD GENERAL FLAGG ABOUT YOUR PLANS TO REQUEST A TRANSFER TO TRUCIAL AS A TRANSLATOR.
HE'S GOING THROUGH BACK CHANNELS TO BLOCK IT.
HE THINKS YOU'RE TOO VALUABLE AT FORT BRAGG.
YOU WHAT?!?!
THUNK
YOU HAD NO RIGHT TO DO THAT!
DAMN YOU, CONRAD HAUSER!
DAMN YOU STRAIGHT TO HELL!!

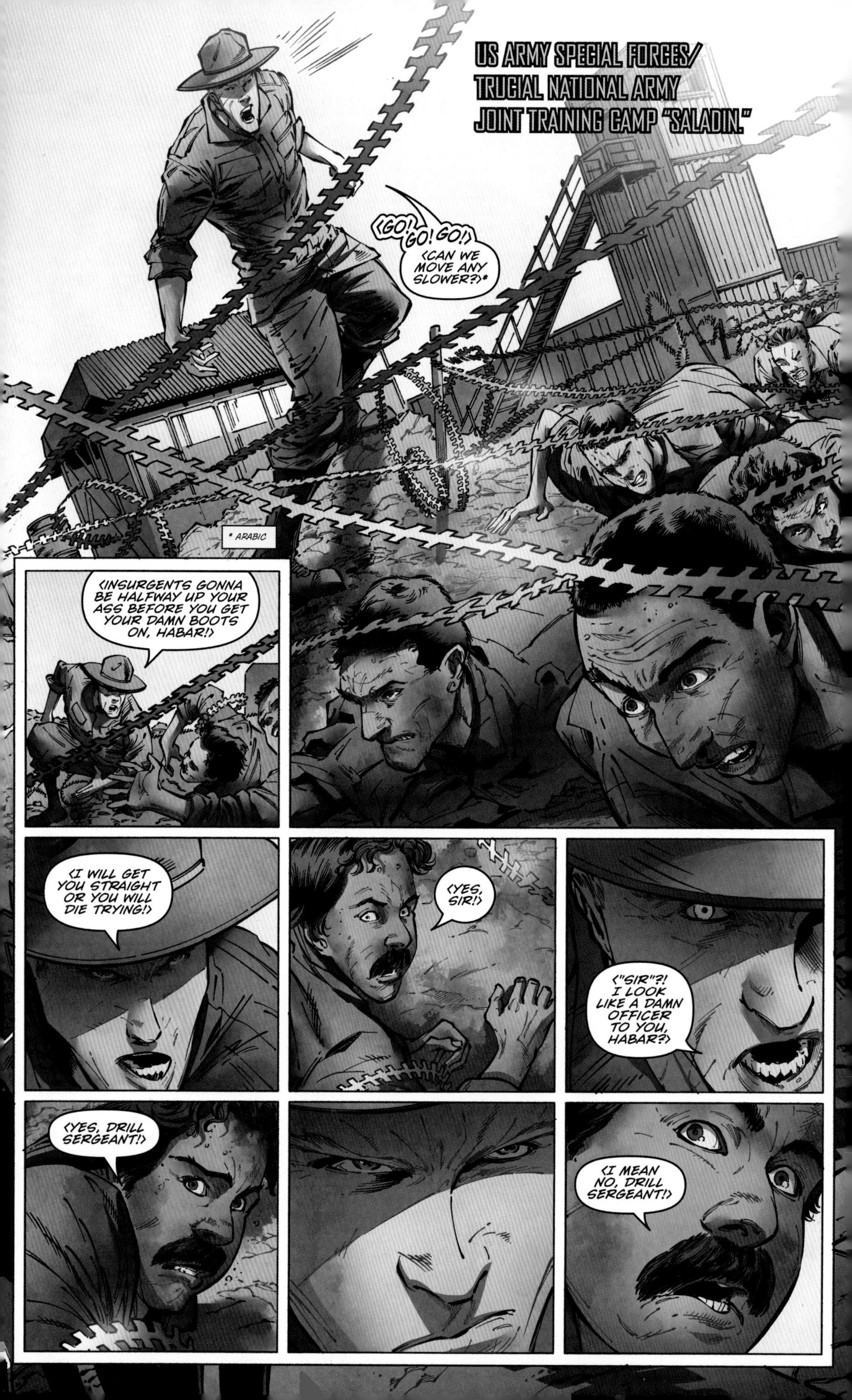
US ARMY SPECIAL FORCES/
TRUCIAL NATIONAL ARMY
JOINT TRAINING CAMP "SALADIN."
<GO! GO! GO!>
<CAN WE MOVE ANY SLOWER?>*
* ARABIC
<INSURGENTS GONNA BE HALFWAY UP YOUR ASS BEFORE YOU GET YOUR DAMN BOOTS ON, HABAR!>
<I WILL GET YOU STRAIGHT OR YOU WILL DIE TRYING!>
<YES, SIR!>
<"SIR"?! I LOOK LIKE A DAMN OFFICER TO YOU, HABAR?>
<YES, DRILL SERGEANT!>
<I MEAN NO, DRILL SERGEANT!>

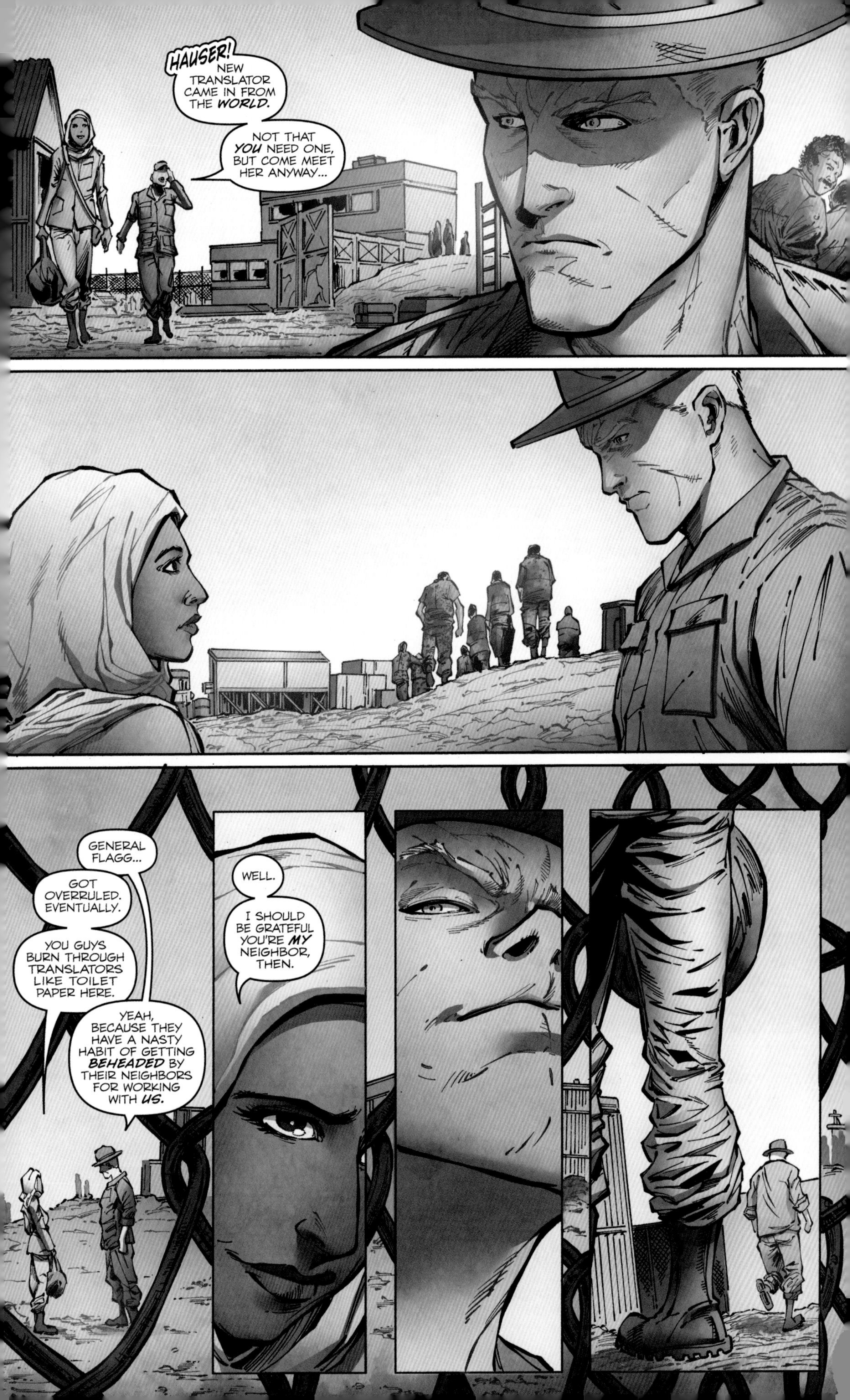
HAUSER! NEW TRANSLATOR CAME IN FROM THE WORLD.
NOT THAT YOU NEED ONE, BUT COME MEET HER ANYWAY...
GENERAL FLAGG...
GOT OVERRULED. EVENTUALLY.
YOU GUYS BURN THROUGH TRANSLATORS LIKE TOILET PAPER HERE.
YEAH, BECAUSE THEY HAVE A NASTY HABIT OF GETTING BEHEADED BY THEIR NEIGHBORS FOR WORKING WITH US.
WELL.
I SHOULD BE GRATEFUL YOU'RE MY NEIGHBOR, THEN.

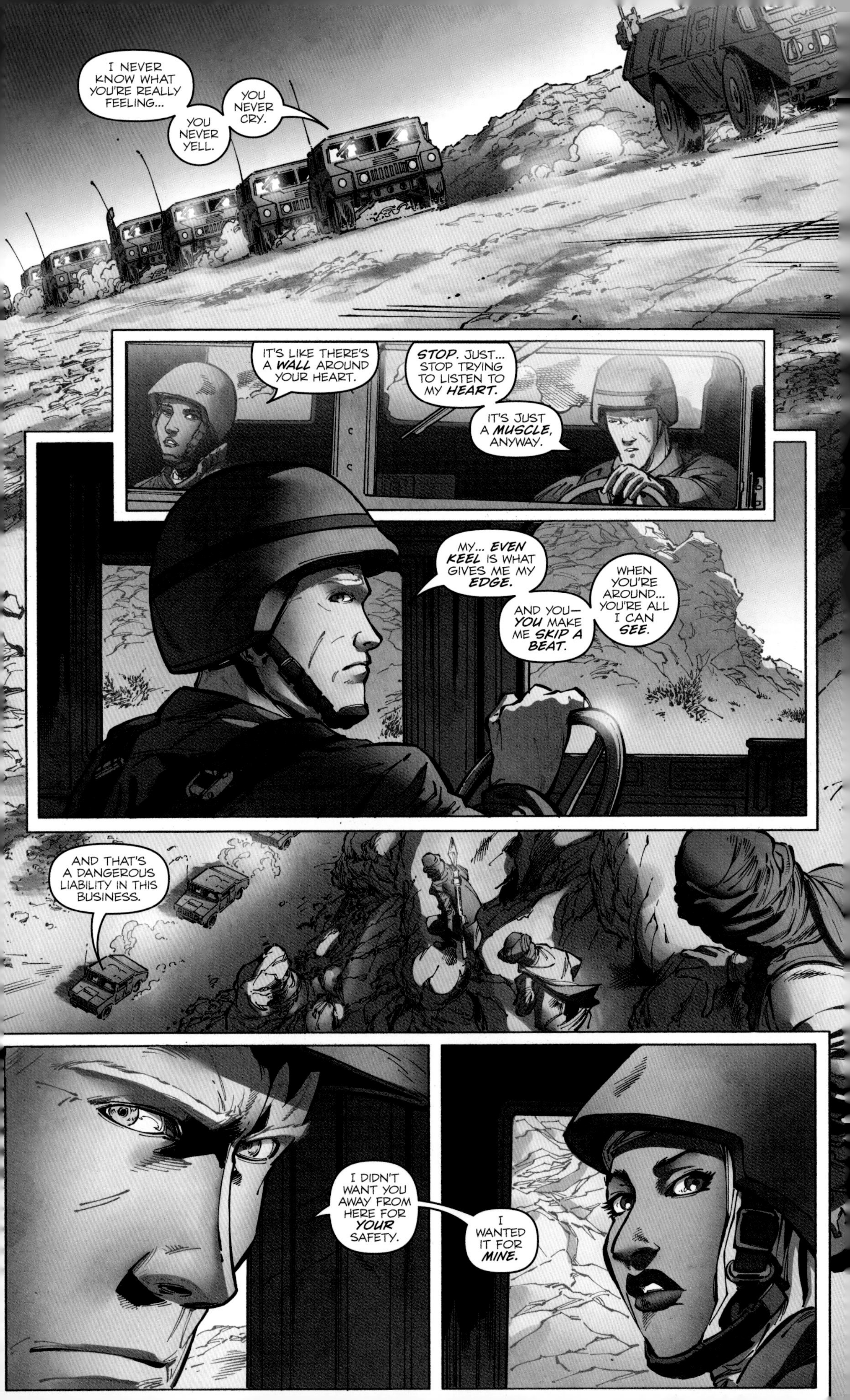
I NEVER KNOW WHAT YOU'RE REALLY FEELING...
YOU NEVER YELL.
YOU NEVER CRY.
IT'S LIKE THERE'S A **WALL** AROUND YOUR HEART.
STOP. JUST... STOP TRYING TO LISTEN TO MY **HEART**.
IT'S JUST A **MUSCLE**, ANYWAY.
MY... **EVEN KEEL** IS WHAT GIVES ME MY **EDGE**.
AND YOU— **YOU** MAKE ME **SKIP A BEAT**.
WHEN YOU'RE AROUND... YOU'RE ALL I CAN **SEE**.
AND THAT'S A DANGEROUS LIABILITY IN THIS BUSINESS.
I DIDN'T WANT YOU AWAY FROM HERE FOR **YOUR** SAFETY.
I WANTED IT FOR **MINE**.

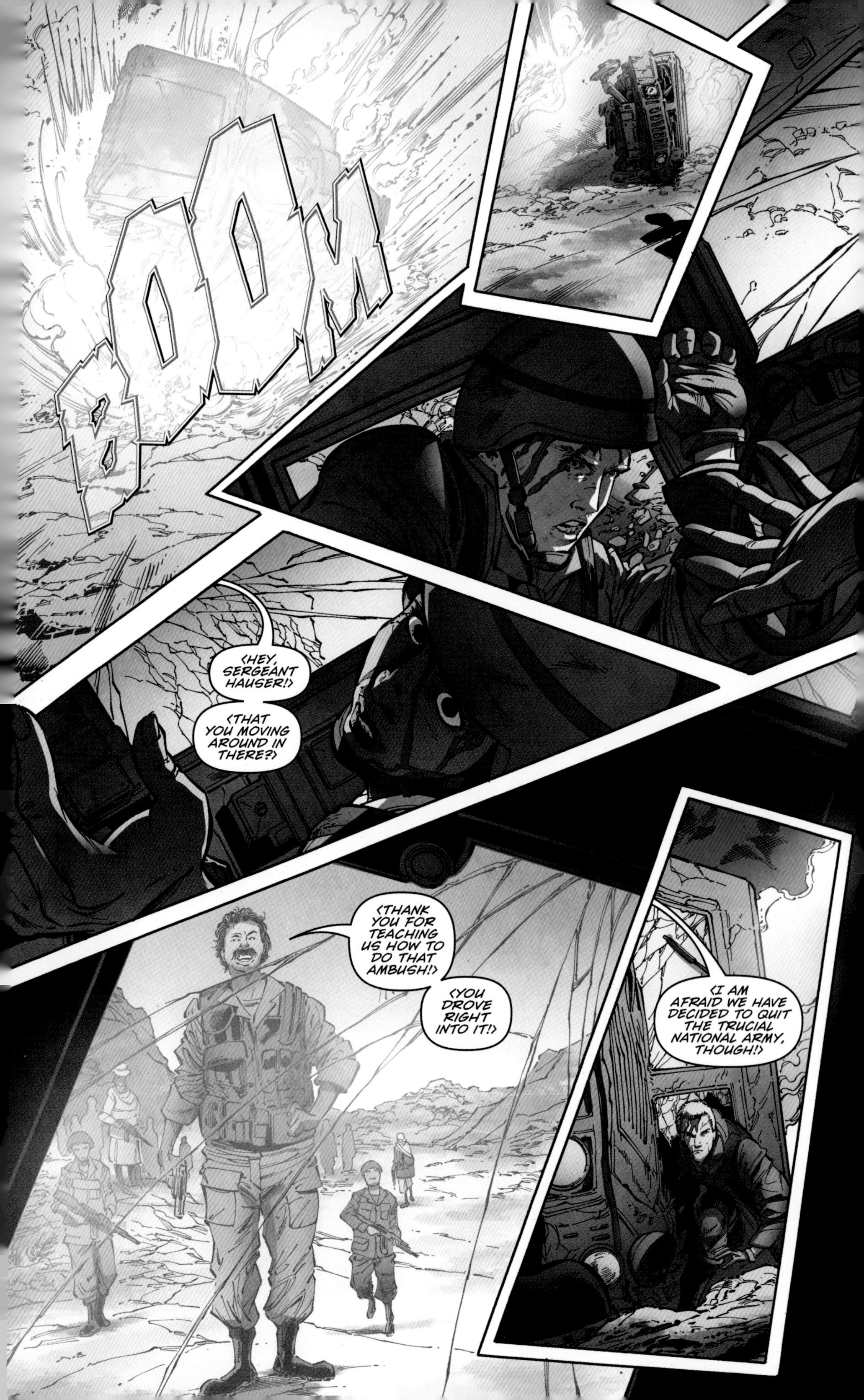
BOOM
<HEY, SERGEANT HAUSER!>
<THAT YOU MOVING AROUND IN THERE?>
<THANK YOU FOR TEACHING US HOW TO DO THAT AMBUSH!>
<YOU DROVE RIGHT INTO IT!>
<I AM AFRAID WE HAVE DECIDED TO QUIT THE TRUCIAL NATIONAL ARMY, THOUGH!>

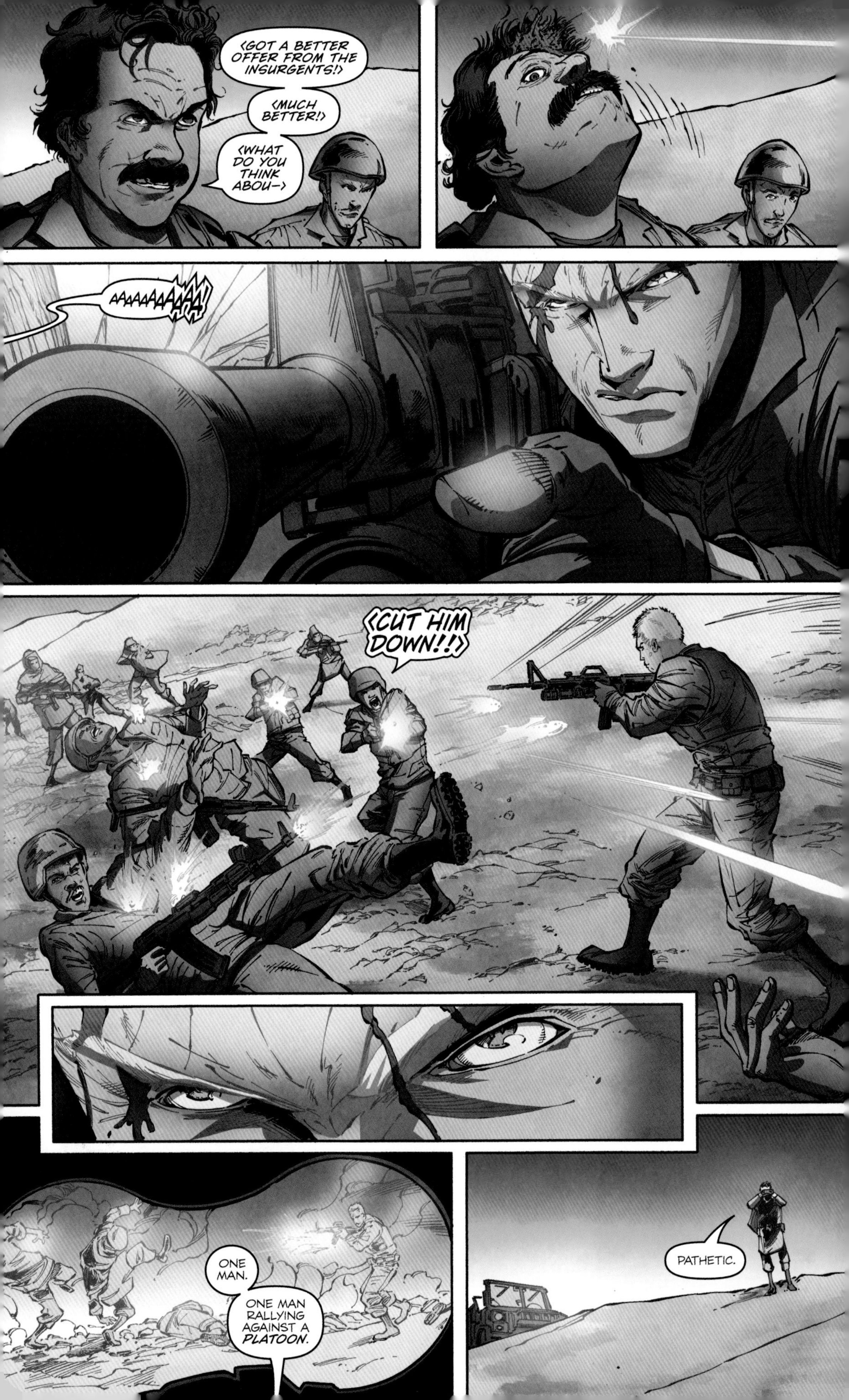

<GOT A BETTER OFFER FROM THE INSURGENTS!>
<MUCH BETTER!>
<WHAT DO YOU THINK ABOU–>
AAAAAAAAAAAA!
<CUT HIM DOWN!!>
ONE MAN.
ONE MAN RALLYING AGAINST A PLATOON.
PATHETIC.

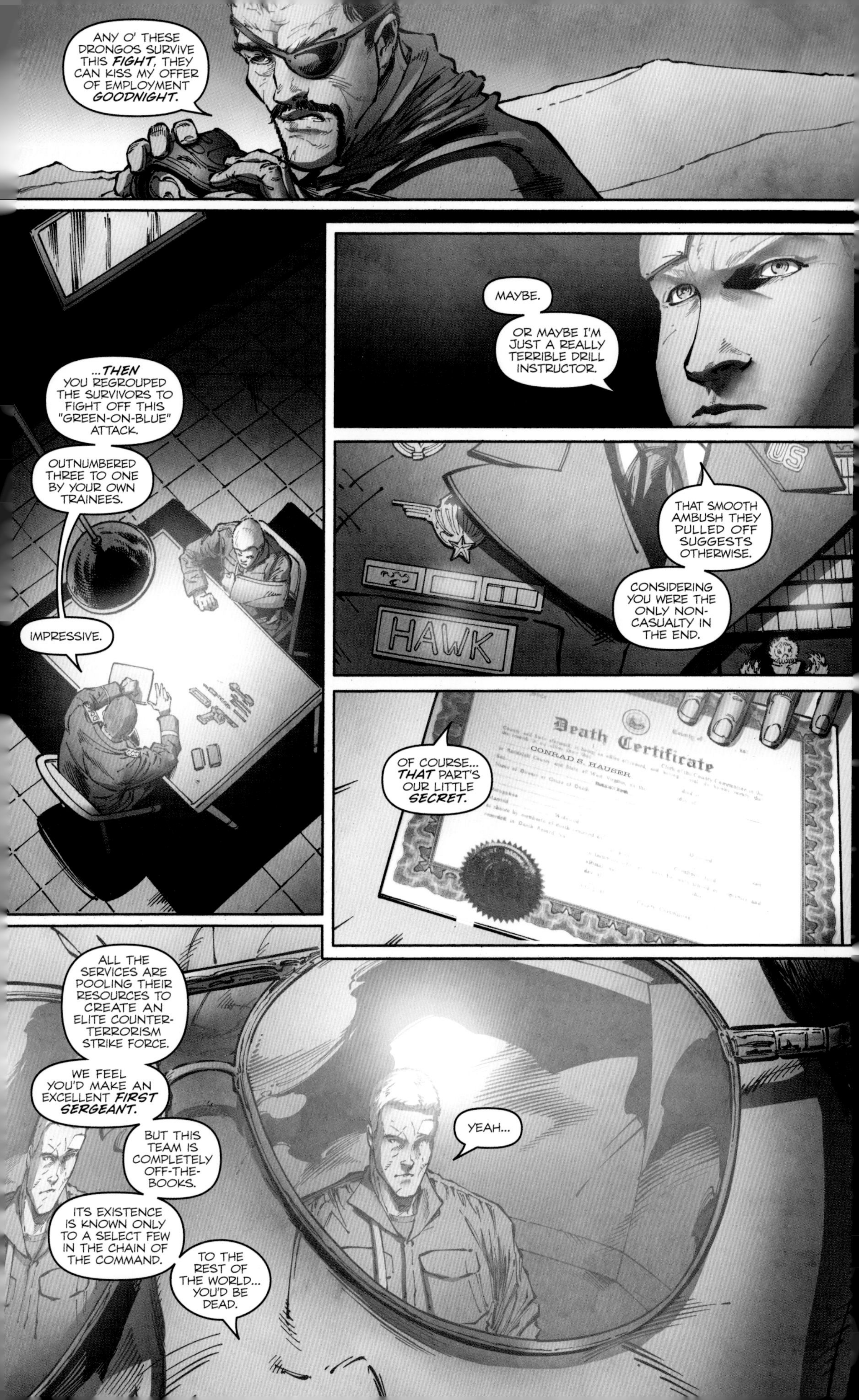
ANY O' THESE DRONGOS SURVIVE THIS FIGHT, THEY CAN KISS MY OFFER OF EMPLOYMENT GOODNIGHT.
...THEN YOU REGROUPED THE SURVIVORS TO FIGHT OFF THIS "GREEN-ON-BLUE" ATTACK.
OUTNUMBERED THREE TO ONE BY YOUR OWN TRAINEES.
IMPRESSIVE.
MAYBE.
OR MAYBE I'M JUST A REALLY TERRIBLE DRILL INSTRUCTOR.
HAWK
THAT SMOOTH AMBUSH THEY PULLED OFF SUGGESTS OTHERWISE.
CONSIDERING YOU WERE THE ONLY NON-CASUALTY IN THE END.
Death Certificate
CONRAD S. HAUSER
OF COURSE... THAT PART'S OUR LITTLE SECRET.
ALL THE SERVICES ARE POOLING THEIR RESOURCES TO CREATE AN ELITE COUNTER-TERRORISM STRIKE FORCE.
WE FEEL YOU'D MAKE AN EXCELLENT FIRST SERGEANT.
YEAH...
BUT THIS TEAM IS COMPLETELY OFF-THE-BOOKS.
ITS EXISTENCE IS KNOWN ONLY TO A SELECT FEW IN THE CHAIN OF THE COMMAND.
TO THE REST OF THE WORLD... YOU'D BE DEAD.

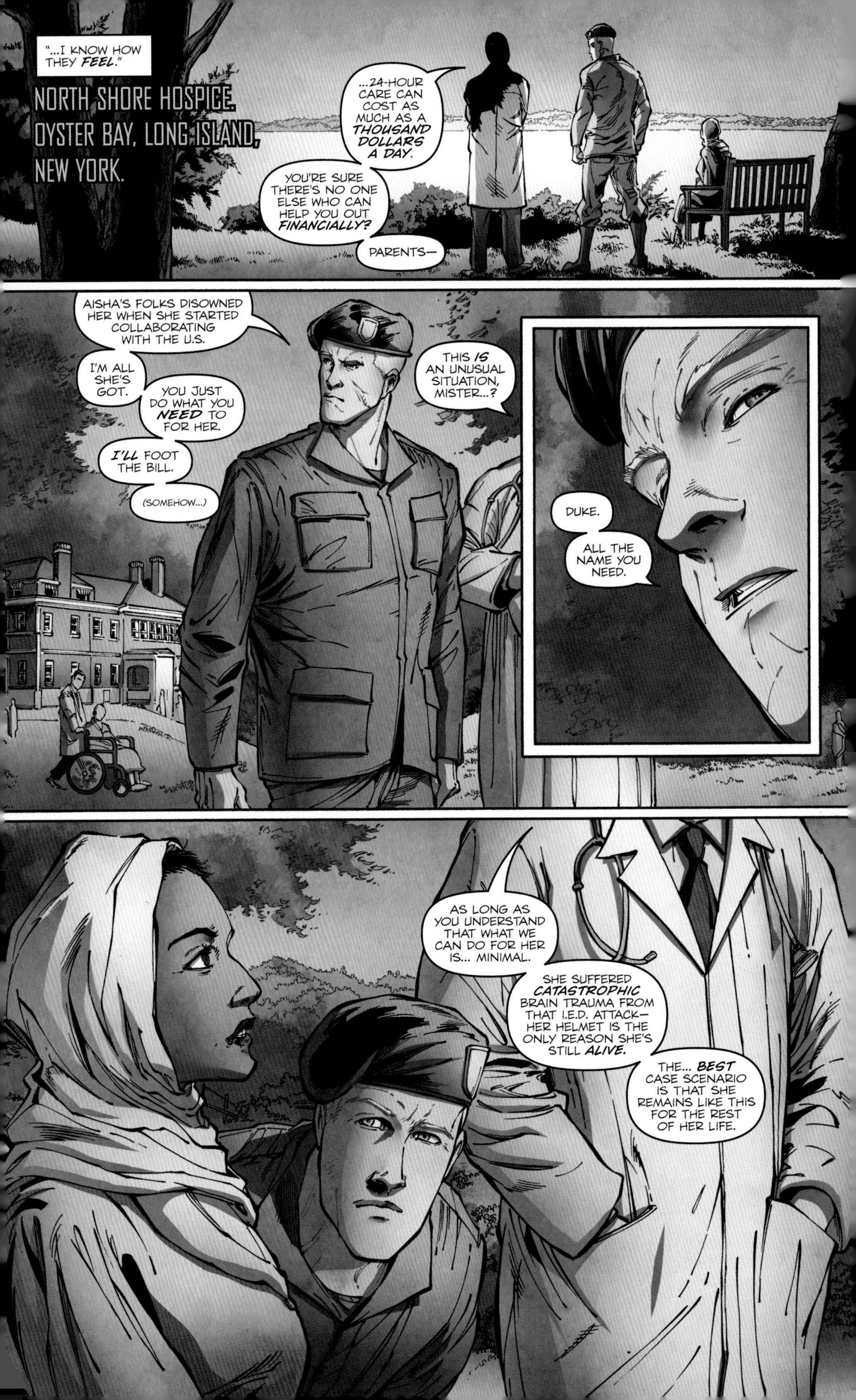
"...I KNOW HOW THEY FEEL."
NORTH SHORE HOSPICE. OYSTER BAY, LONG ISLAND, NEW YORK.
...24-HOUR CARE CAN COST AS MUCH AS A THOUSAND DOLLARS A DAY.
YOU'RE SURE THERE'S NO ONE ELSE WHO CAN HELP YOU OUT FINANCIALLY?
PARENTS—
AISHA'S FOLKS DISOWNED HER WHEN SHE STARTED COLLABORATING WITH THE U.S.
I'M ALL SHE'S GOT.
YOU JUST DO WHAT YOU NEED TO FOR HER.
I'LL FOOT THE BILL.
(SOMEHOW...)
THIS IS AN UNUSUAL SITUATION, MISTER...?
DUKE.
ALL THE NAME YOU NEED.
AS LONG AS YOU UNDERSTAND THAT WHAT WE CAN DO FOR HER IS... MINIMAL.
SHE SUFFERED CATASTROPHIC BRAIN TRAUMA FROM THAT I.E.D. ATTACK—HER HELMET IS THE ONLY REASON SHE'S STILL ALIVE.
THE... BEST CASE SCENARIO IS THAT SHE REMAINS LIKE THIS FOR THE REST OF HER LIFE.

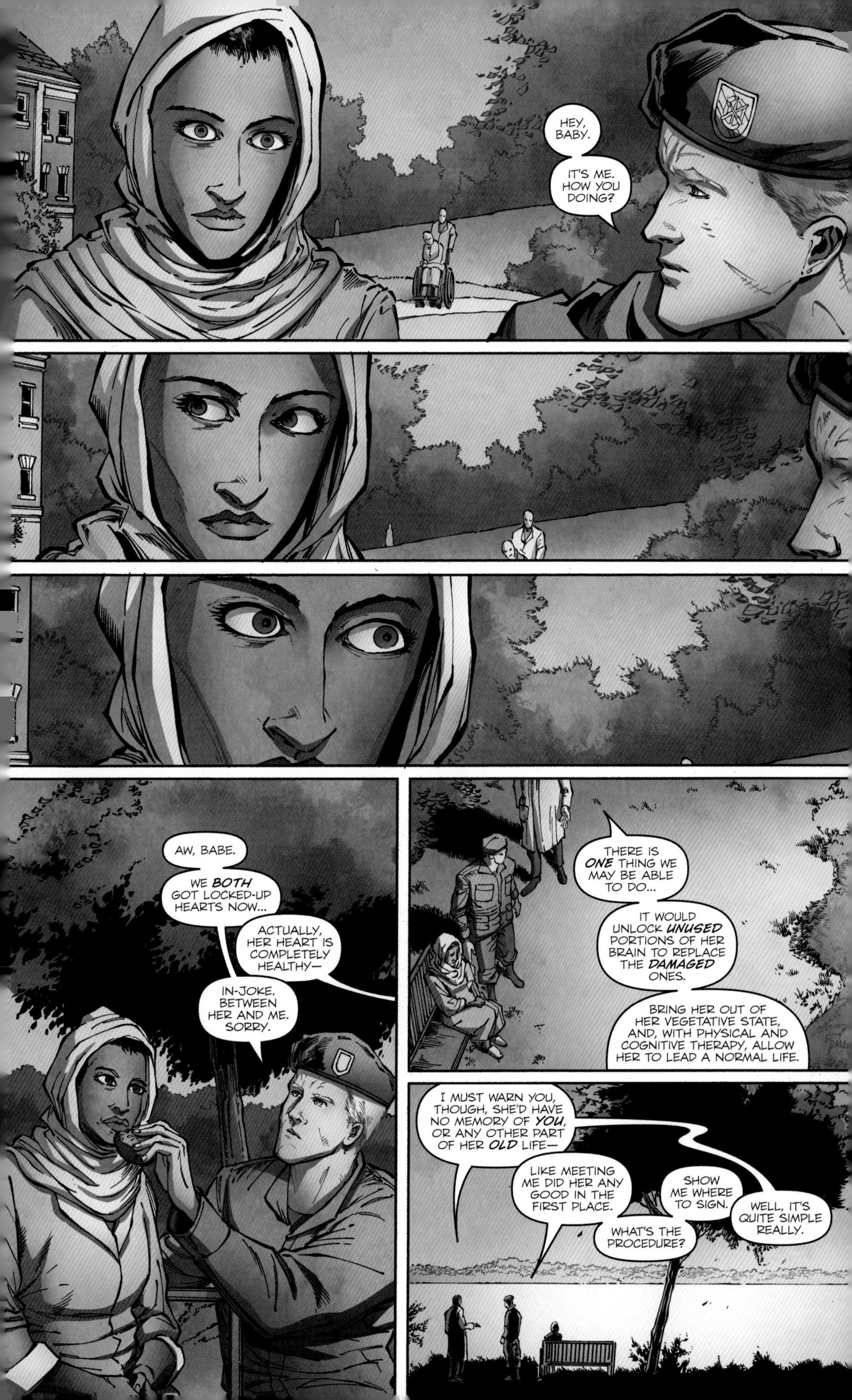

HEY, BABY.
IT'S ME. HOW YOU DOING?
AW, BABE.
WE BOTH GOT LOCKED-UP HEARTS NOW...
ACTUALLY, HER HEART IS COMPLETELY HEALTHY—
IN-JOKE. BETWEEN HER AND ME. SORRY.
THERE IS ONE THING WE MAY BE ABLE TO DO...
IT WOULD UNLOCK UNUSED PORTIONS OF HER BRAIN TO REPLACE THE DAMAGED ONES.
BRING HER OUT OF HER VEGETATIVE STATE, AND, WITH PHYSICAL AND COGNITIVE THERAPY, ALLOW HER TO LEAD A NORMAL LIFE.
I MUST WARN YOU, THOUGH, SHE'D HAVE NO MEMORY OF YOU, OR ANY OTHER PART OF HER OLD LIFE—
LIKE MEETING ME DID HER ANY GOOD IN THE FIRST PLACE.
SHOW ME WHERE TO SIGN.
WHAT'S THE PROCEDURE?
WELL, IT'S QUITE SIMPLE REALLY.

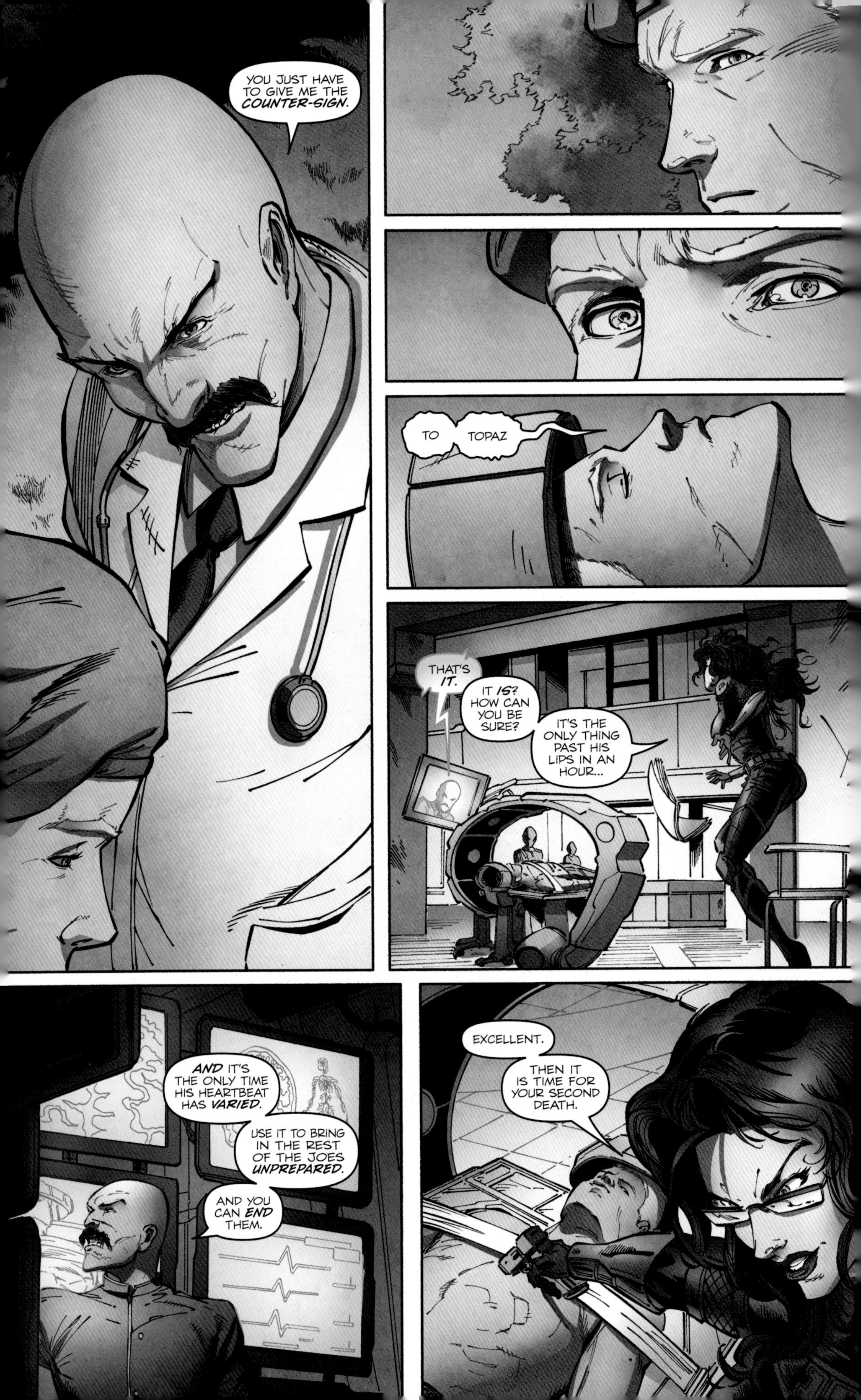
YOU JUST HAVE TO GIVE ME THE COUNTER-SIGN.
TO
TOPAZ
THAT'S IT.
IT IS? HOW CAN YOU BE SURE?
IT'S THE ONLY THING PAST HIS LIPS IN AN HOUR...
AND IT'S THE ONLY TIME HIS HEARTBEAT HAS VARIED.
USE IT TO BRING IN THE REST OF THE JOES UNPREPARED.
AND YOU CAN END THEM.
EXCELLENT.
THEN IT IS TIME FOR YOUR SECOND DEATH.

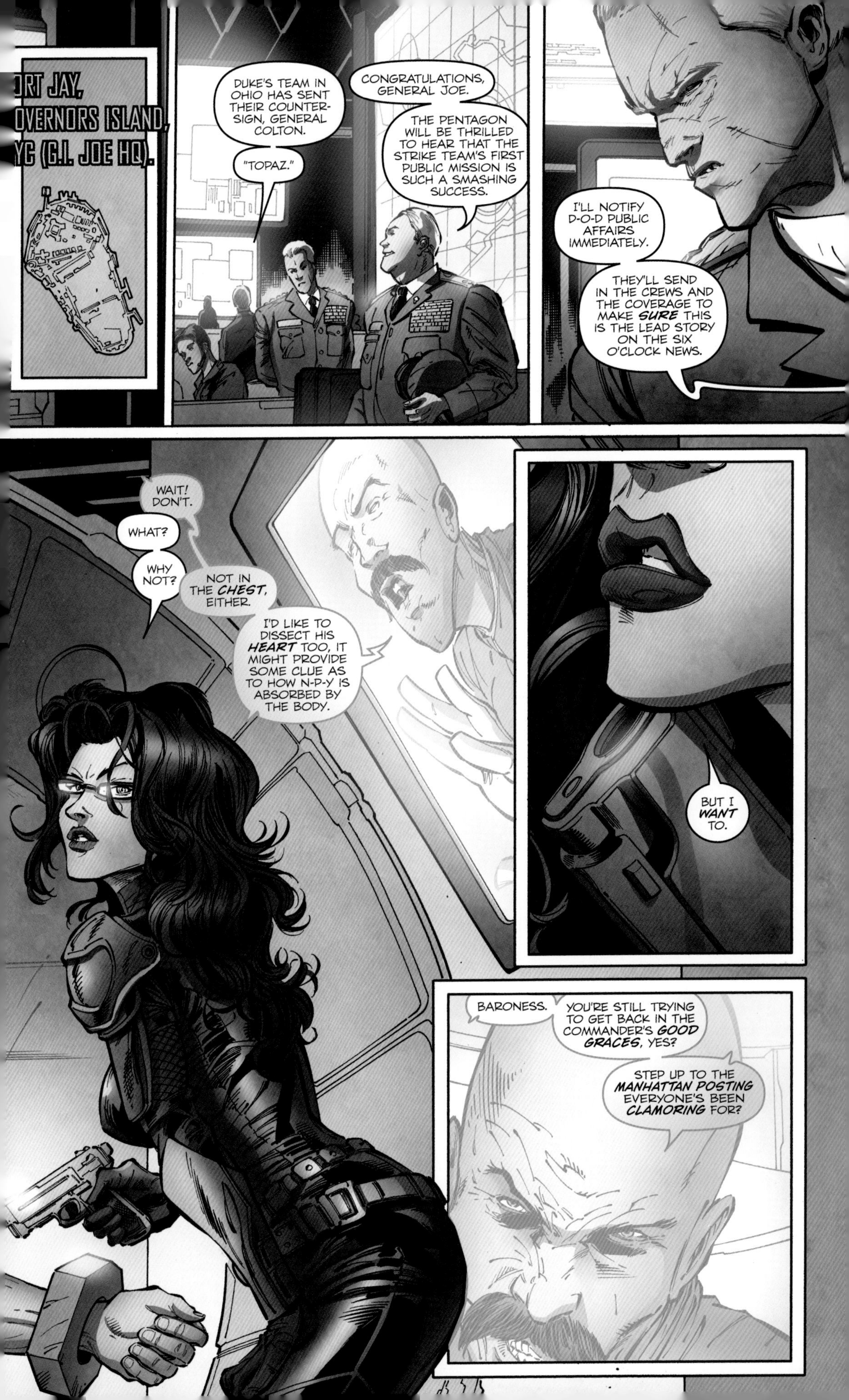

ORT JAY, OVERNORS ISLAND, YC (G.I. JOE HQ).
DUKE'S TEAM IN OHIO HAS SENT THEIR COUNTER-SIGN, GENERAL COLTON.
"TOPAZ."
CONGRATULATIONS, GENERAL JOE.
THE PENTAGON WILL BE THRILLED TO HEAR THAT THE STRIKE TEAM'S FIRST PUBLIC MISSION IS SUCH A SMASHING SUCCESS.
I'LL NOTIFY D-O-D PUBLIC AFFAIRS IMMEDIATELY.
THEY'LL SEND IN THE CREWS AND THE COVERAGE TO MAKE SURE THIS IS THE LEAD STORY ON THE SIX O'CLOCK NEWS.
WAIT! DON'T.
WHAT?
WHY NOT?
NOT IN THE CHEST, EITHER.
I'D LIKE TO DISSECT HIS HEART TOO, IT MIGHT PROVIDE SOME CLUE AS TO HOW N-P-Y IS ABSORBED BY THE BODY.
BUT I WANT TO.
BARONESS.
YOU'RE STILL TRYING TO GET BACK IN THE COMMANDER'S GOOD GRACES, YES?
STEP UP TO THE MANHATTAN POSTING EVERYONE'S BEEN CLAMORING FOR?

THEN DON'T MAKE ME *TELL* HIM YOU RUINED RESEARCH THAT COULD BE *INVALUABLE* TO HIS *CRIMSON GUARDSMEN* PROJECT.

FINE.

I'LL GO GET MY COMBAT KNIFE AND *BLEED* HIM OUT.

SIR... "TOPAZ" ISN'T ON THE LIST OF COUNTER-SIGNS...

I KNOW.

IT'S FROM THE OLD ADVENTURE TEAM LINE.

SOMETHING'S GONE WRONG IN WARRENTON.

GENERAL?

THE STUPID *TOYS.*

I RECORDED ALL OF MY OWN DIALOGUE.

MADE ME NERVOUS AS HELL. HAD TO DO TWENTY TAKES EACH.

TOPAZ ISN'T ALL-CLEAR.

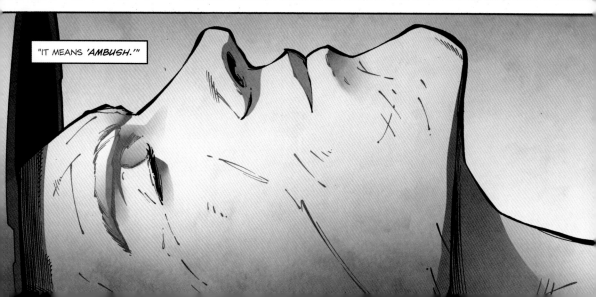

"IT MEANS *'AMBUSH.'*"

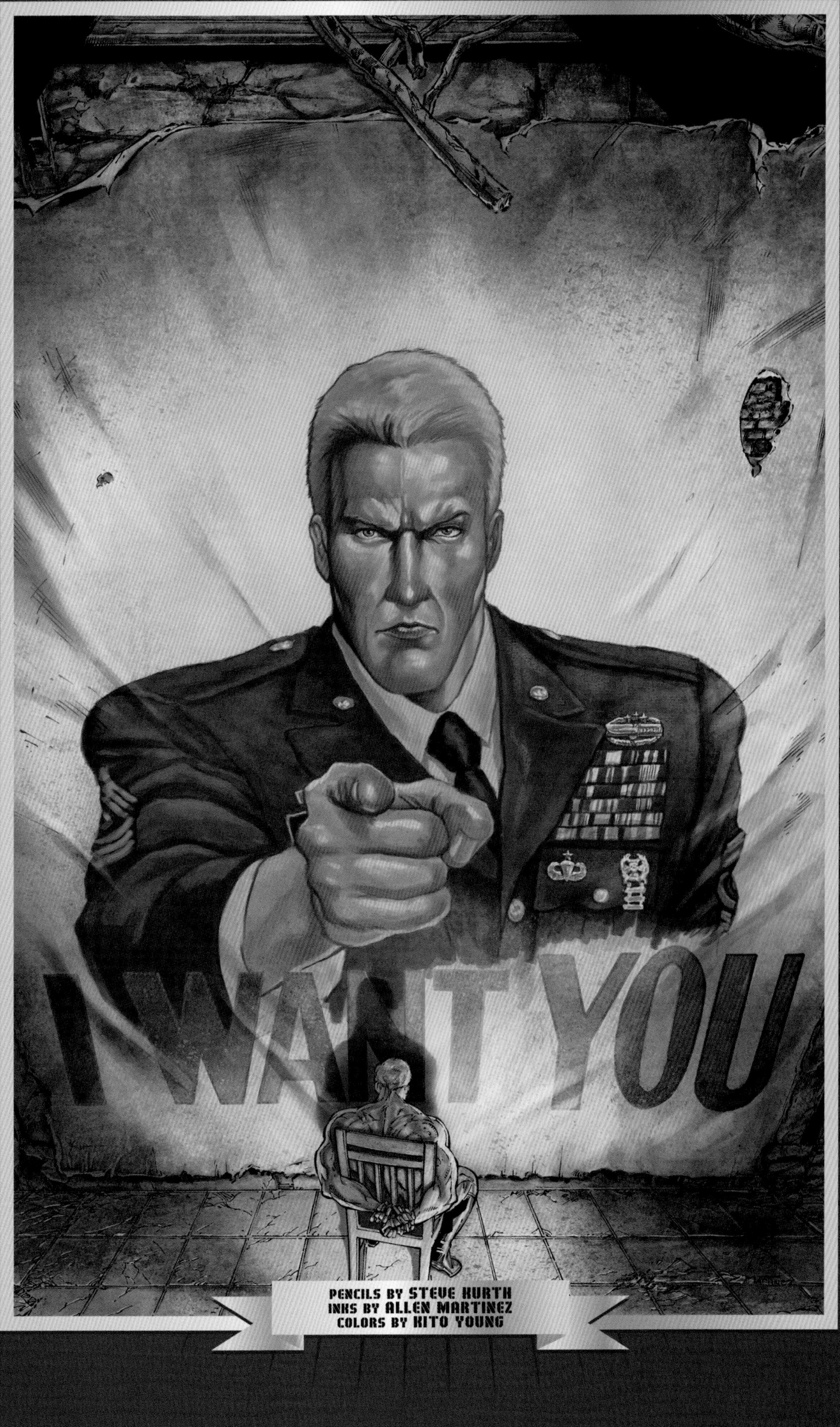
PENCILS BY STEVE KURTH
INKS BY ALLEN MARTINEZ
COLORS BY KITO YOUNG

CHAPTER FOUR

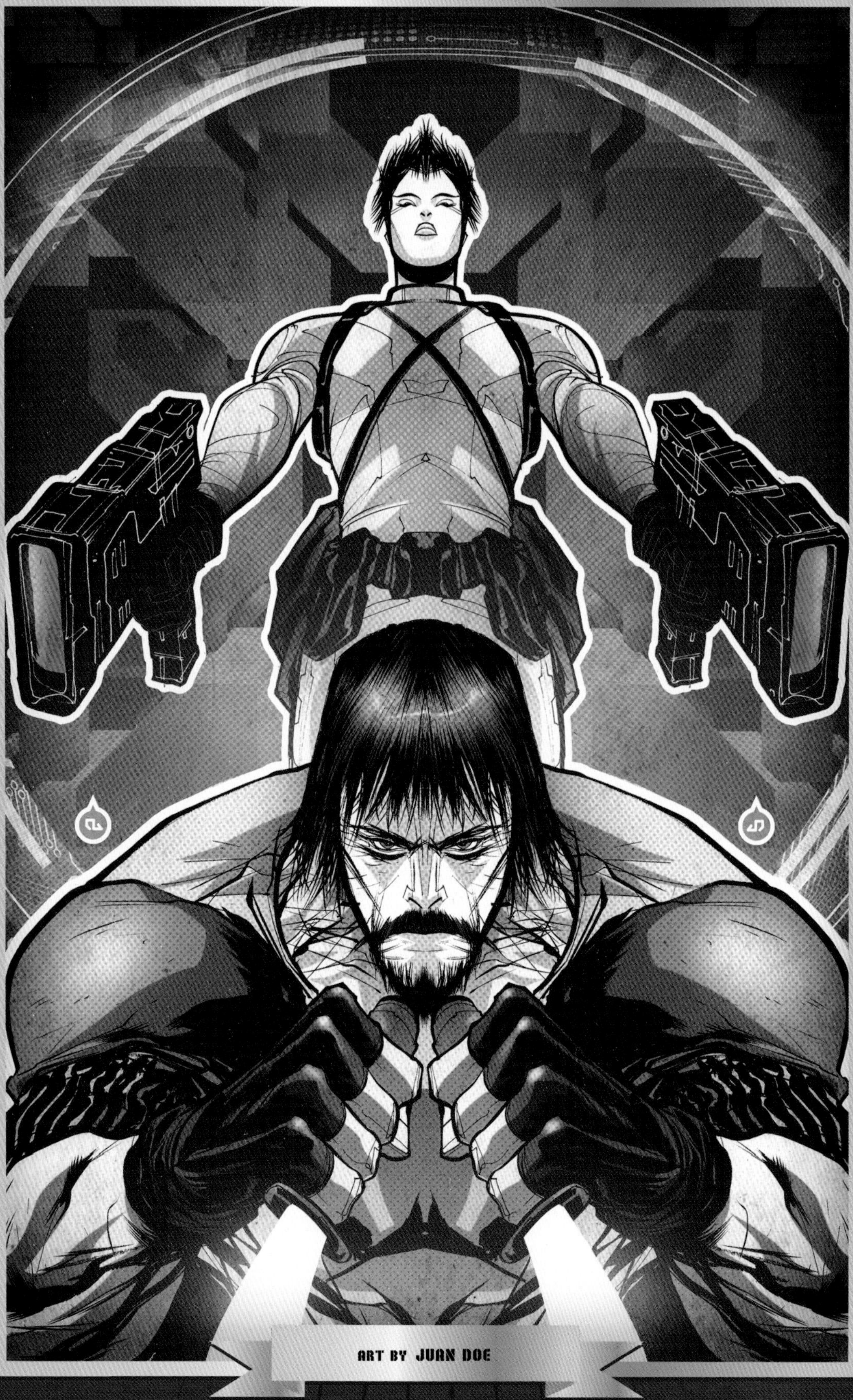
ART BY JUAN DOE

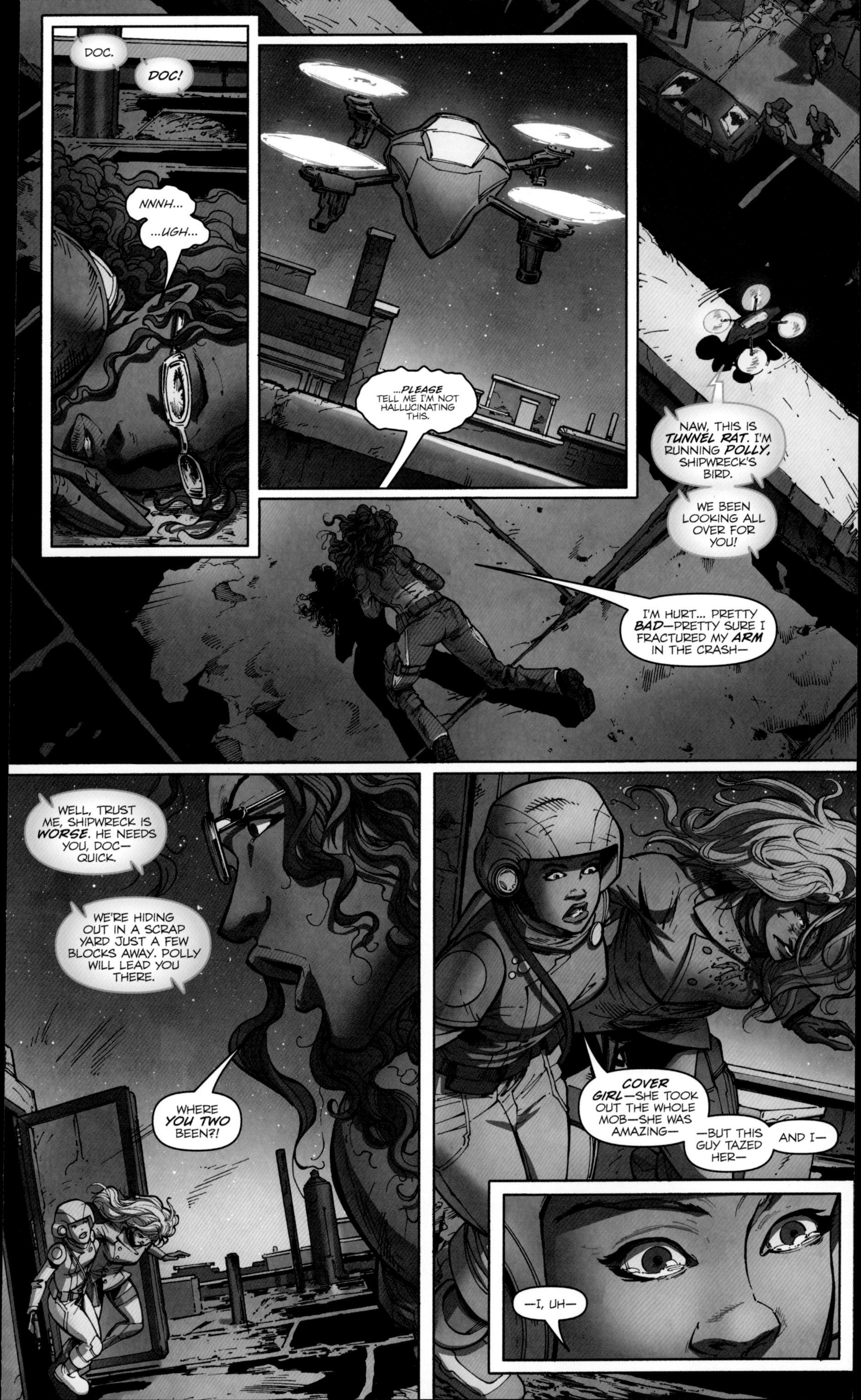
DOC.
DOC!
NNNH...
...UGH...
...PLEASE TELL ME I'M NOT HALLUCINATING THIS.
NAW, THIS IS TUNNEL RAT. I'M RUNNING POLLY, SHIPWRECK'S BIRD.
WE BEEN LOOKING ALL OVER FOR YOU!
I'M HURT... PRETTY BAD—PRETTY SURE I FRACTURED MY ARM IN THE CRASH—
WELL, TRUST ME, SHIPWRECK IS WORSE. HE NEEDS YOU, DOC—QUICK.
WE'RE HIDING OUT IN A SCRAP YARD JUST A FEW BLOCKS AWAY. POLLY WILL LEAD YOU THERE.
WHERE YOU TWO BEEN?!
COVER GIRL—SHE TOOK OUT THE WHOLE MOB—SHE WAS AMAZING—
—BUT THIS GUY TAZED HER—
AND I—
—I, UH—

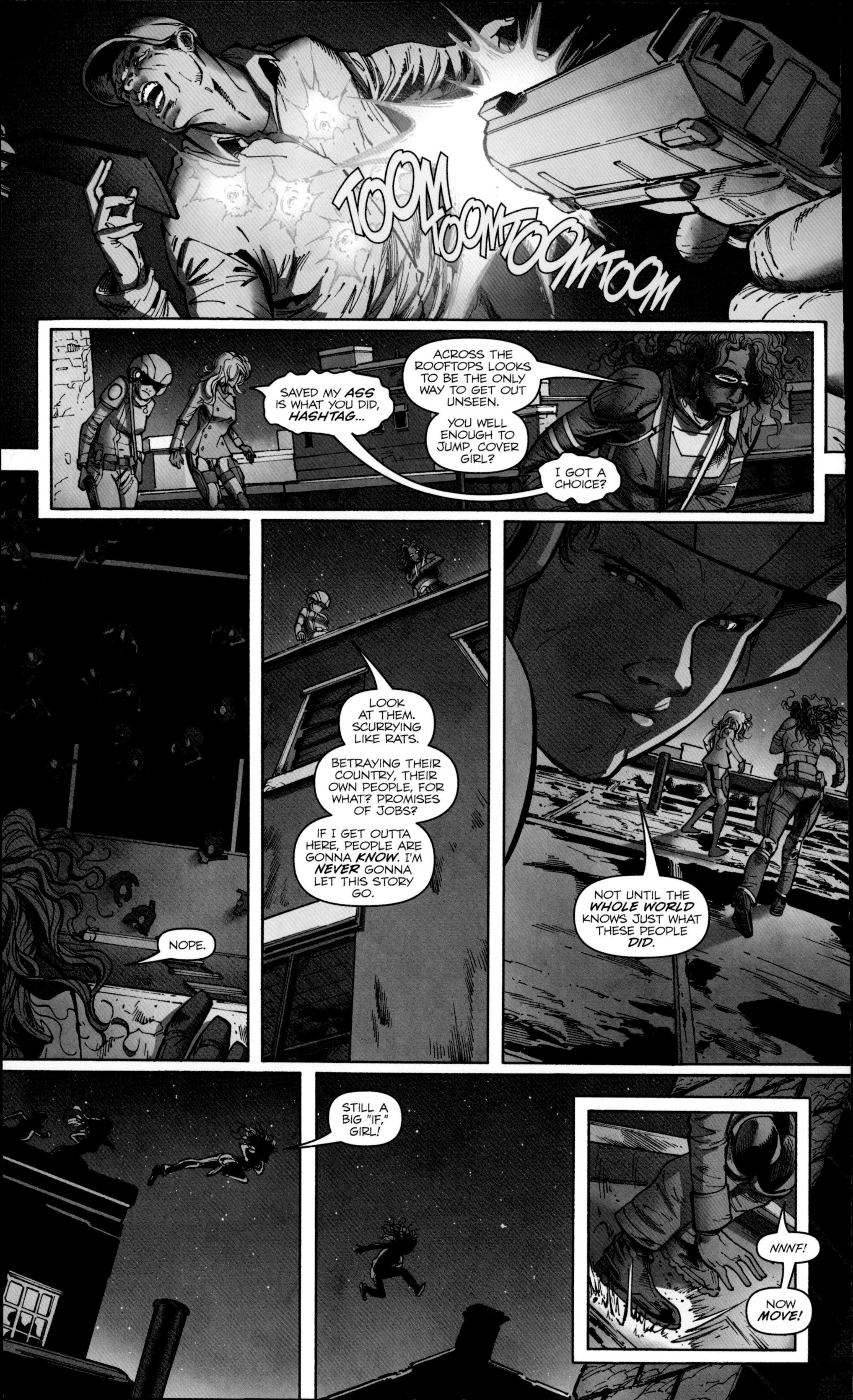
TOOM TOOM TOOM TOOM
ACROSS THE ROOFTOPS LOOKS TO BE THE ONLY WAY TO GET OUT UNSEEN.
YOU WELL ENOUGH TO JUMP, COVER GIRL?
SAVED MY **ASS** IS WHAT YOU DID, ***HASHTAG...***
I GOT A CHOICE?
NOPE.
LOOK AT THEM. SCURRYING LIKE RATS.
BETRAYING THEIR COUNTRY, THEIR OWN PEOPLE, FOR WHAT? PROMISES OF JOBS?
IF I GET OUTTA HERE, PEOPLE ARE GONNA ***KNOW***. I'M ***NEVER*** GONNA LET THIS STORY GO.
NOT UNTIL THE ***WHOLE WORLD*** KNOWS JUST WHAT THESE PEOPLE ***DID***.
STILL A BIG "IF," GIRL!
NNNF!
NOW ***MOVE!***

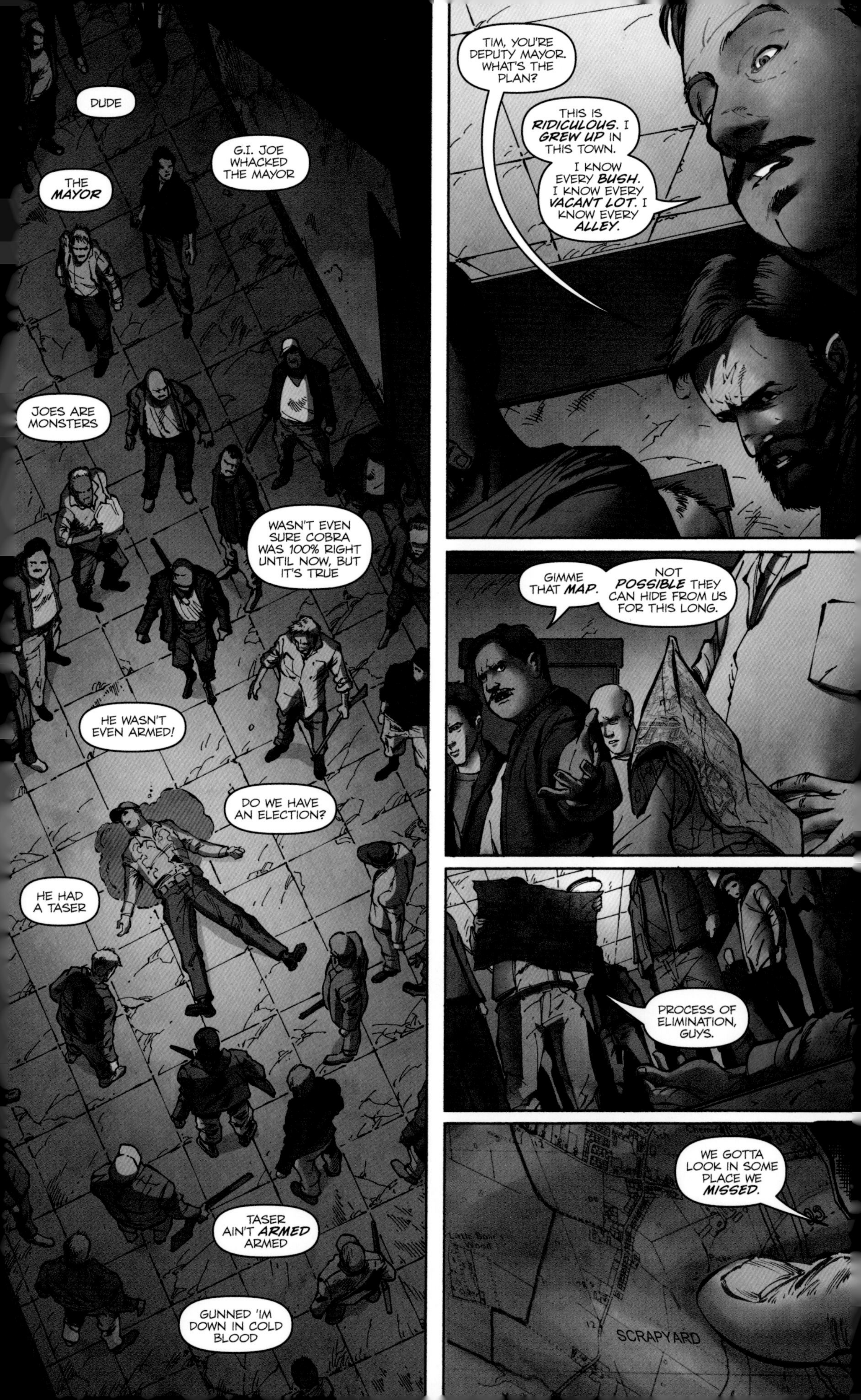
DUDE
THE *MAYOR*
G.I. JOE WHACKED THE MAYOR
JOES ARE MONSTERS
WASN'T EVEN SURE COBRA WAS 100% RIGHT UNTIL NOW, BUT IT'S TRUE
HE WASN'T EVEN ARMED!
DO WE HAVE AN ELECTION?
HE HAD A TASER
TASER AIN'T ***ARMED*** ARMED
GUNNED 'IM DOWN IN COLD BLOOD
TIM, YOU'RE DEPUTY MAYOR. WHAT'S THE PLAN?
THIS IS ***RIDICULOUS***. I ***GREW UP*** IN THIS TOWN.
I KNOW EVERY ***BUSH***. I KNOW EVERY ***VACANT LOT***. I KNOW EVERY ***ALLEY***.
GIMME THAT ***MAP***.
NOT ***POSSIBLE*** THEY CAN HIDE FROM US FOR THIS LONG.
PROCESS OF ELIMINATION, GUYS.
WE GOTTA LOOK IN SOME PLACE WE ***MISSED***.
SCRAPYARD

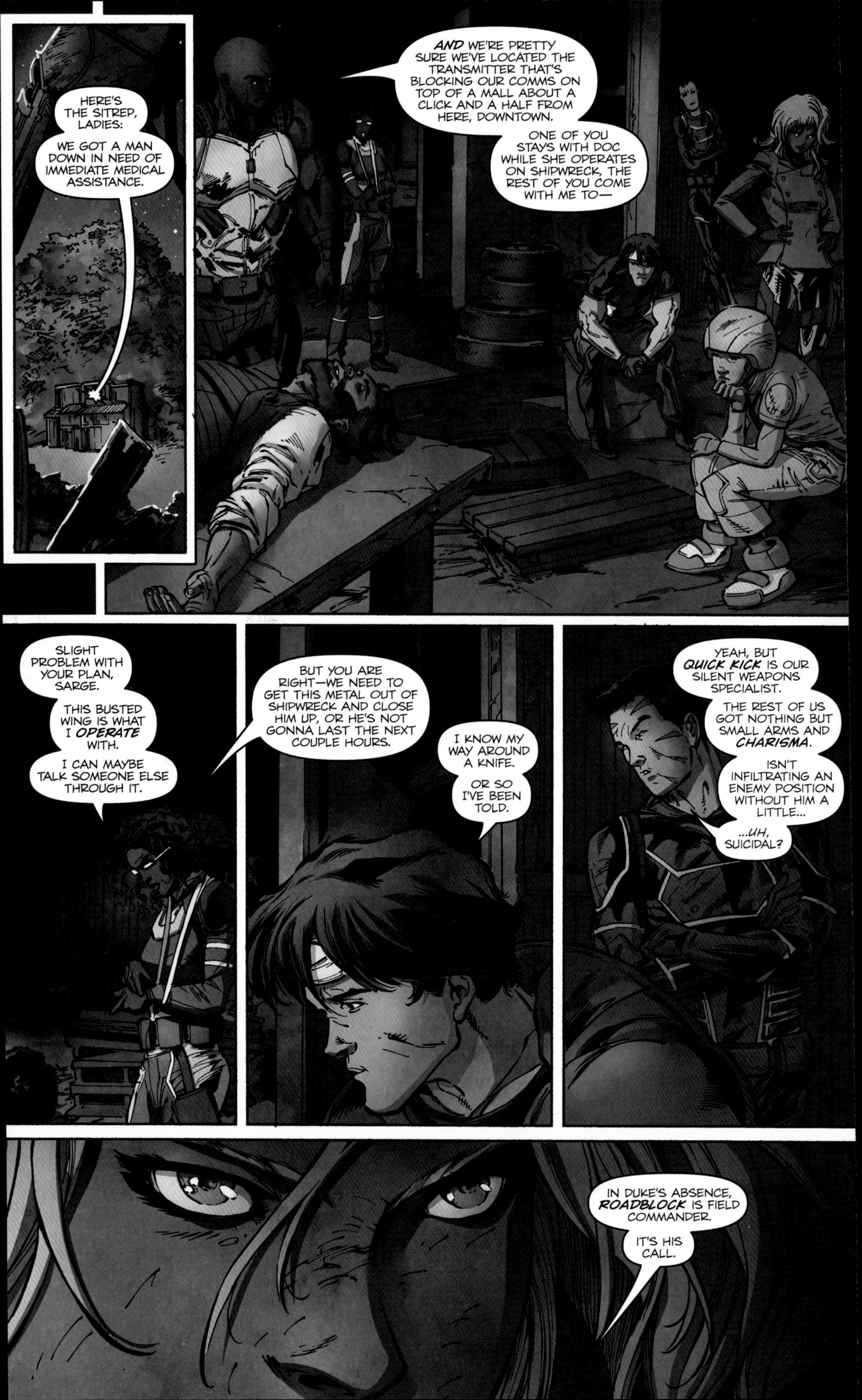
HERE'S THE SITREP, LADIES:
WE GOT A MAN DOWN IN NEED OF IMMEDIATE MEDICAL ASSISTANCE.
AND WE'RE PRETTY SURE WE'VE LOCATED THE TRANSMITTER THAT'S BLOCKING OUR COMMS ON TOP OF A MALL ABOUT A CLICK AND A HALF FROM HERE, DOWNTOWN.
ONE OF YOU STAYS WITH DOC WHILE SHE OPERATES ON SHIPWRECK, THE REST OF YOU COME WITH ME TO—
SLIGHT PROBLEM WITH YOUR PLAN, SARGE.
THIS BUSTED WING IS WHAT I OPERATE WITH.
I CAN MAYBE TALK SOMEONE ELSE THROUGH IT.
BUT YOU ARE RIGHT—WE NEED TO GET THIS METAL OUT OF SHIPWRECK AND CLOSE HIM UP, OR HE'S NOT GONNA LAST THE NEXT COUPLE HOURS.
I KNOW MY WAY AROUND A KNIFE.
OR SO I'VE BEEN TOLD.
YEAH, BUT QUICK KICK IS OUR SILENT WEAPONS SPECIALIST.
THE REST OF US GOT NOTHING BUT SMALL ARMS AND CHARISMA.
ISN'T INFILTRATING AN ENEMY POSITION WITHOUT HIM A LITTLE...
...UH, SUICIDAL?
IN DUKE'S ABSENCE, ROADBLOCK IS FIELD COMMANDER.
IT'S HIS CALL.

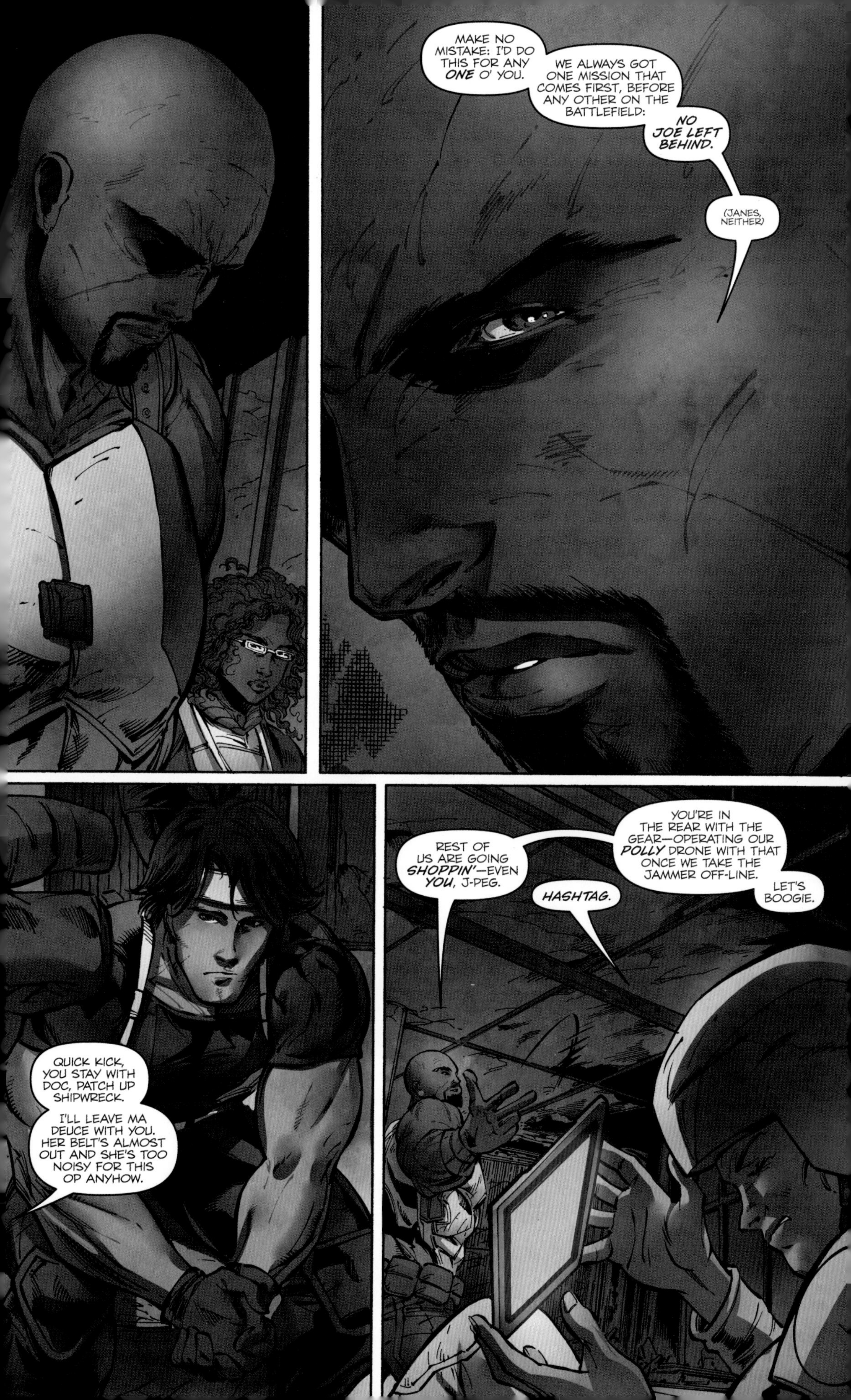
MAKE NO MISTAKE: I'D DO THIS FOR ANY *ONE* O' YOU.
WE ALWAYS GOT ONE MISSION THAT COMES FIRST, BEFORE ANY OTHER ON THE BATTLEFIELD:
NO JOE LEFT BEHIND.
(JANES, NEITHER)
QUICK KICK, YOU STAY WITH DOC, PATCH UP SHIPWRECK.
I'LL LEAVE MA DEUCE WITH YOU. HER BELT'S ALMOST OUT AND SHE'S TOO NOISY FOR THIS OP ANYHOW.
REST OF US ARE GOING ***SHOPPIN'***—EVEN ***YOU***, J-PEG.
YOU'RE IN THE REAR WITH THE GEAR—OPERATING OUR ***POLLY*** DRONE WITH THAT ONCE WE TAKE THE JAMMER OFF-LINE.
HASHTAG.
LET'S BOOGIE.

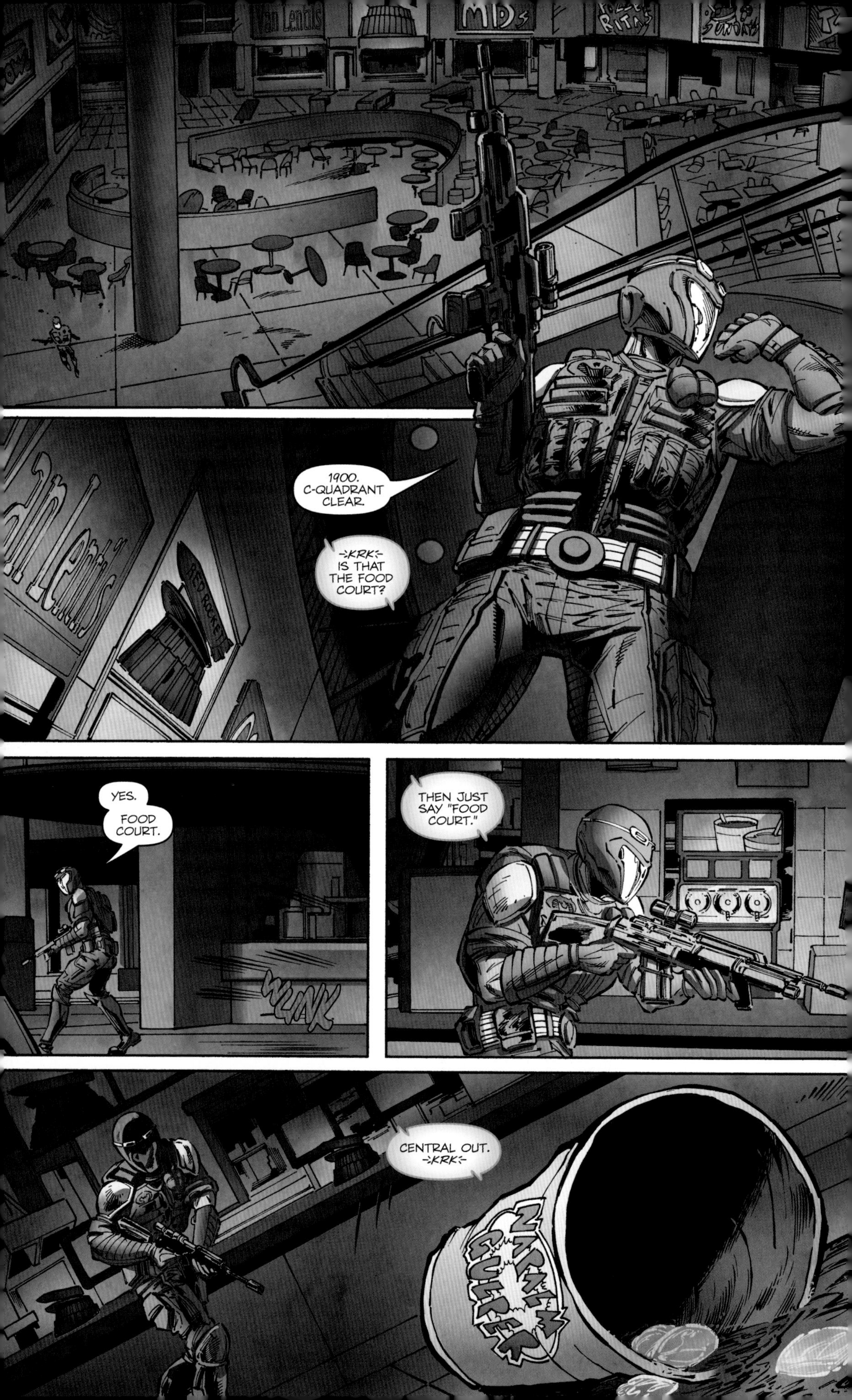
Van Lentils
MDs
Sundays
1900. C-QUADRANT CLEAR.
-KRK- IS THAT THE FOOD COURT?
RED ROCKET
YES. FOOD COURT.
WUNK
THEN JUST SAY "FOOD COURT."
CENTRAL OUT. -KRK-

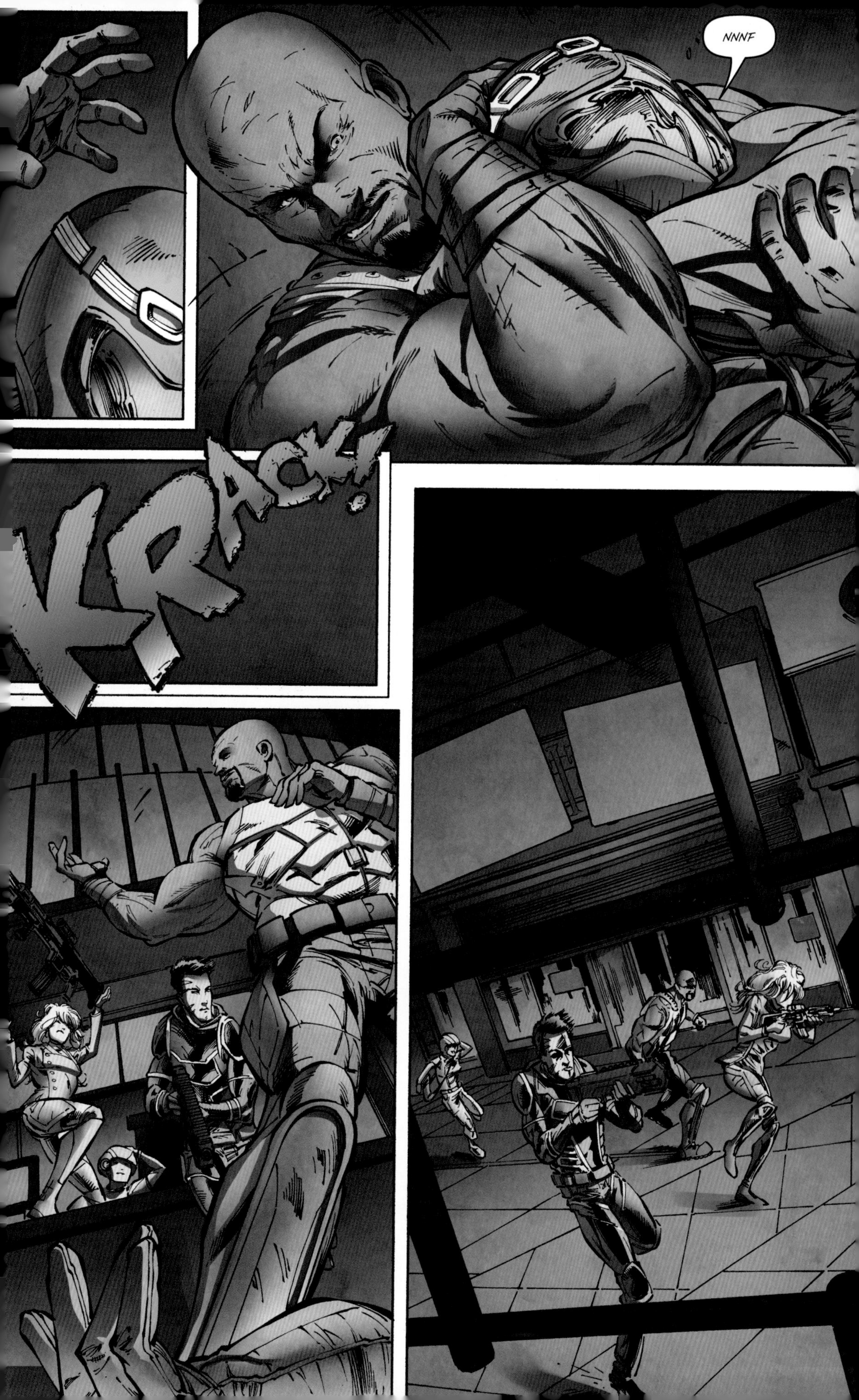
NNNF
KRACK!

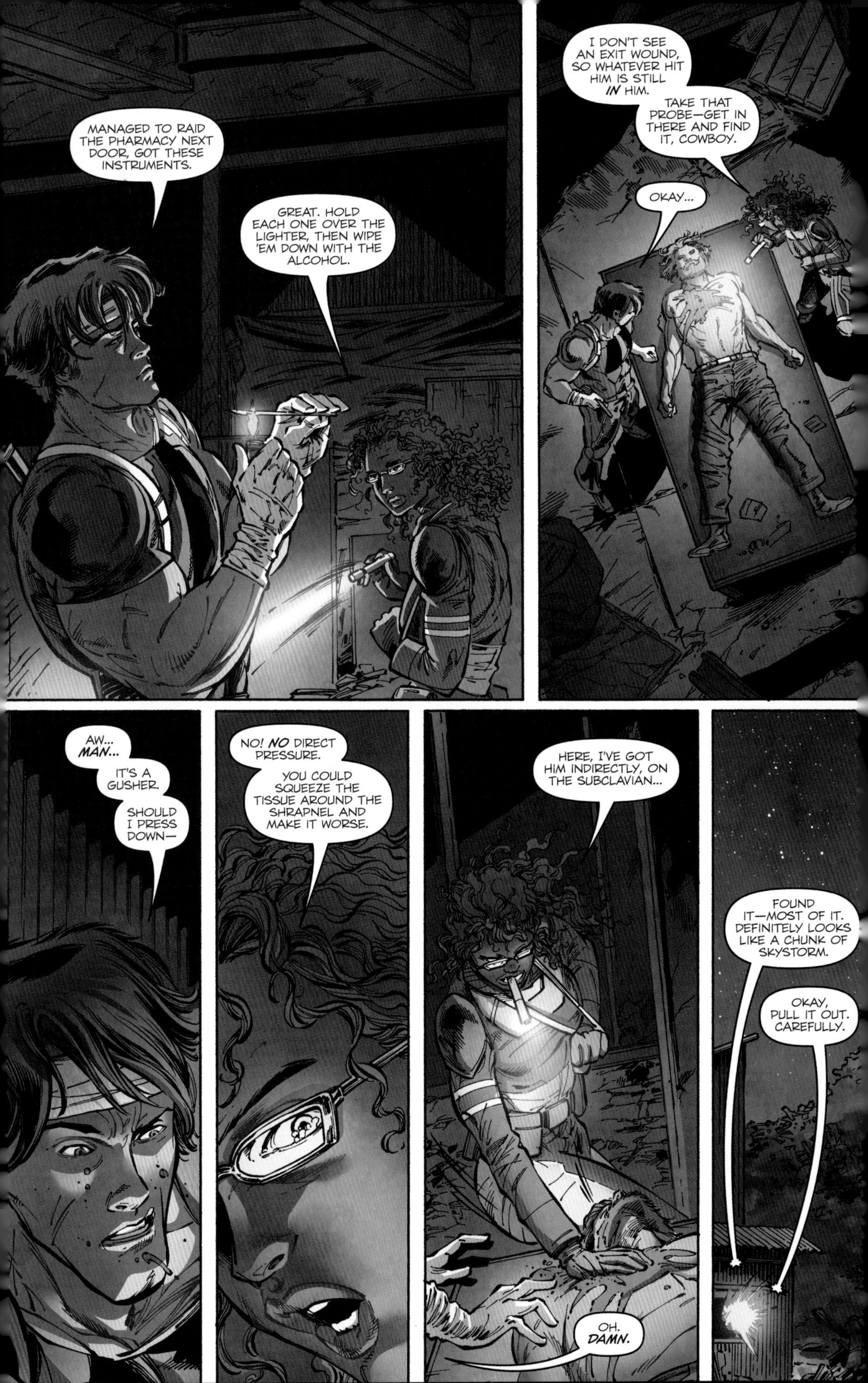
MANAGED TO RAID THE PHARMACY NEXT DOOR, GOT THESE INSTRUMENTS.
GREAT. HOLD EACH ONE OVER THE LIGHTER, THEN WIPE 'EM DOWN WITH THE ALCOHOL.
I DON'T SEE AN EXIT WOUND, SO WHATEVER HIT HIM IS STILL *IN* HIM.
TAKE THAT PROBE—GET IN THERE AND FIND IT, COWBOY.
OKAY...
AW... *MAN*...
IT'S A GUSHER.
SHOULD I PRESS DOWN—
NO! *NO* DIRECT PRESSURE.
YOU COULD SQUEEZE THE TISSUE AROUND THE SHRAPNEL AND MAKE IT WORSE.
HERE, I'VE GOT HIM INDIRECTLY, ON THE SUBCLAVIAN...
OH. *DAMN.*
FOUND IT—MOST OF IT. DEFINITELY LOOKS LIKE A CHUNK OF SKYSTORM.
OKAY, PULL IT OUT. CAREFULLY.

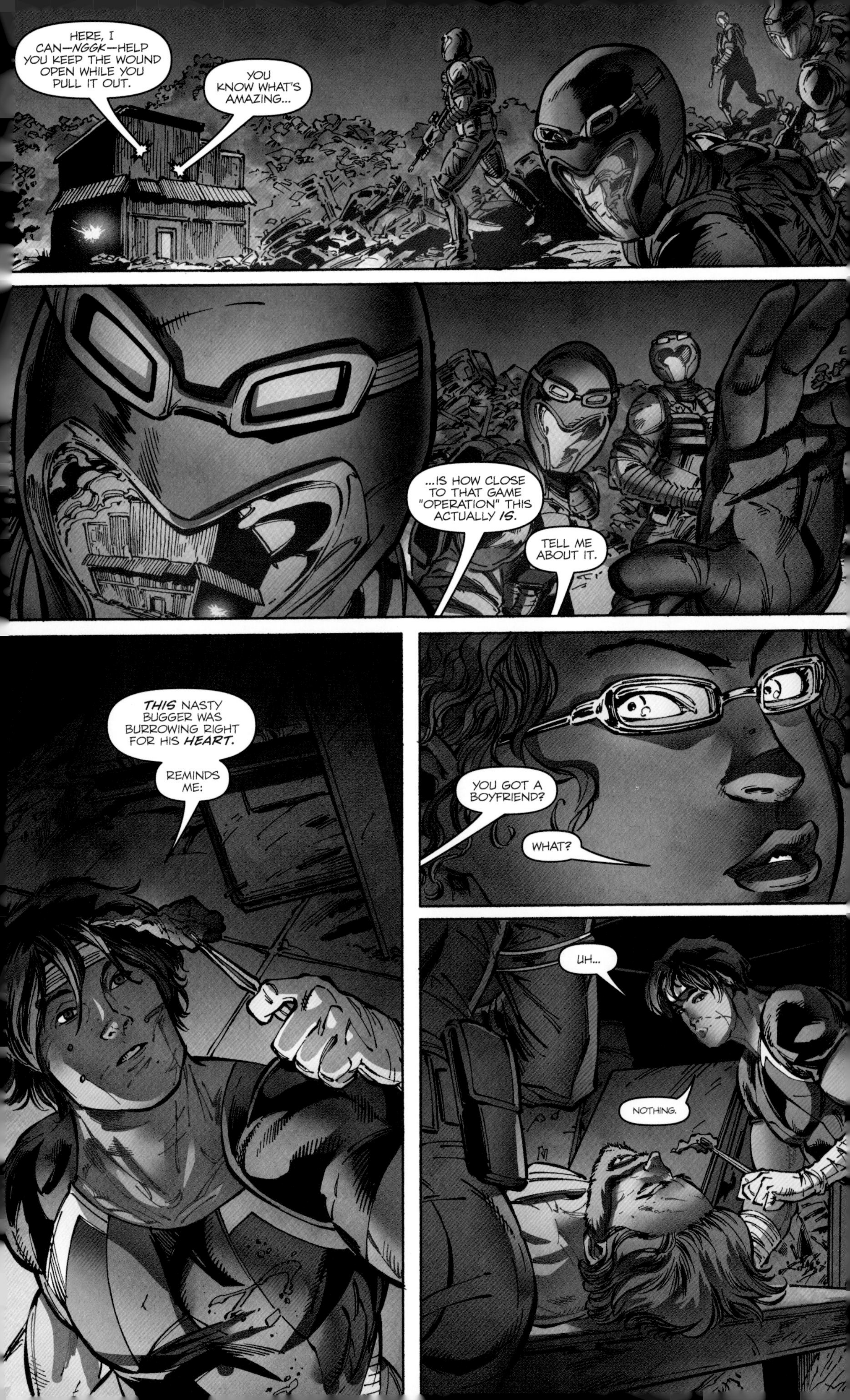

HERE, I CAN—NGGK—HELP YOU KEEP THE WOUND OPEN WHILE YOU PULL IT OUT.
YOU KNOW WHAT'S AMAZING...
...IS HOW CLOSE TO THAT GAME "OPERATION" THIS ACTUALLY IS.
TELL ME ABOUT IT.
THIS NASTY BUGGER WAS BURROWING RIGHT FOR HIS HEART.
REMINDS ME:
YOU GOT A BOYFRIEND?
WHAT?
UH...
NOTHING.

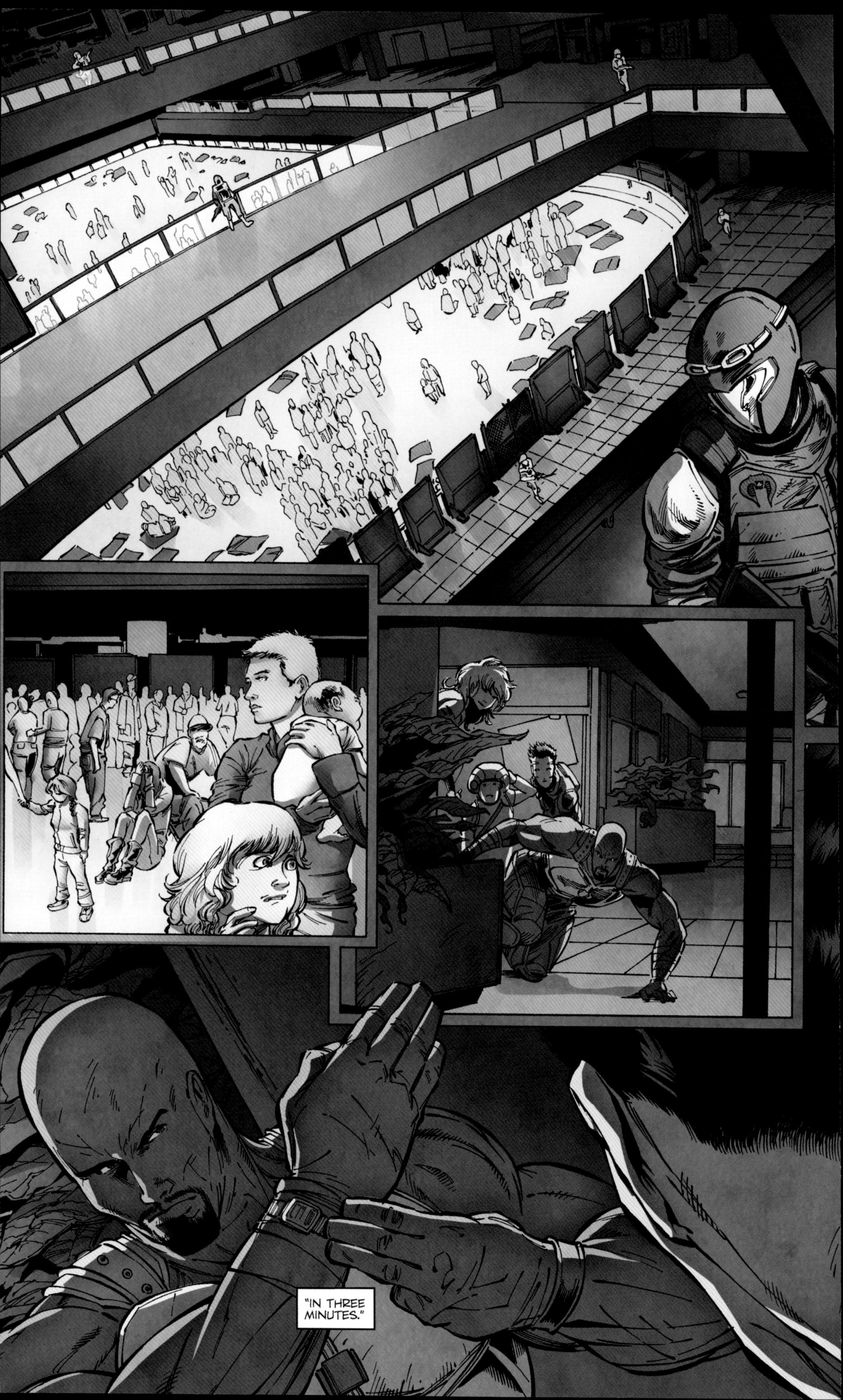
"IN THREE MINUTES."

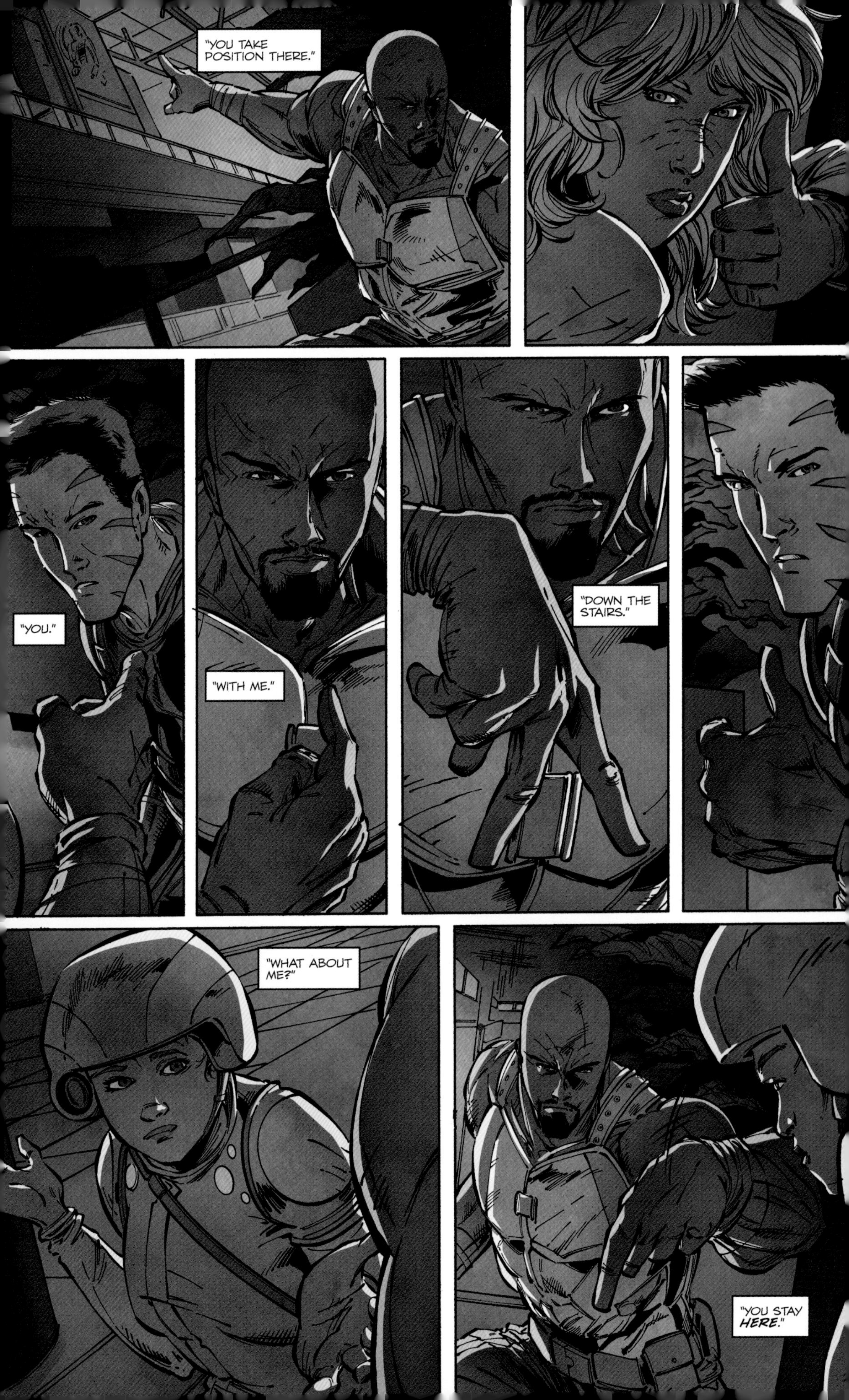
"YOU TAKE POSITION THERE."
"YOU."
"WITH ME."
"DOWN THE STAIRS."
"WHAT ABOUT ME?"
"YOU STAY *HERE*."

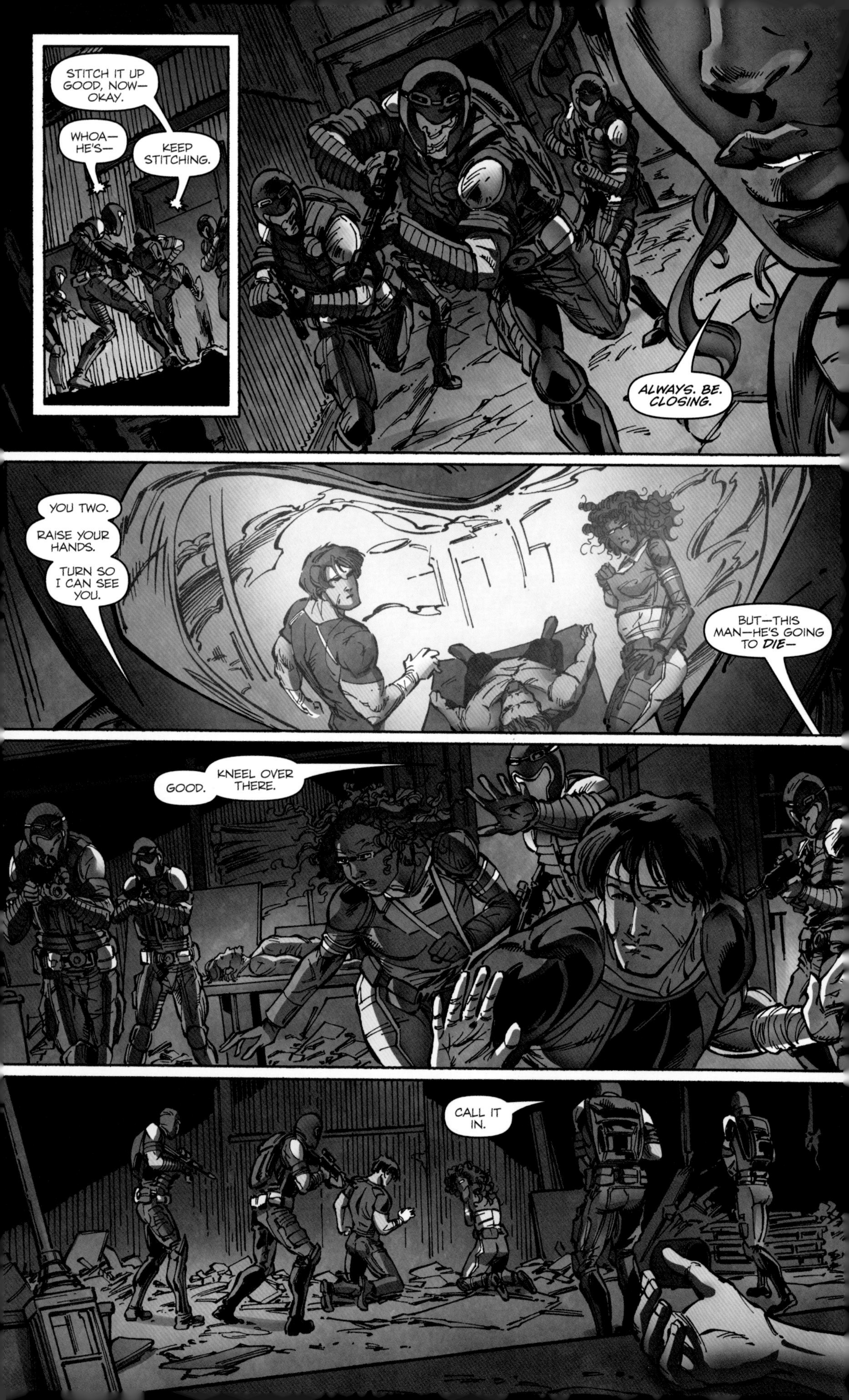
STITCH IT UP GOOD, NOW—OKAY.
WHOA—HE'S—
KEEP STITCHING.
ALWAYS. BE. CLOSING.
YOU TWO.
RAISE YOUR HANDS.
TURN SO I CAN SEE YOU.
BUT—THIS MAN—HE'S GOING TO DIE—
GOOD.
KNEEL OVER THERE.
CALL IT IN.

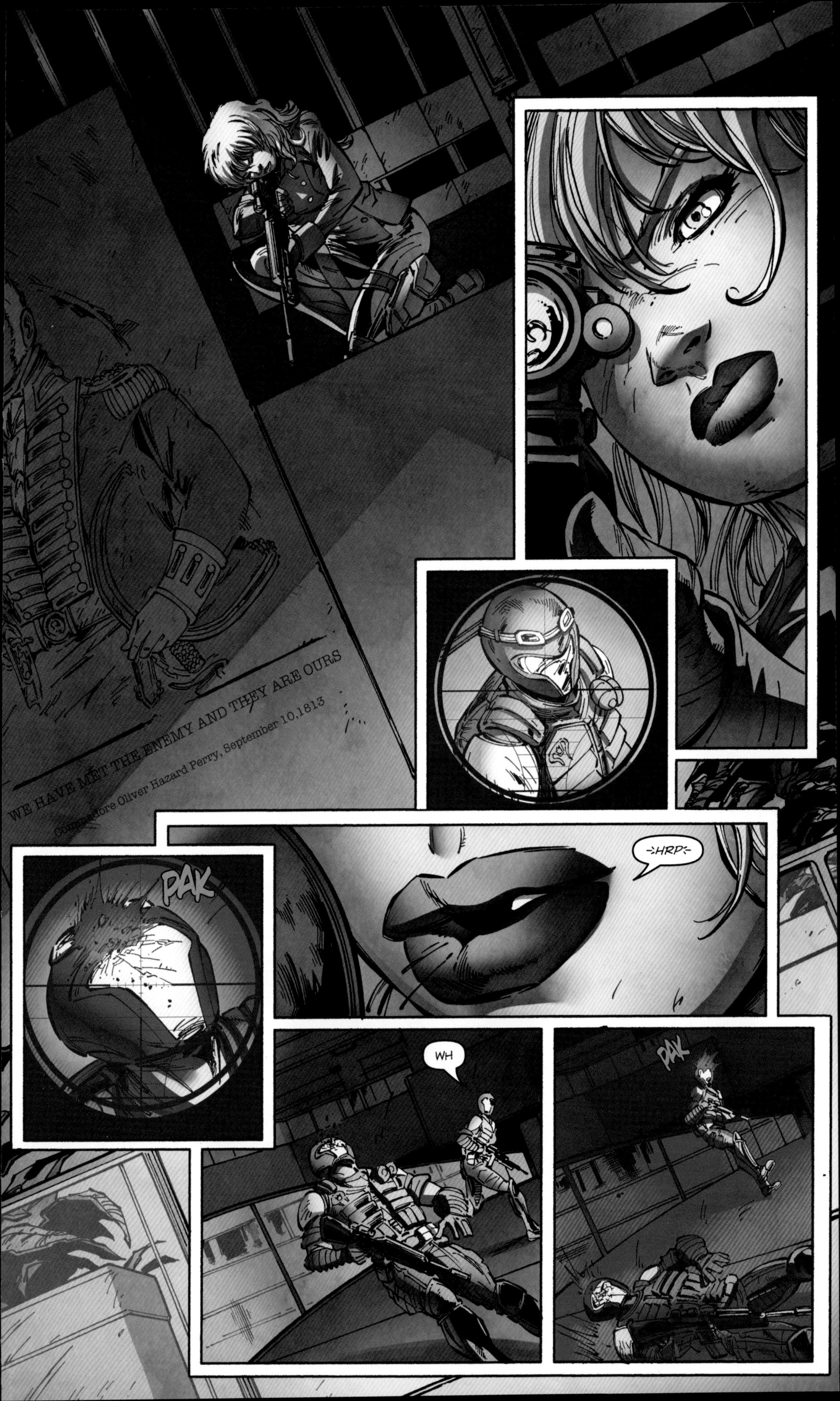
WE HAVE MET THE ENEMY AND THEY ARE OURS
Commodore Oliver Hazard Perry, September 10,1813
-HRP-
PAK
WH
PAK

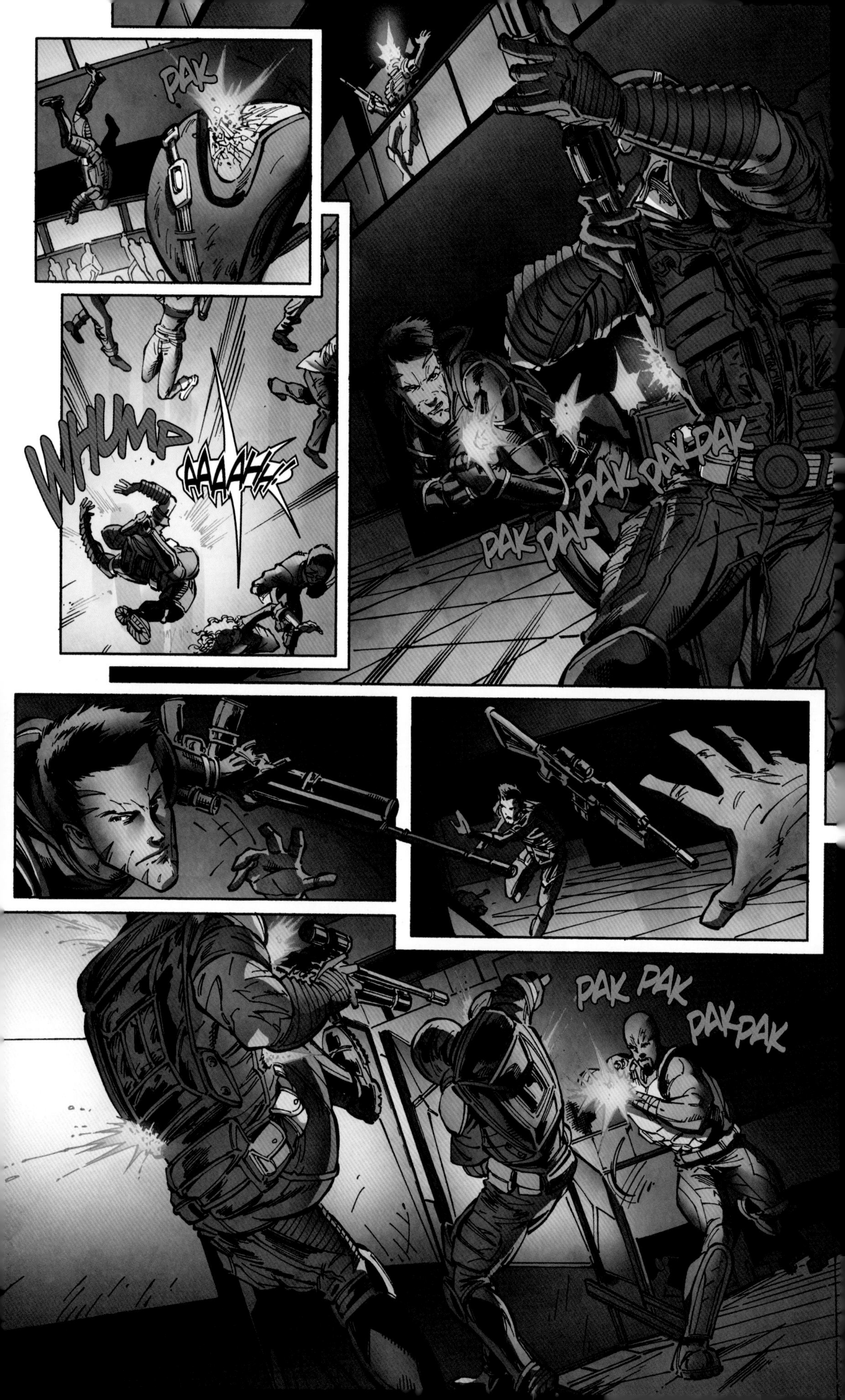
PAK
WHUMP
AAAAHH!
PAK PAK PAK PAK PAK PAK
PAK PAK
PAK PAK

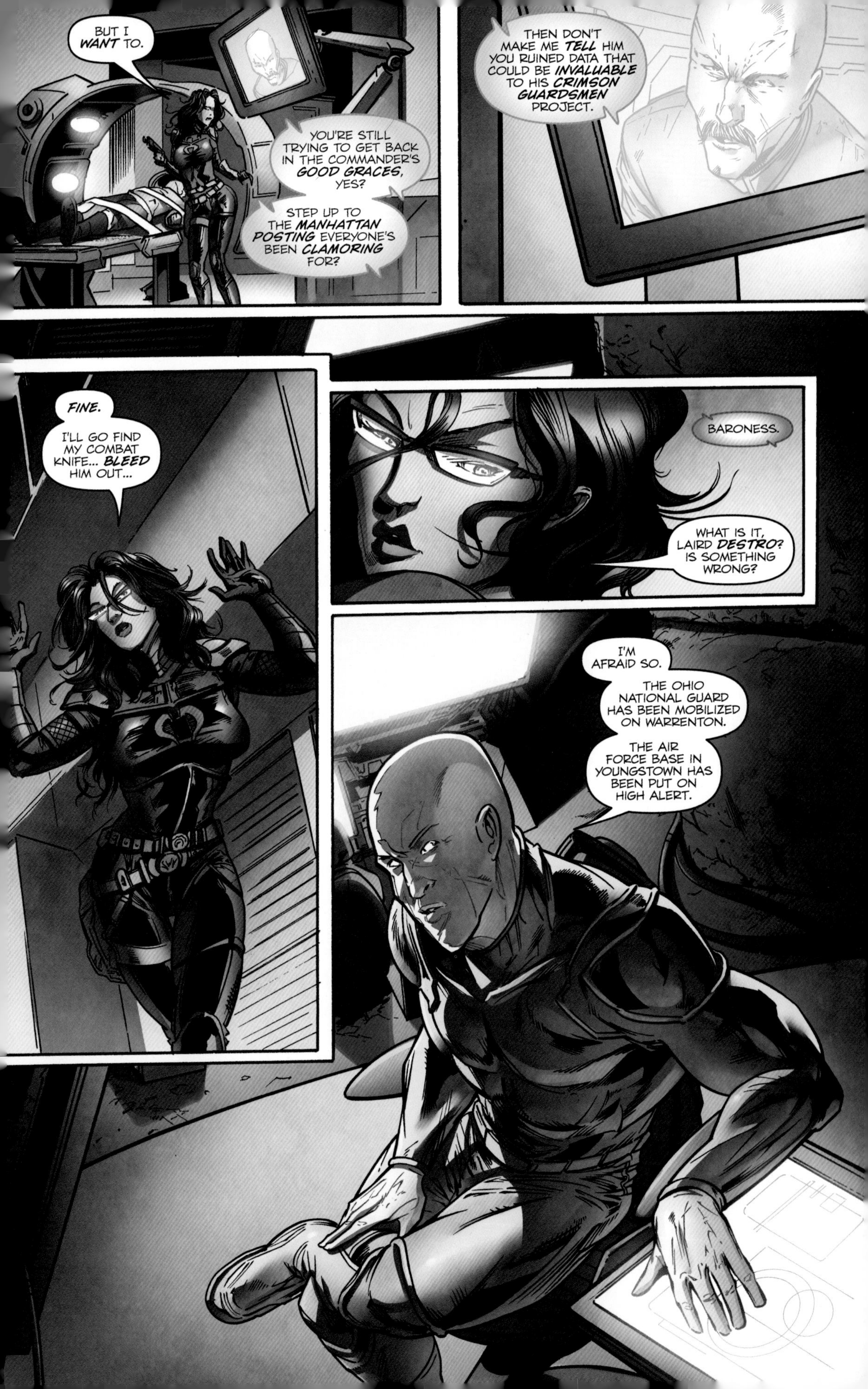

BUT I WANT TO.
YOU'RE STILL TRYING TO GET BACK IN THE COMMANDER'S GOOD GRACES, YES?
STEP UP TO THE MANHATTAN POSTING EVERYONE'S BEEN CLAMORING FOR?
THEN DON'T MAKE ME TELL HIM YOU RUINED DATA THAT COULD BE INVALUABLE TO HIS CRIMSON GUARDSMEN PROJECT.
FINE.
I'LL GO FIND MY COMBAT KNIFE... BLEED HIM OUT...
BARONESS.
WHAT IS IT, LAIRD DESTRO? IS SOMETHING WRONG?
I'M AFRAID SO.
THE OHIO NATIONAL GUARD HAS BEEN MOBILIZED ON WARRENTON.
THE AIR FORCE BASE IN YOUNGSTOWN HAS BEEN PUT ON HIGH ALERT.

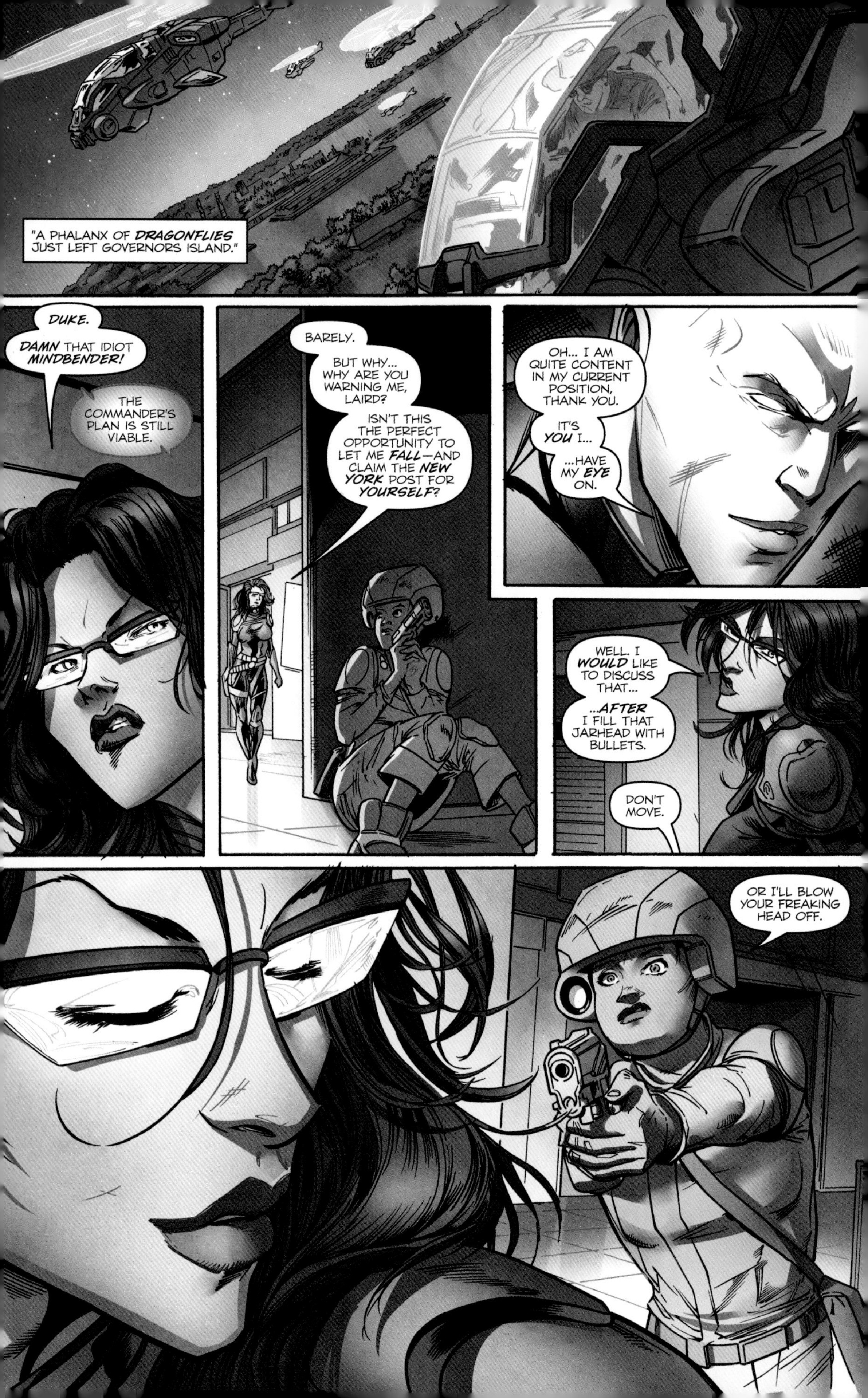
"A PHALANX OF DRAGONFLIES JUST LEFT GOVERNORS ISLAND."
DUKE.
DAMN THAT IDIOT MINDBENDER!
THE COMMANDER'S PLAN IS STILL VIABLE.
BARELY.
BUT WHY... WHY ARE YOU WARNING ME, LAIRD?
ISN'T THIS THE PERFECT OPPORTUNITY TO LET ME FALL—AND CLAIM THE NEW YORK POST FOR YOURSELF?
OH... I AM QUITE CONTENT IN MY CURRENT POSITION, THANK YOU.
IT'S YOU I...
...HAVE MY EYE ON.
WELL. I WOULD LIKE TO DISCUSS THAT...
...AFTER I FILL THAT JARHEAD WITH BULLETS.
DON'T MOVE.
OR I'LL BLOW YOUR FREAKING HEAD OFF.

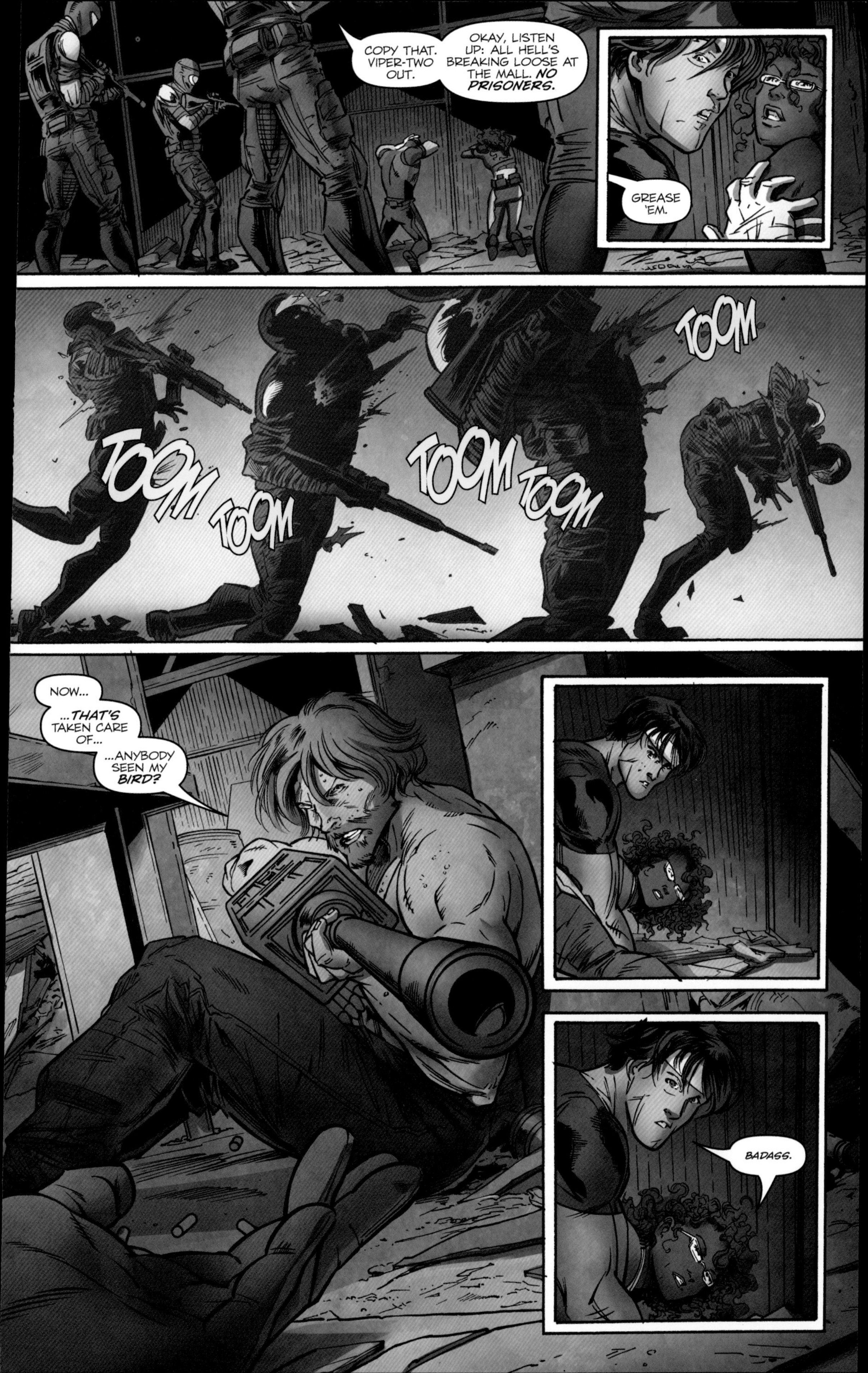
COPY THAT. VIPER-TWO OUT.
OKAY, LISTEN UP: ALL HELL'S BREAKING LOOSE AT THE MALL. *NO PRISONERS.*
GREASE 'EM.
TOOM
TOOM
TOOM
TOOM
TOOM
NOW...
...*THAT'S* TAKEN CARE OF...
...ANYBODY SEEN MY *BIRD?*
BADASS.

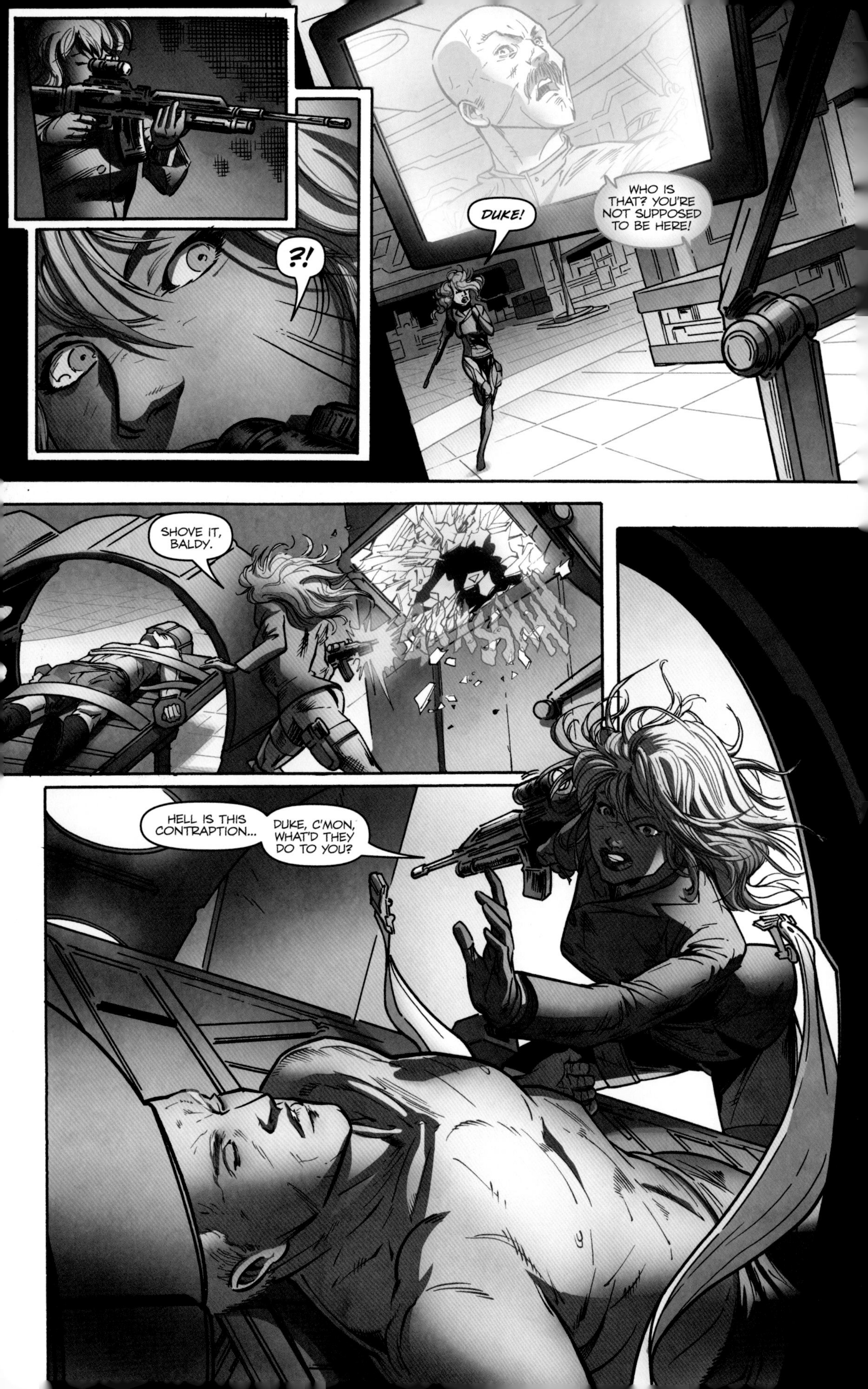
?!
DUKE!
WHO IS THAT? YOU'RE NOT SUPPOSED TO BE HERE!
SHOVE IT, BALDY.
HELL IS THIS CONTRAPTION...
DUKE, C'MON, WHAT'D THEY DO TO YOU?

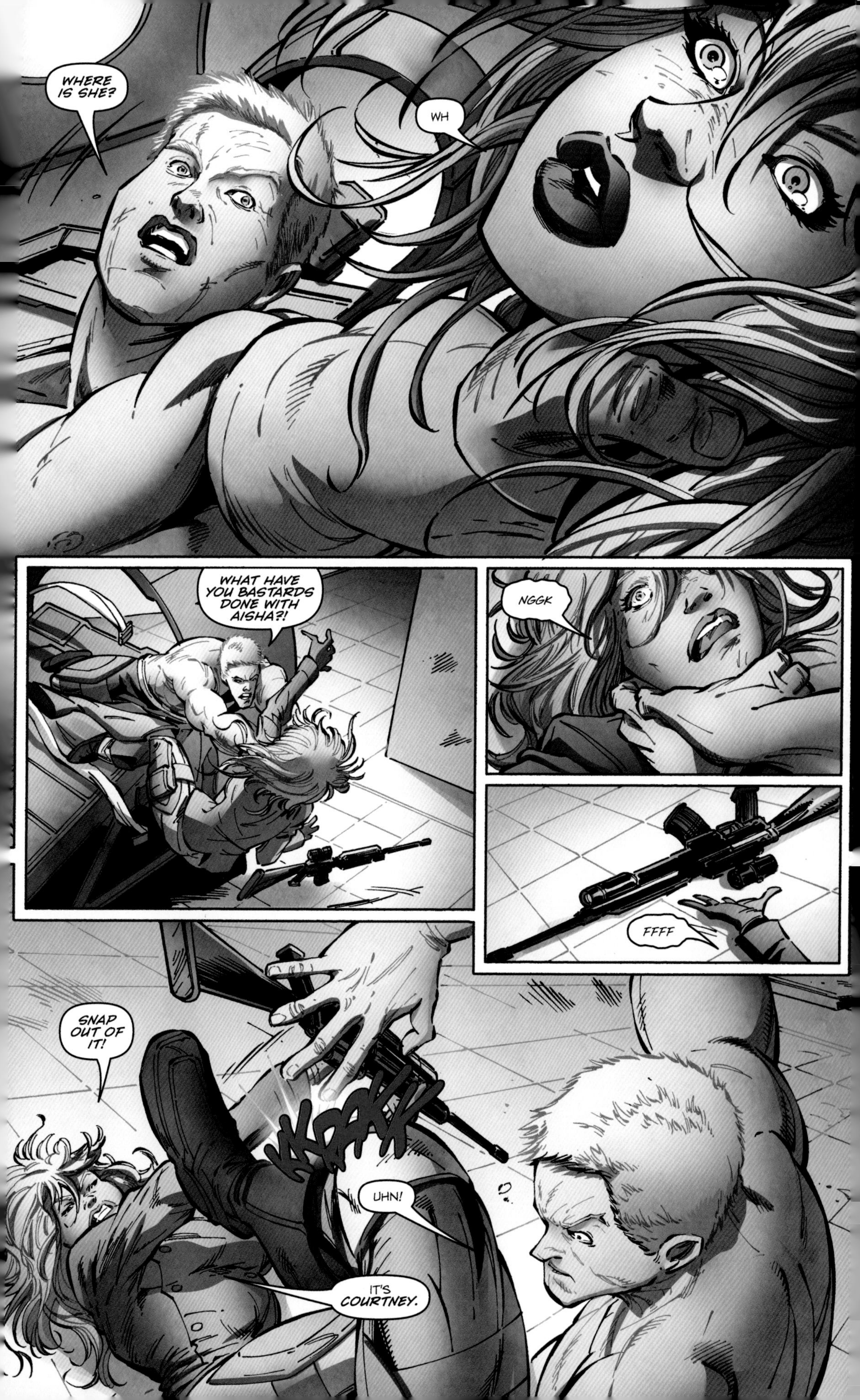
WHERE IS SHE?
WH
WHAT HAVE YOU BASTARDS DONE WITH AISHA?!
NGGK
FFFF
SNAP OUT OF IT!
UHN!
IT'S COURTNEY.

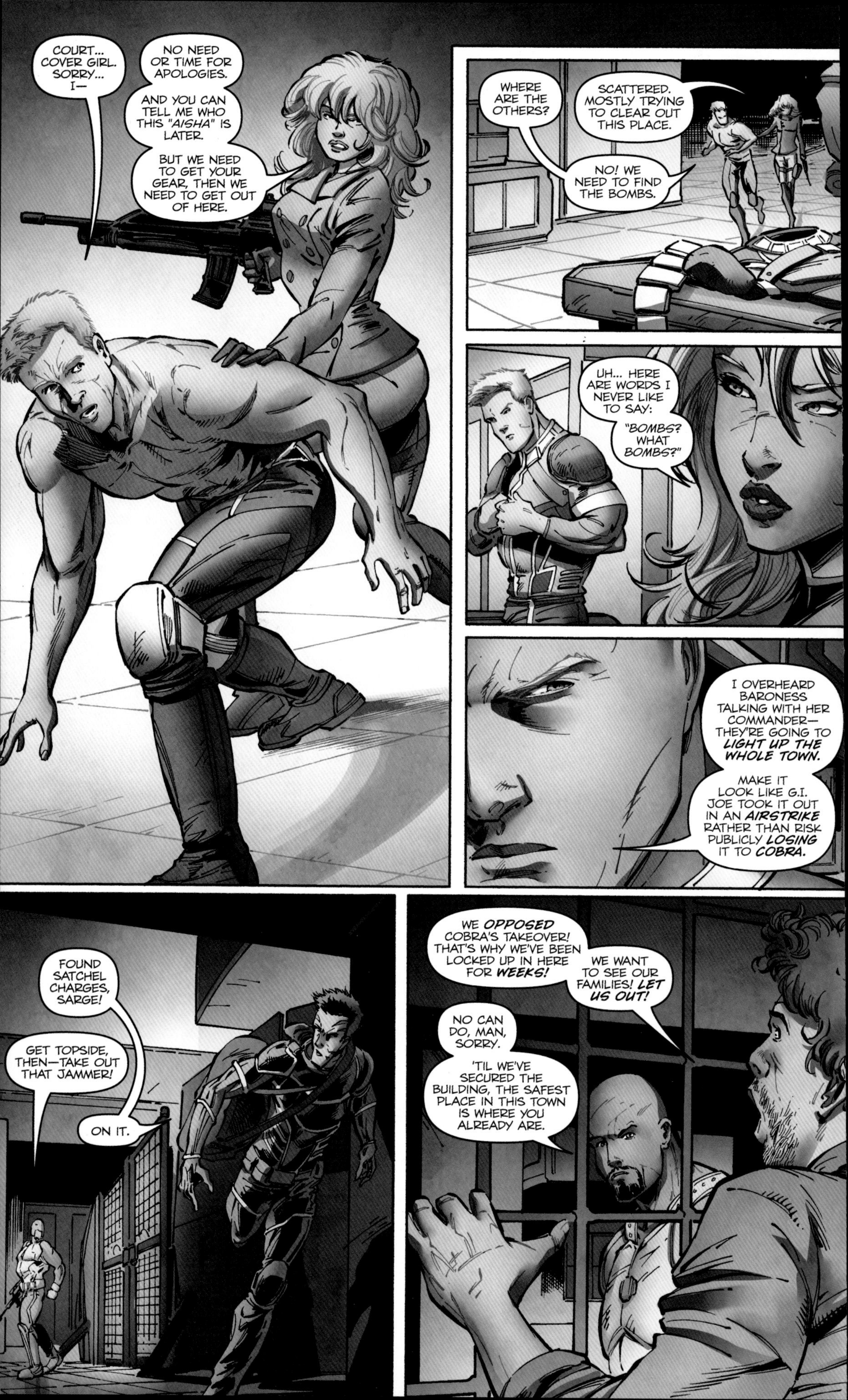
COURT... COVER GIRL. SORRY... I—
NO NEED OR TIME FOR APOLOGIES.
AND YOU CAN TELL ME WHO THIS "AISHA" IS LATER.
BUT WE NEED TO GET YOUR GEAR, THEN WE NEED TO GET OUT OF HERE.
WHERE ARE THE OTHERS?
SCATTERED. MOSTLY TRYING TO CLEAR OUT THIS PLACE.
NO! WE NEED TO FIND THE BOMBS.
UH... HERE ARE WORDS I NEVER LIKE TO SAY:
"BOMBS? WHAT BOMBS?"
I OVERHEARD BARONESS TALKING WITH HER COMMANDER—THEY'RE GOING TO LIGHT UP THE WHOLE TOWN.
MAKE IT LOOK LIKE G.I. JOE TOOK IT OUT IN AN AIRSTRIKE RATHER THAN RISK PUBLICLY LOSING IT TO COBRA.
FOUND SATCHEL CHARGES, SARGE!
GET TOPSIDE, THEN—TAKE OUT THAT JAMMER!
ON IT.
WE OPPOSED COBRA'S TAKEOVER! THAT'S WHY WE'VE BEEN LOCKED UP IN HERE FOR WEEKS!
WE WANT TO SEE OUR FAMILIES! LET US OUT!
NO CAN DO, MAN, SORRY.
'TIL WE'VE SECURED THE BUILDING, THE SAFEST PLACE IN THIS TOWN IS WHERE YOU ALREADY ARE.

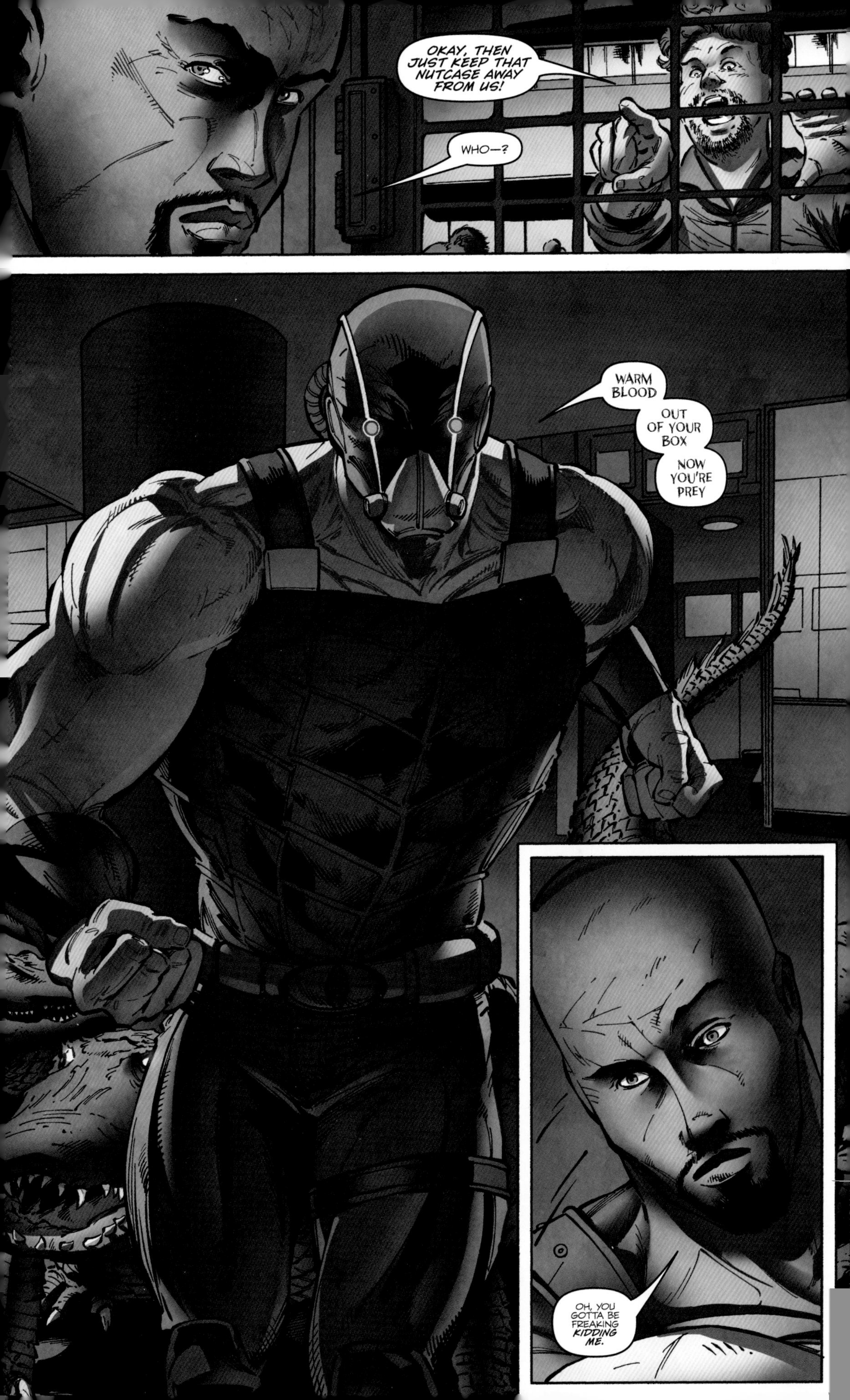
OKAY, THEN JUST KEEP THAT NUTCASE AWAY FROM US!
WHO--?
WARM BLOOD
OUT OF YOUR BOX
NOW YOU'RE PREY
OH, YOU GOTTA BE FREAKING *KIDDING ME.*

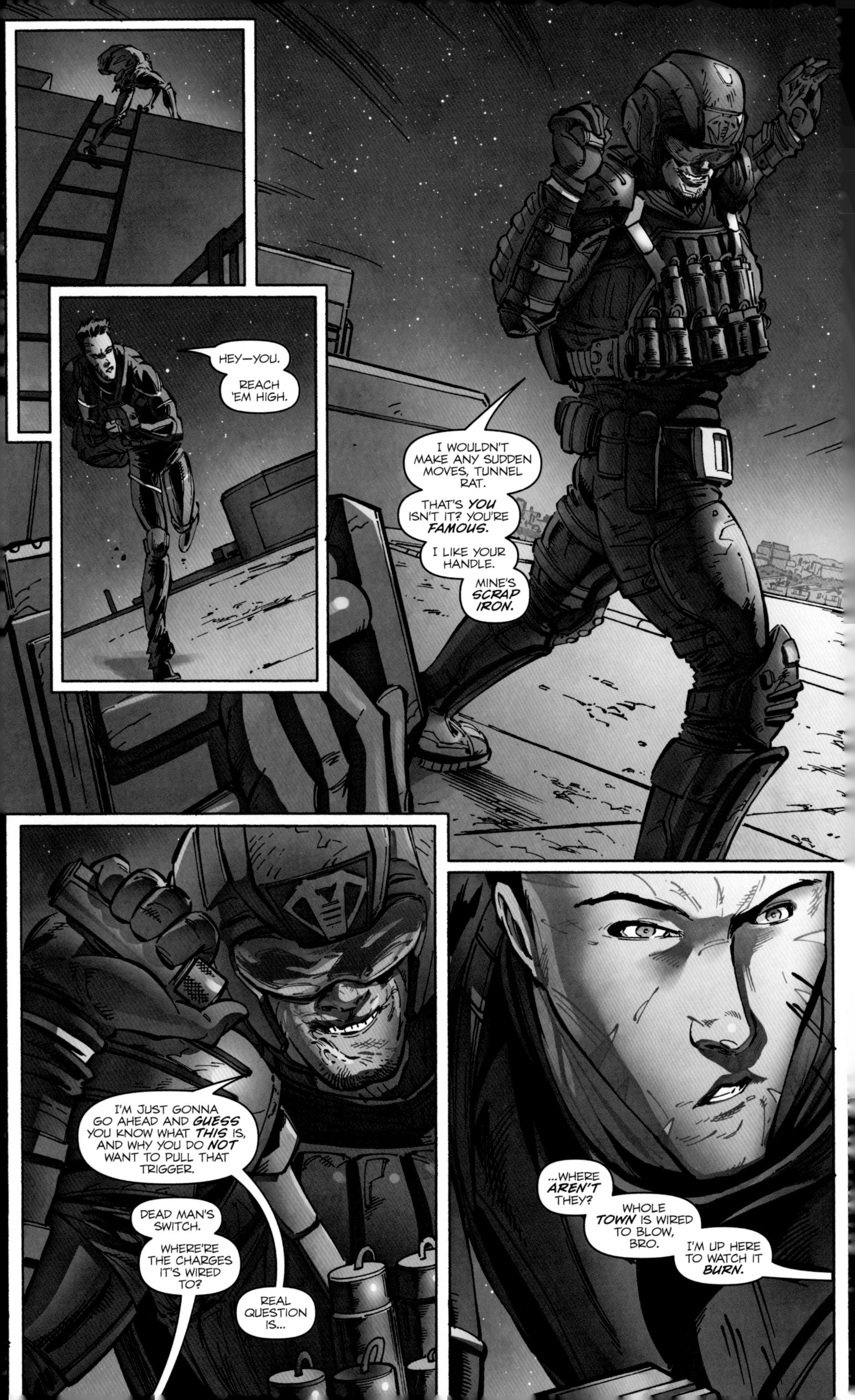
HEY—YOU.
REACH 'EM HIGH.
I WOULDN'T MAKE ANY SUDDEN MOVES, TUNNEL RAT.
THAT'S *YOU* ISN'T IT? YOU'RE *FAMOUS.*
I LIKE YOUR HANDLE.
MINE'S *SCRAP IRON.*
I'M JUST GONNA GO AHEAD AND *GUESS* YOU KNOW WHAT *THIS* IS, AND WHY YOU DO *NOT* WANT TO PULL THAT TRIGGER.
DEAD MAN'S SWITCH.
WHERE'RE THE CHARGES IT'S WIRED TO?
REAL QUESTION IS...
...WHERE *AREN'T* THEY?
WHOLE *TOWN* IS WIRED TO BLOW, BRO.
I'M UP HERE TO WATCH IT *BURN.*

CHAPTER FIVE

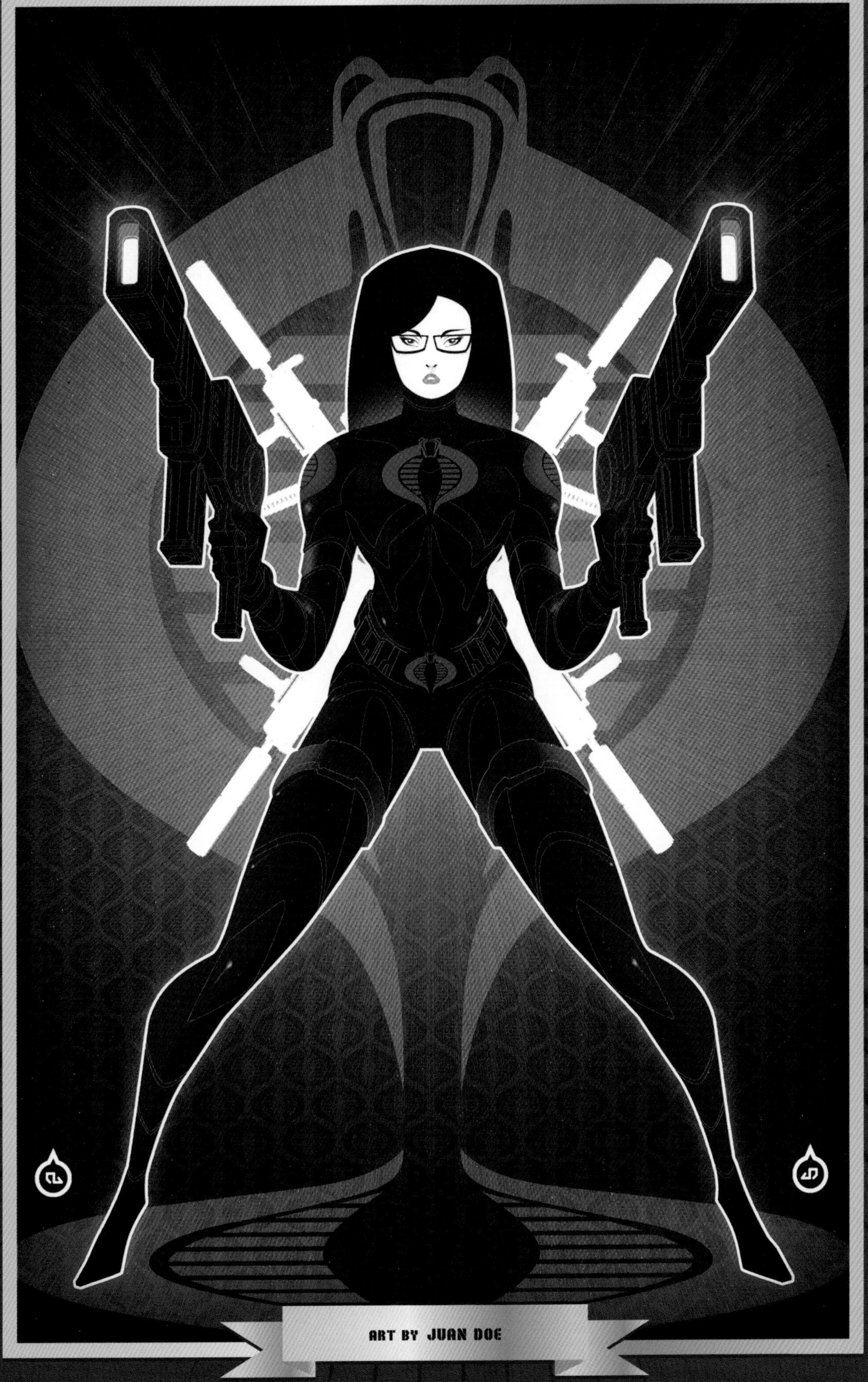
ART BY JUAN DOE

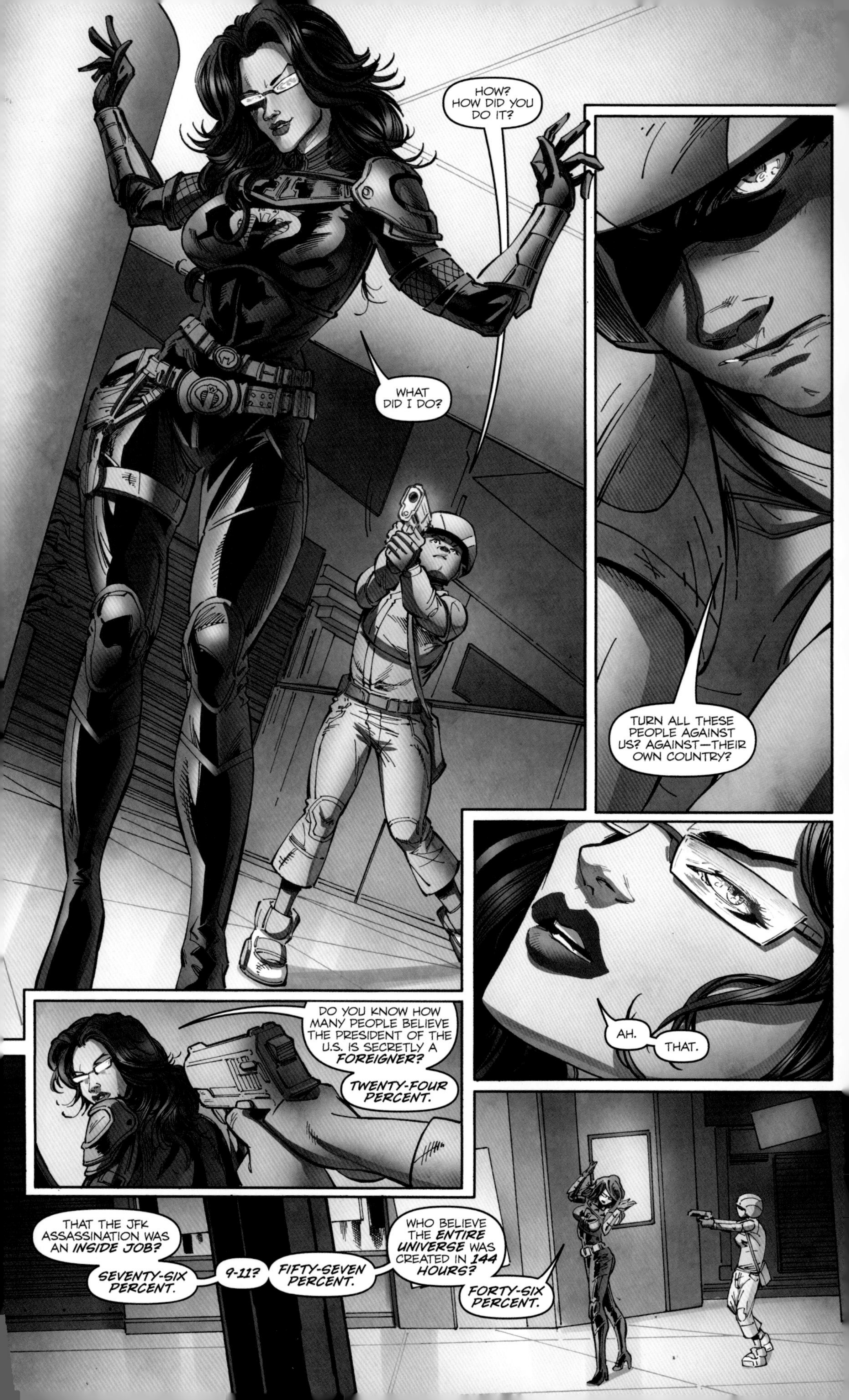
HOW? HOW DID YOU DO IT?
WHAT DID I DO?
TURN ALL THESE PEOPLE AGAINST US? AGAINST—THEIR OWN COUNTRY?
AH.
THAT.
DO YOU KNOW HOW MANY PEOPLE BELIEVE THE PRESIDENT OF THE U.S. IS SECRETLY A FOREIGNER?
TWENTY-FOUR PERCENT.
THAT THE JFK ASSASSINATION WAS AN INSIDE JOB?
SEVENTY-SIX PERCENT.
9-11?
FIFTY-SEVEN PERCENT.
WHO BELIEVE THE ENTIRE UNIVERSE WAS CREATED IN 144 HOURS?
FORTY-SIX PERCENT.

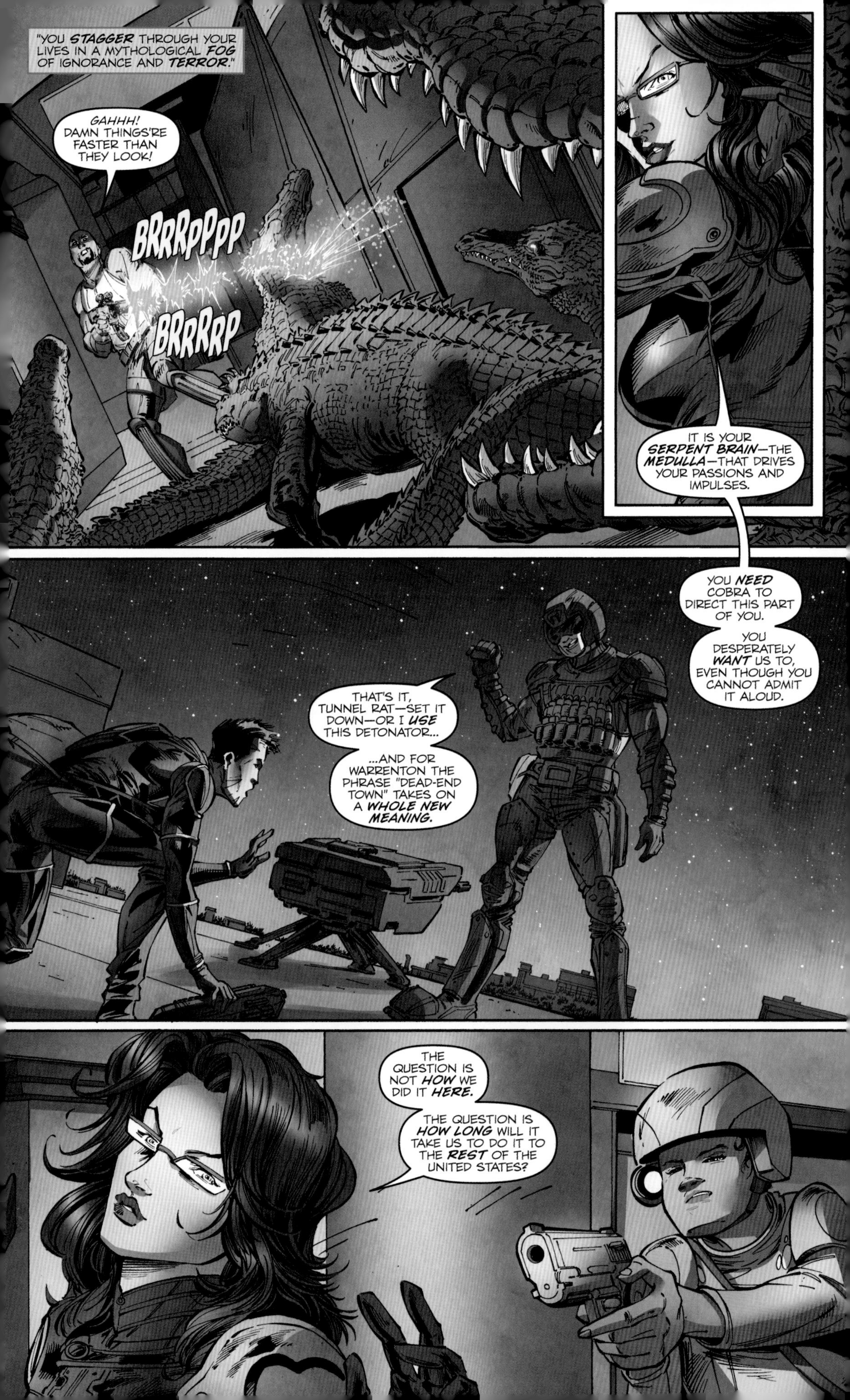
"YOU STAGGER THROUGH YOUR LIVES IN A MYTHOLOGICAL FOG OF IGNORANCE AND TERROR."
GAHHH! DAMN THINGS'RE FASTER THAN THEY LOOK!
BRRRPPPP
BRRRRP
IT IS YOUR SERPENT BRAIN—THE MEDULLA—THAT DRIVES YOUR PASSIONS AND IMPULSES.
YOU NEED COBRA TO DIRECT THIS PART OF YOU.
YOU DESPERATELY WANT US TO, EVEN THOUGH YOU CANNOT ADMIT IT ALOUD.
THAT'S IT, TUNNEL RAT—SET IT DOWN—OR I USE THIS DETONATOR...
...AND FOR WARRENTON THE PHRASE "DEAD-END TOWN" TAKES ON A WHOLE NEW MEANING.
THE QUESTION IS NOT HOW WE DID IT HERE.
THE QUESTION IS HOW LONG WILL IT TAKE US TO DO IT TO THE REST OF THE UNITED STATES?

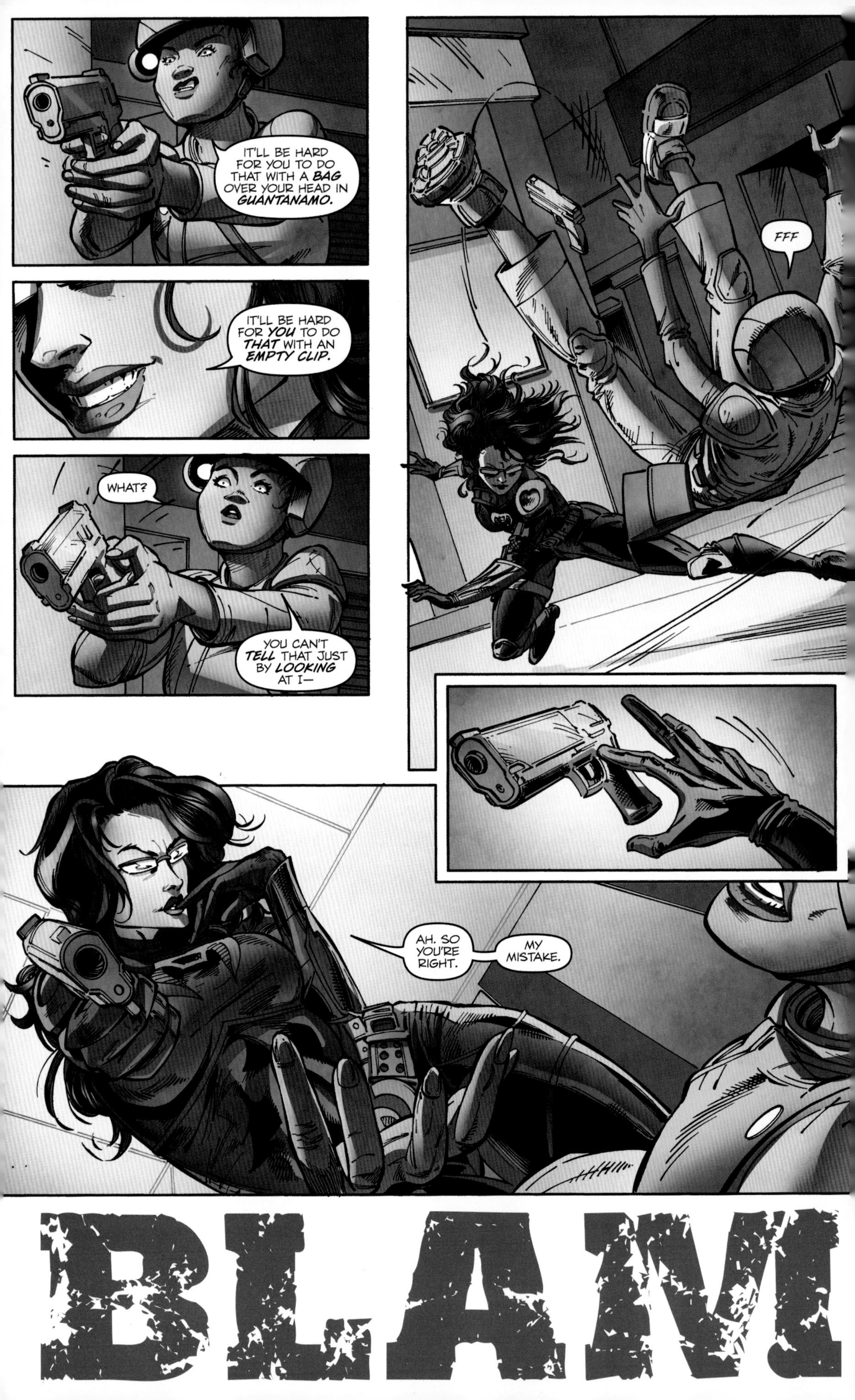
IT'LL BE HARD FOR YOU TO DO THAT WITH A BAG OVER YOUR HEAD IN GUANTANAMO.
IT'LL BE HARD FOR YOU TO DO THAT WITH AN EMPTY CLIP.
WHAT?
YOU CAN'T TELL THAT JUST BY LOOKING AT I—
FFF
AH. SO YOU'RE RIGHT.
MY MISTAKE.
BLAM!

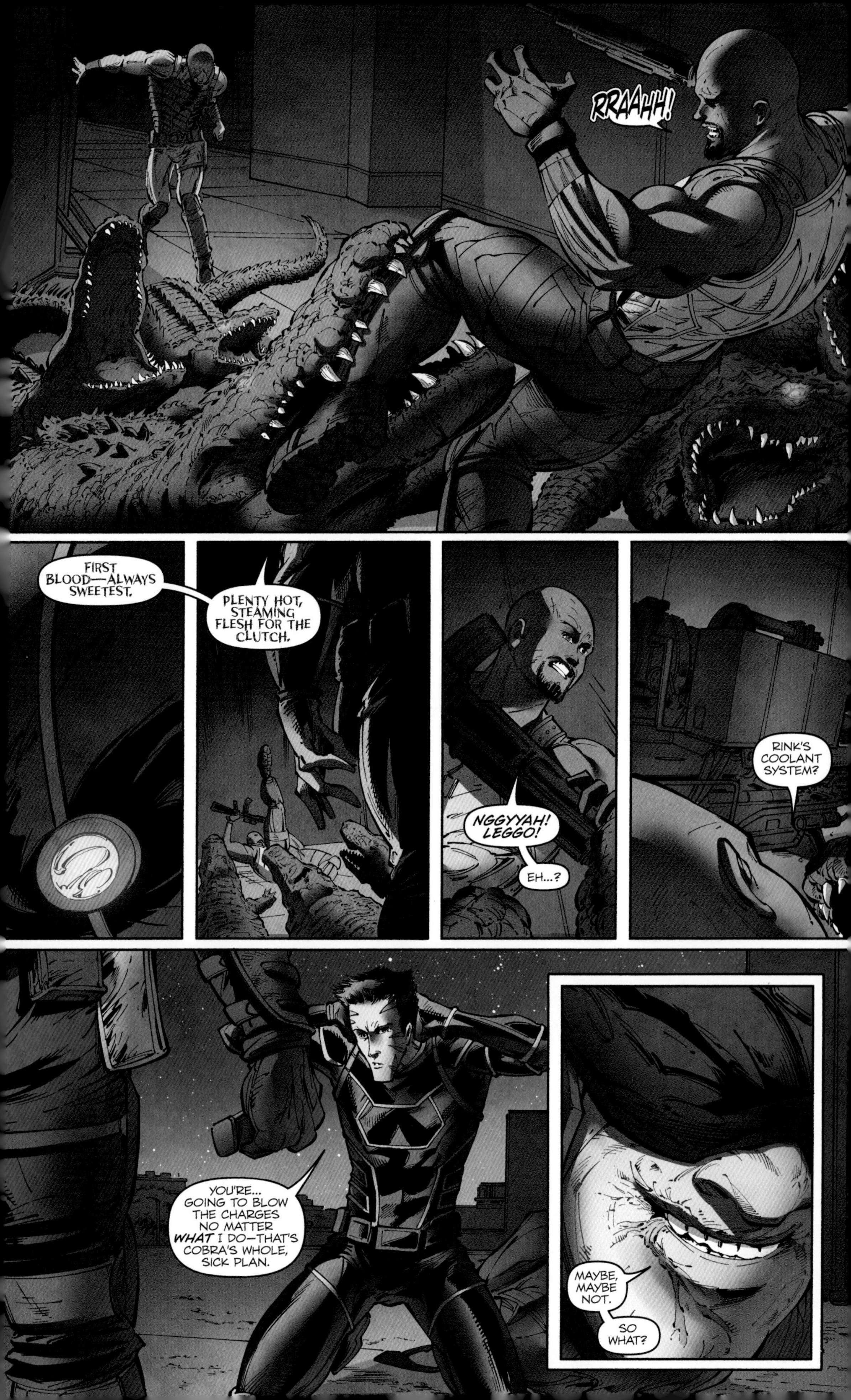
RRAAHH!
FIRST BLOOD—ALWAYS SWEETEST.
PLENTY HOT, STEAMING FLESH FOR THE CLUTCH.
NGGYYAH! LEGGO!
EH...?
RINK'S COOLANT SYSTEM?
YOU'RE... GOING TO BLOW THE CHARGES NO MATTER WHAT I DO—THAT'S COBRA'S WHOLE, SICK PLAN.
MAYBE, MAYBE NOT.
SO WHAT?

SO LEVERAGE, SCRAP IRON.

TKK

YOU *GOT* NONE.

KKRRRRKKKKKKKKRRRKKKK

BRRRPPPP BRRRRP

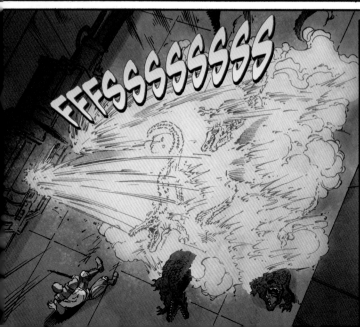

FFFSSSSSSSS

NOOOOO— NO!

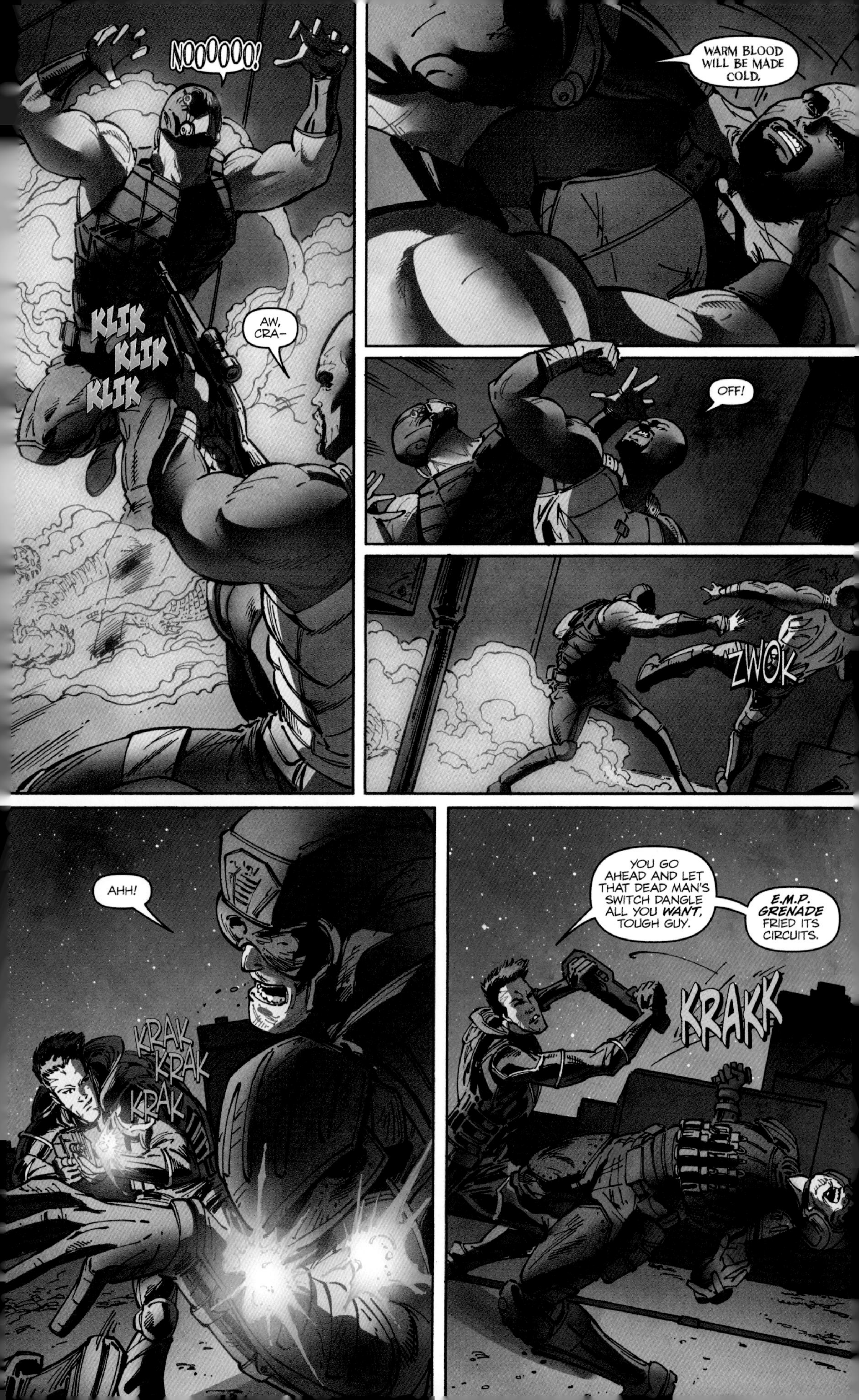
NOOOOOO!
KLIK
KLIK
KLIK
AW, CRA–
WARM BLOOD WILL BE MADE COLD.
OFF!
ZWOK
AHH!
KRAK
KRAK
KRAK
YOU GO AHEAD AND LET THAT DEAD MAN'S SWITCH DANGLE ALL YOU WANT, TOUGH GUY.
E.M.P. GRENADE FRIED ITS CIRCUITS.
KRAKK

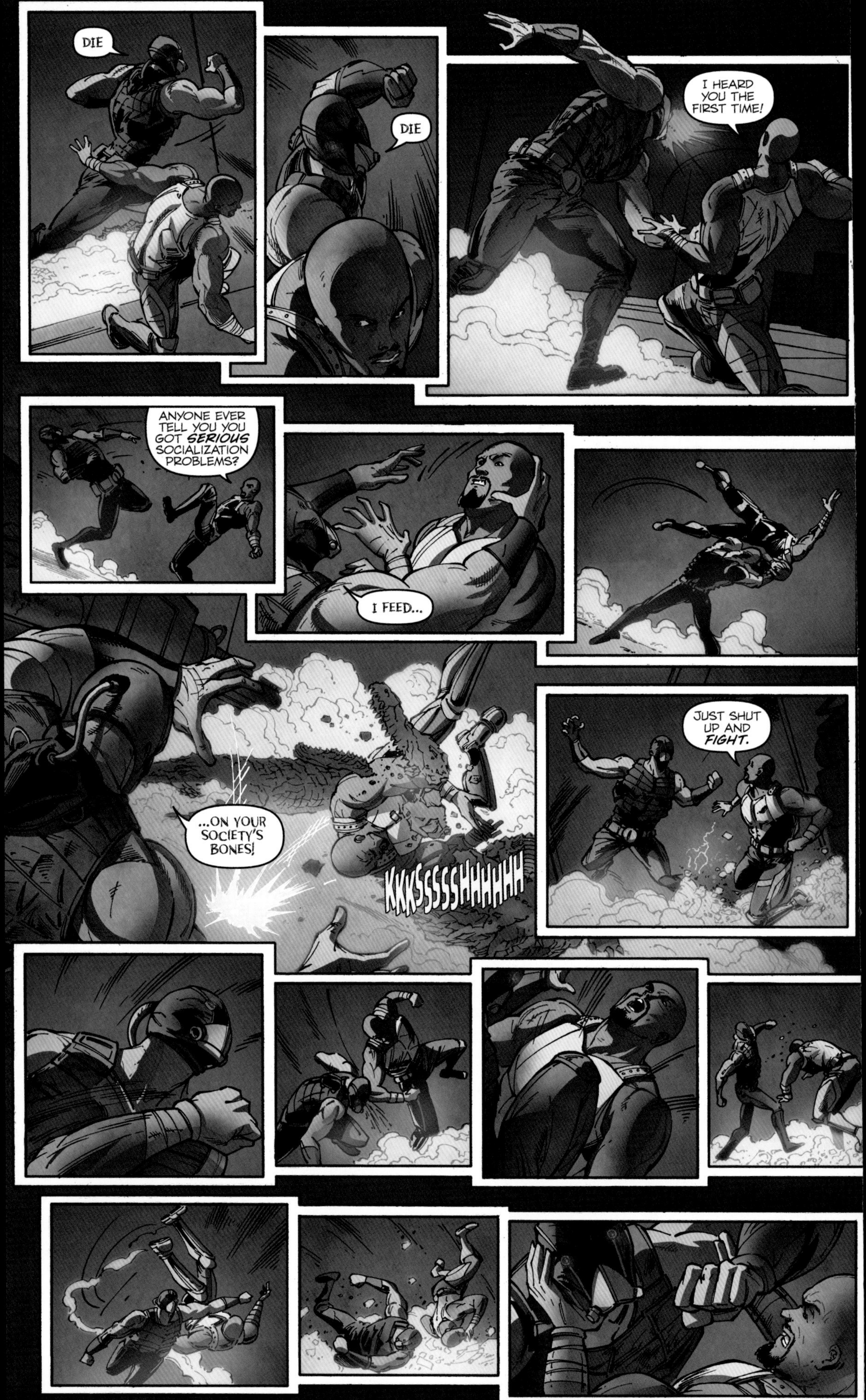
DIE
DIE
I HEARD YOU THE FIRST TIME!
ANYONE EVER TELL YOU YOU GOT SERIOUS SOCIALIZATION PROBLEMS?
I FEED...
...ON YOUR SOCIETY'S BONES!
KKKSSSSSHHHHHH
JUST SHUT UP AND FIGHT.

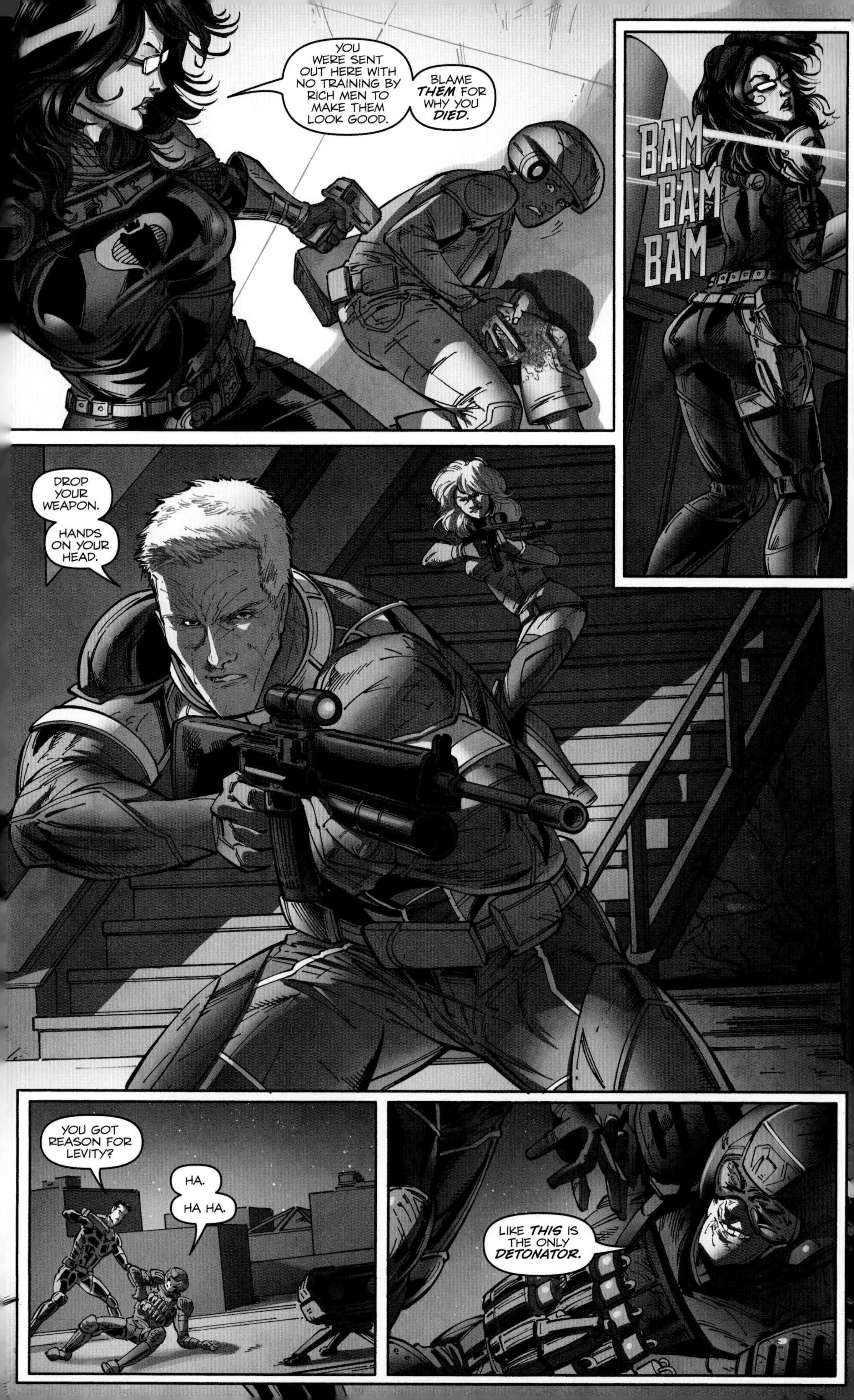
YOU WERE SENT OUT HERE WITH NO TRAINING BY RICH MEN TO MAKE THEM LOOK GOOD.
BLAME THEM FOR WHY YOU DIED.
BAM BAM BAM
DROP YOUR WEAPON.
HANDS ON YOUR HEAD.
YOU GOT REASON FOR LEVITY?
HA.
HA HA.
LIKE THIS IS THE ONLY DETONATOR.

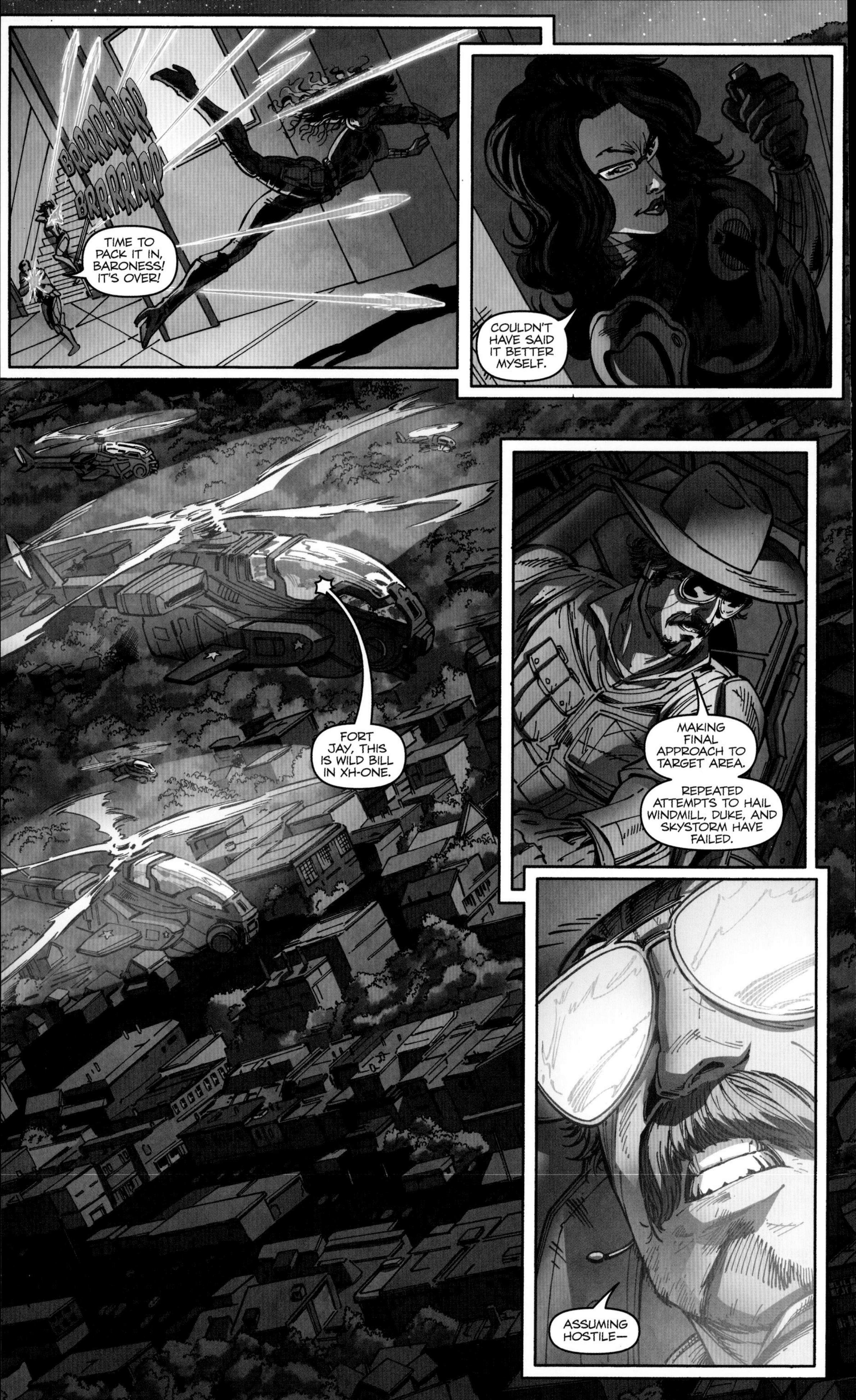
BRRRRRRRP
BRRRRRRP
TIME TO PACK IT IN, BARONESS! IT'S OVER!
COULDN'T HAVE SAID IT BETTER MYSELF.
FORT JAY, THIS IS WILD BILL IN XH-ONE.
MAKING FINAL APPROACH TO TARGET AREA.
REPEATED ATTEMPTS TO HAIL WINDMILL, DUKE, AND SKYSTORM HAVE FAILED.
ASSUMING HOSTILE—

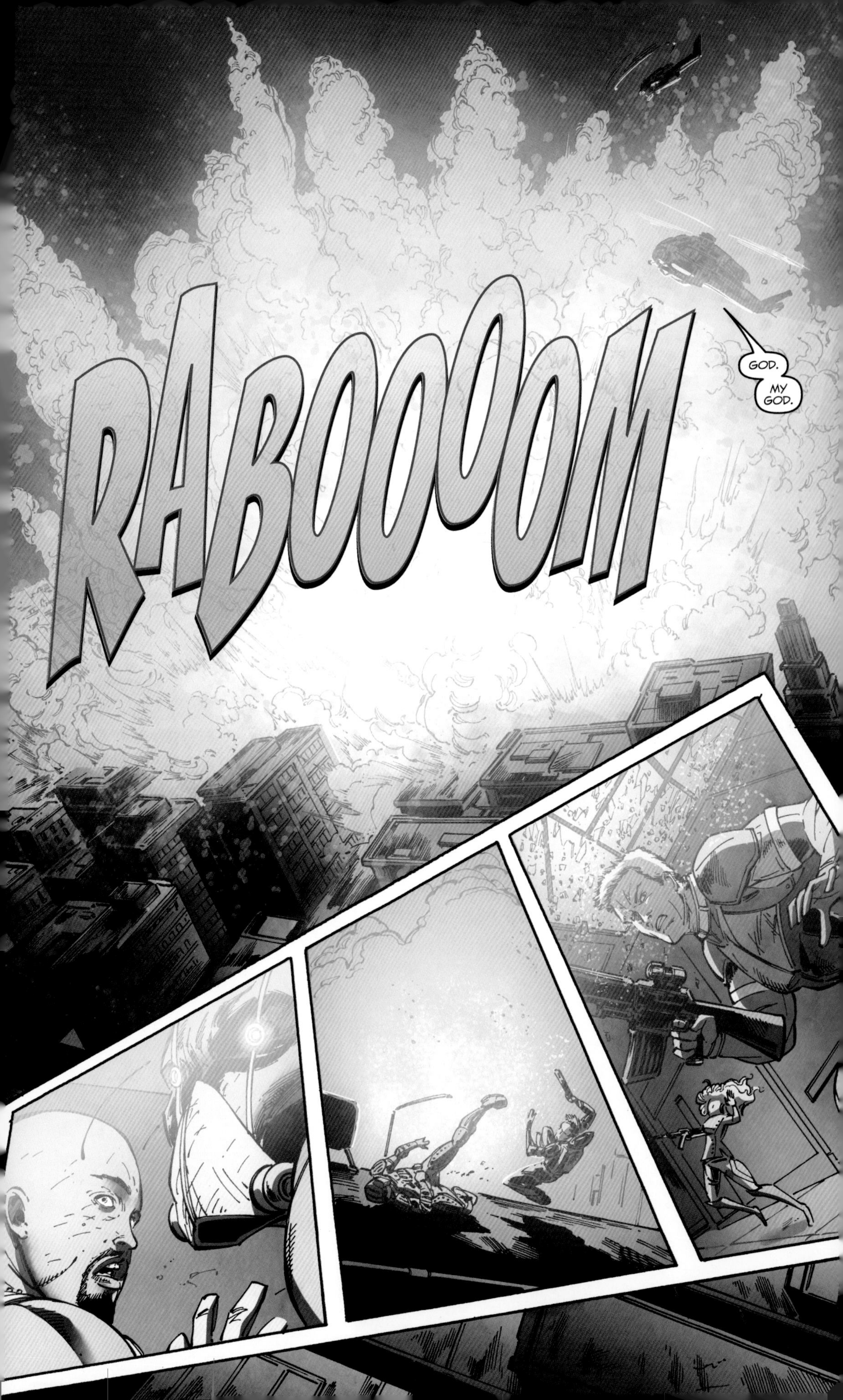
RABOOOOM
GOD.
MY GOD.

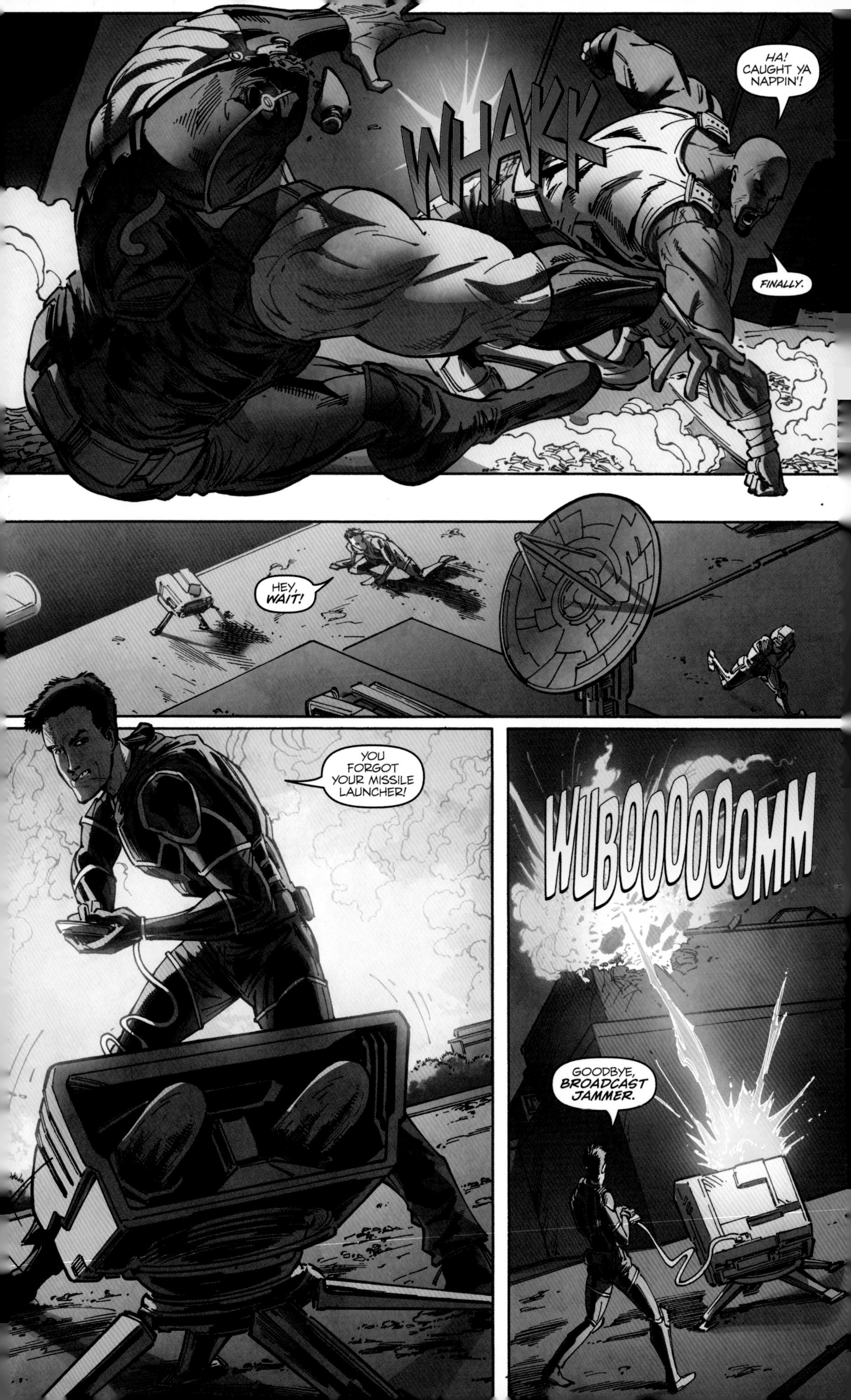

HA! CAUGHT YA NAPPIN'!
WHAKK
FINALLY.
HEY, WAIT!
YOU FORGOT YOUR MISSILE LAUNCHER!
WUBOOOOOOMM
GOODBYE, BROADCAST JAMMER.

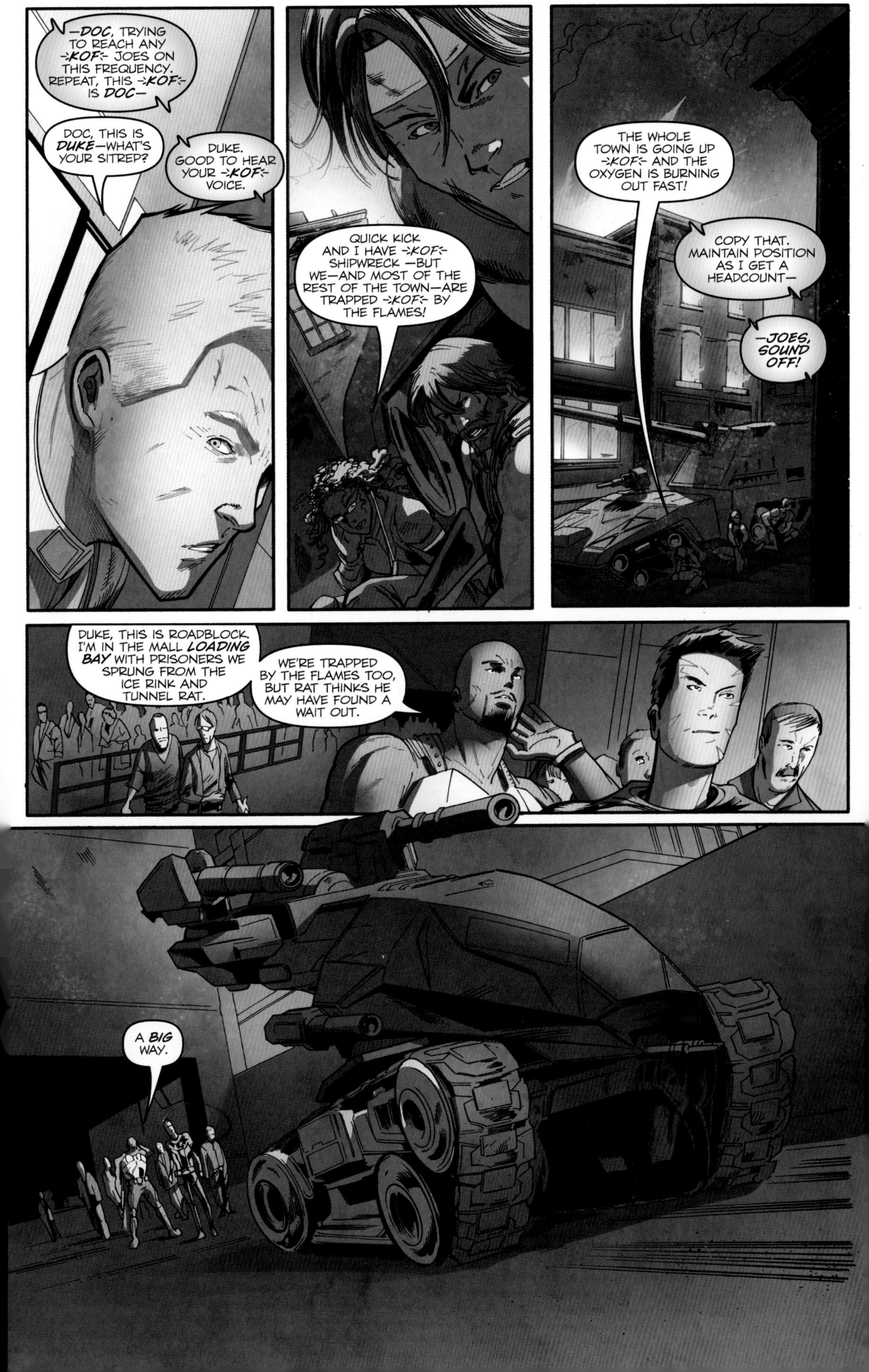
—DOC, TRYING TO REACH ANY -KOF- JOES ON THIS FREQUENCY. REPEAT, THIS -KOF- IS DOC—
DOC, THIS IS DUKE—WHAT'S YOUR SITREP?
DUKE. GOOD TO HEAR YOUR -KOF- VOICE.
QUICK KICK AND I HAVE -KOF- SHIPWRECK —BUT WE—AND MOST OF THE REST OF THE TOWN—ARE TRAPPED -KOF- BY THE FLAMES!
THE WHOLE TOWN IS GOING UP -KOF- AND THE OXYGEN IS BURNING OUT FAST!
COPY THAT. MAINTAIN POSITION AS I GET A HEADCOUNT—
—JOES, SOUND OFF!
DUKE, THIS IS ROADBLOCK. I'M IN THE MALL LOADING BAY WITH PRISONERS WE SPRUNG FROM THE ICE RINK AND TUNNEL RAT.
WE'RE TRAPPED BY THE FLAMES TOO, BUT RAT THINKS HE MAY HAVE FOUND A WAIT OUT.
A BIG WAY.

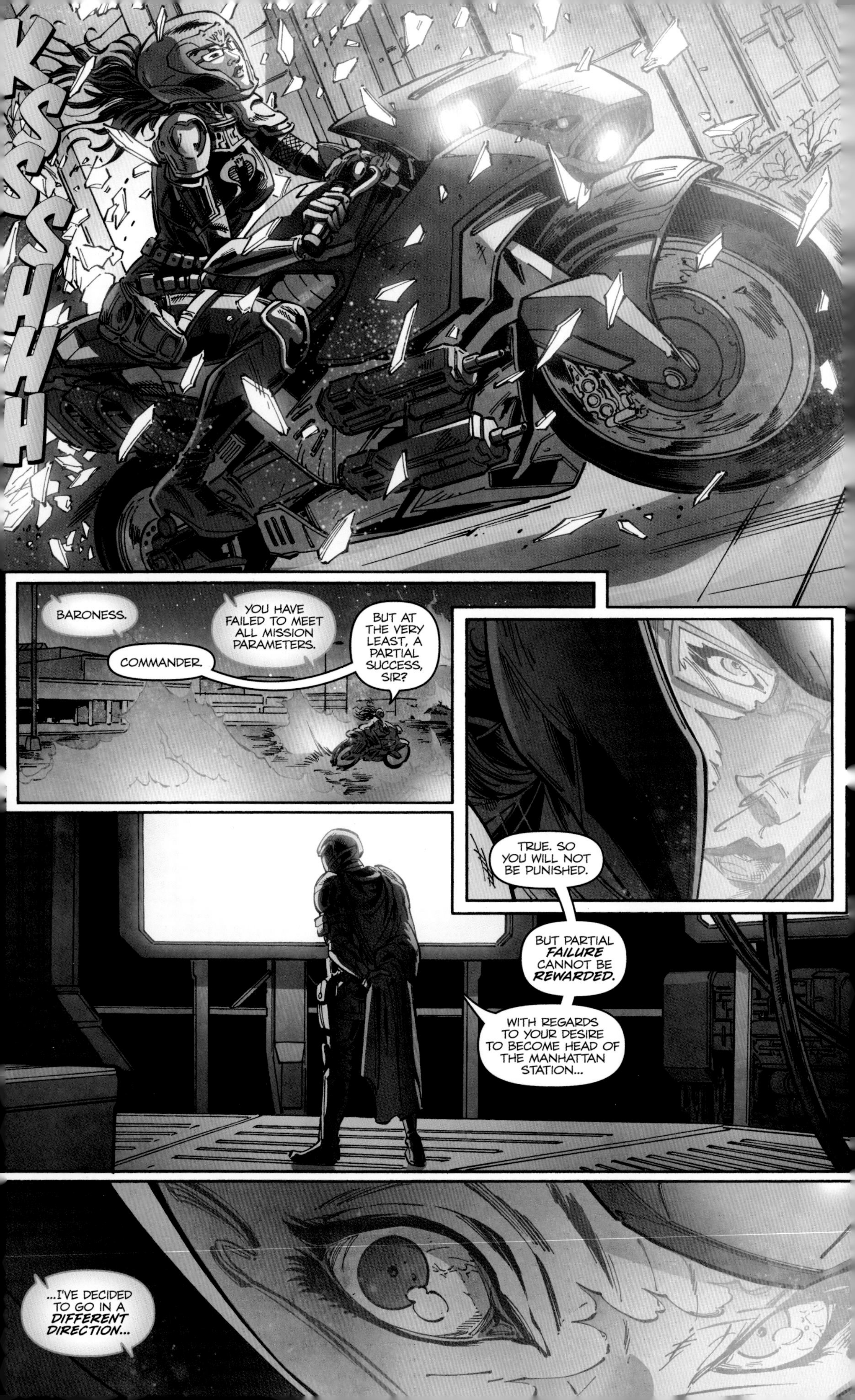
KSSSHHH
BARONESS.
COMMANDER.
YOU HAVE FAILED TO MEET ALL MISSION PARAMETERS.
BUT AT THE VERY LEAST, A PARTIAL SUCCESS, SIR?
TRUE. SO YOU WILL NOT BE PUNISHED.
BUT PARTIAL *FAILURE* CANNOT BE *REWARDED.*
WITH REGARDS TO YOUR DESIRE TO BECOME HEAD OF THE MANHATTAN STATION...
...I'VE DECIDED TO GO IN A *DIFFERENT DIRECTION...*

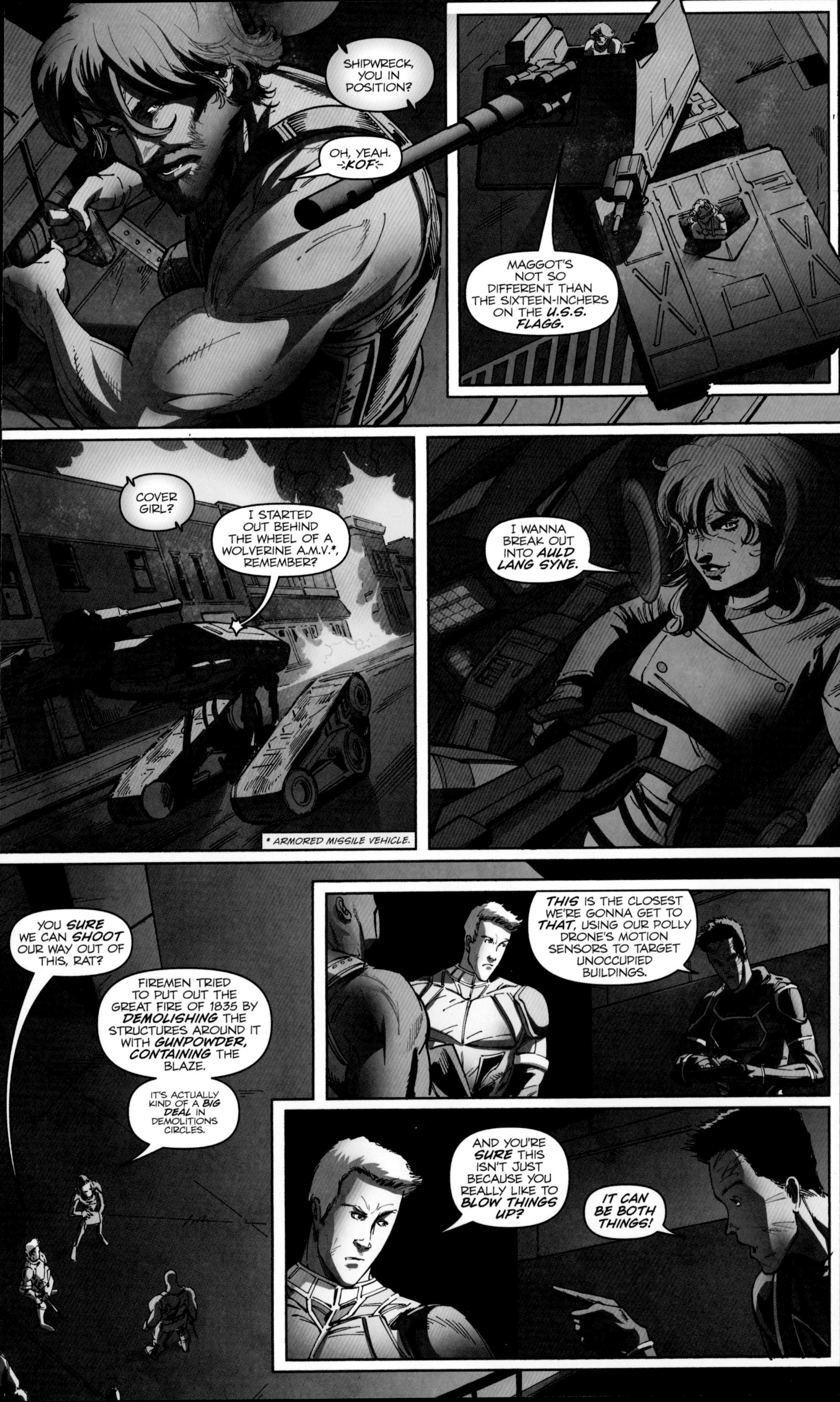

SHIPWRECK, YOU IN POSITION?
OH, YEAH. -KOF-
MAGGOT'S NOT SO DIFFERENT THAN THE SIXTEEN-INCHERS ON THE U.S.S. FLAGG.
COVER GIRL?
I STARTED OUT BEHIND THE WHEEL OF A WOLVERINE A.M.V.*, REMEMBER?
* ARMORED MISSILE VEHICLE.
I WANNA BREAK OUT INTO AULD LANG SYNE.
YOU SURE WE CAN SHOOT OUR WAY OUT OF THIS, RAT?
FIREMEN TRIED TO PUT OUT THE GREAT FIRE OF 1835 BY DEMOLISHING THE STRUCTURES AROUND IT WITH GUNPOWDER, CONTAINING THE BLAZE.
IT'S ACTUALLY KIND OF A BIG DEAL IN DEMOLITIONS CIRCLES.
THIS IS THE CLOSEST WE'RE GONNA GET TO THAT, USING OUR POLLY DRONE'S MOTION SENSORS TO TARGET UNOCCUPIED BUILDINGS.
AND YOU'RE SURE THIS ISN'T JUST BECAUSE YOU REALLY LIKE TO BLOW THINGS UP?
IT CAN BE BOTH THINGS!

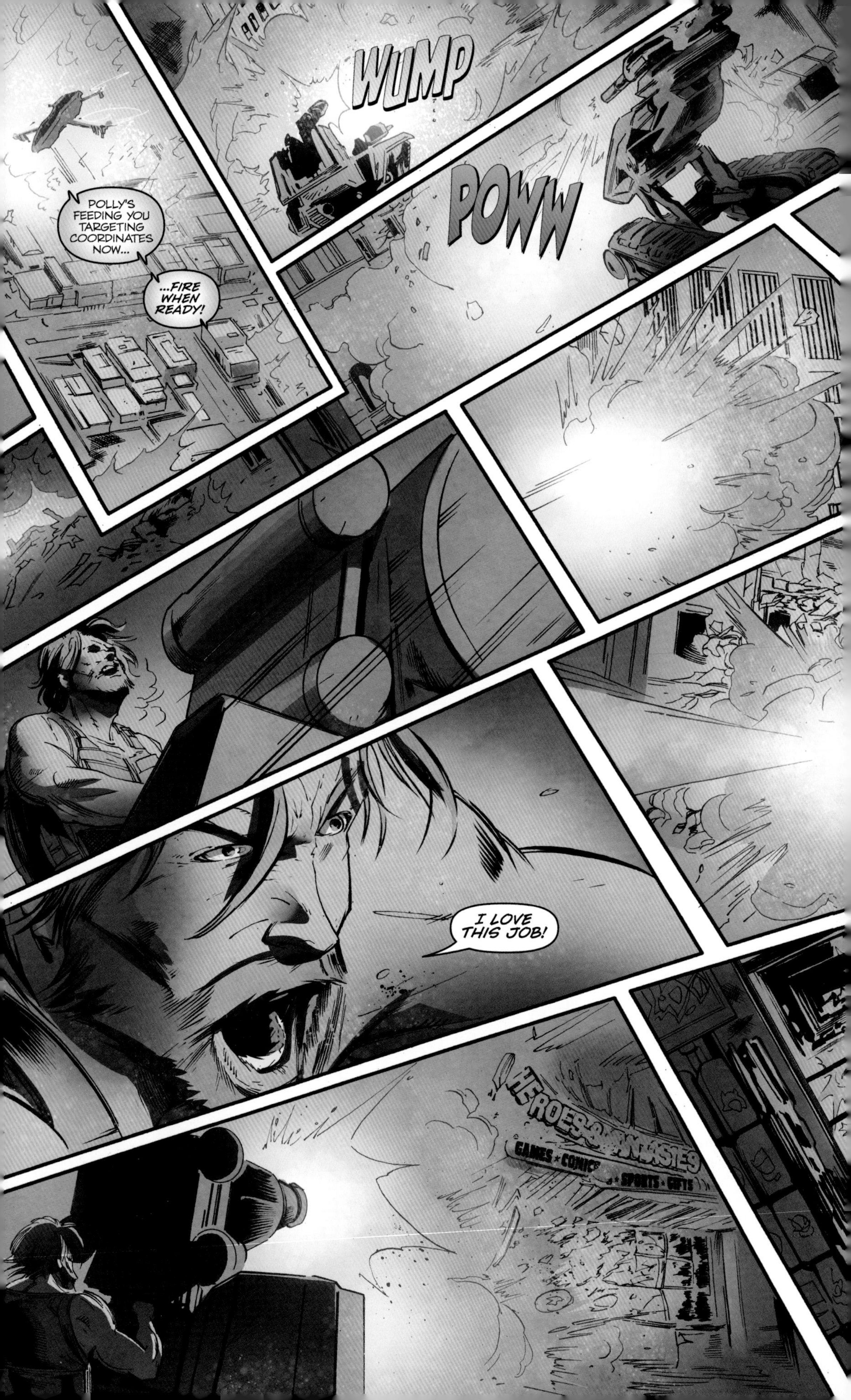
POLLY'S FEEDING YOU TARGETING COORDINATES NOW...
...FIRE WHEN READY!
WUMP
POWW
I LOVE THIS JOB!

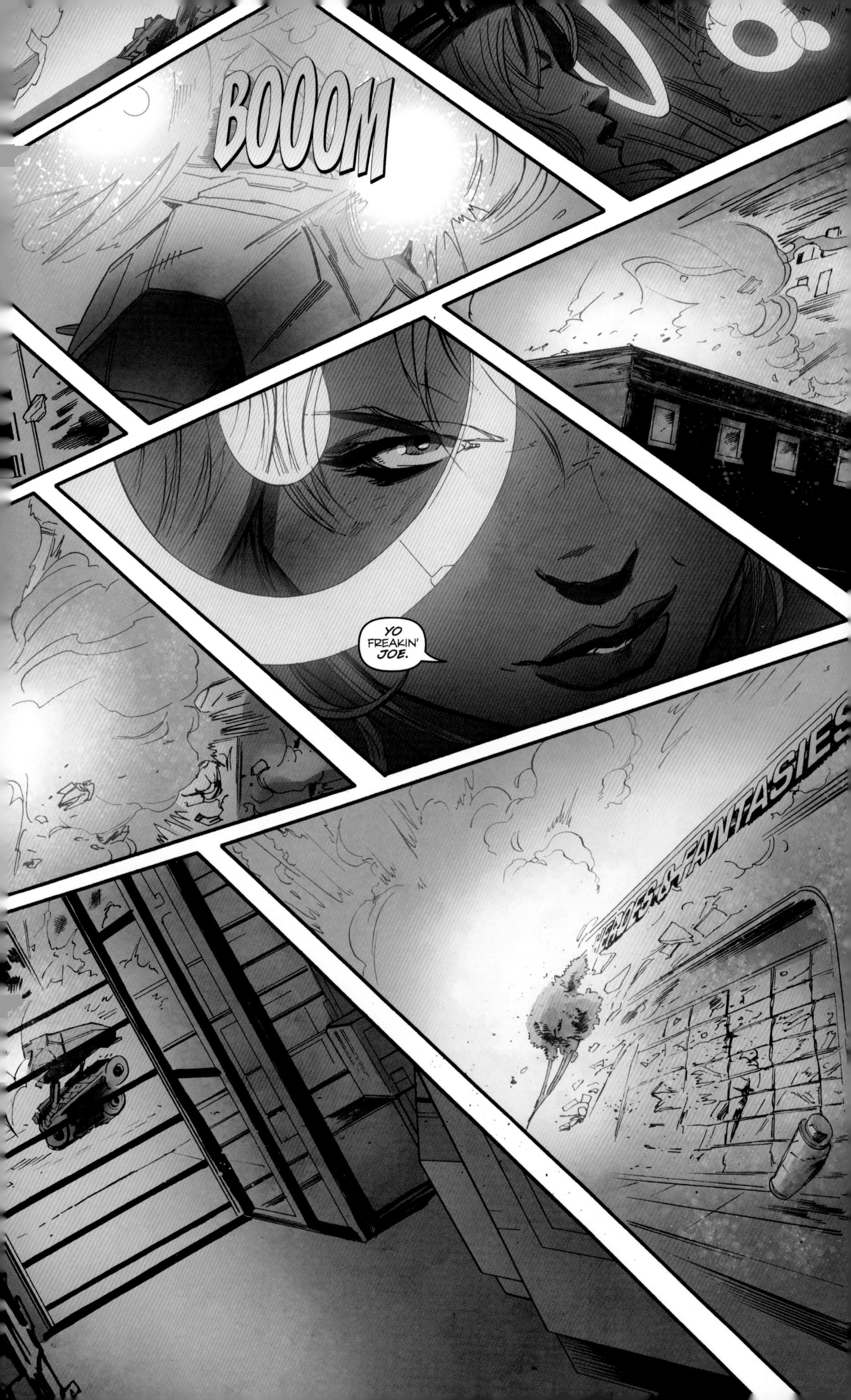
BOOOM
YO FREAKIN' JOE.
FANTASIES

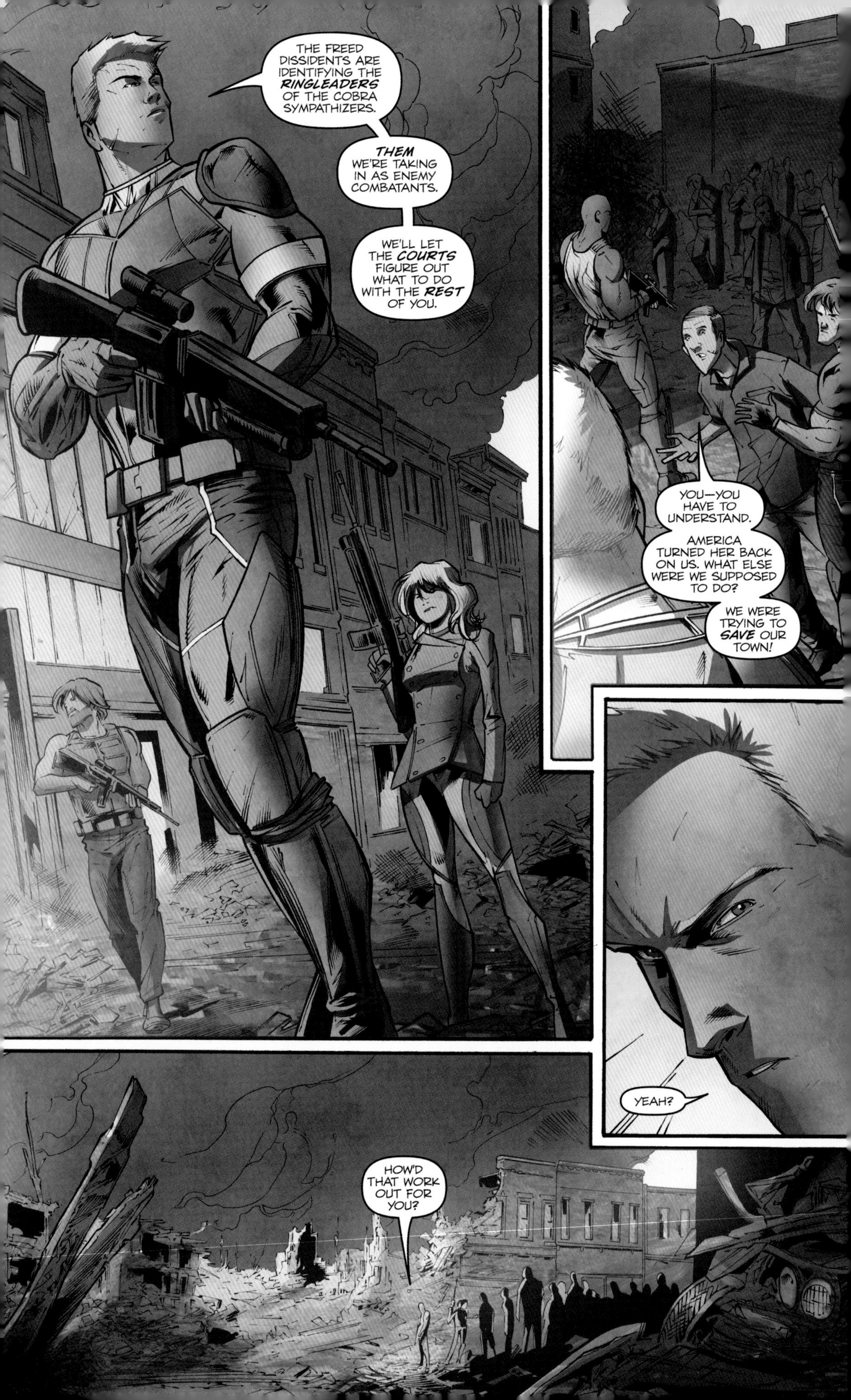
THE FREED DISSIDENTS ARE IDENTIFYING THE RINGLEADERS OF THE COBRA SYMPATHIZERS.
THEM WE'RE TAKING IN AS ENEMY COMBATANTS.
WE'LL LET THE COURTS FIGURE OUT WHAT TO DO WITH THE REST OF YOU.
YOU—YOU HAVE TO UNDERSTAND.
AMERICA TURNED HER BACK ON US. WHAT ELSE WERE WE SUPPOSED TO DO?
WE WERE TRYING TO SAVE OUR TOWN!
YEAH?
HOW'D THAT WORK OUT FOR YOU?

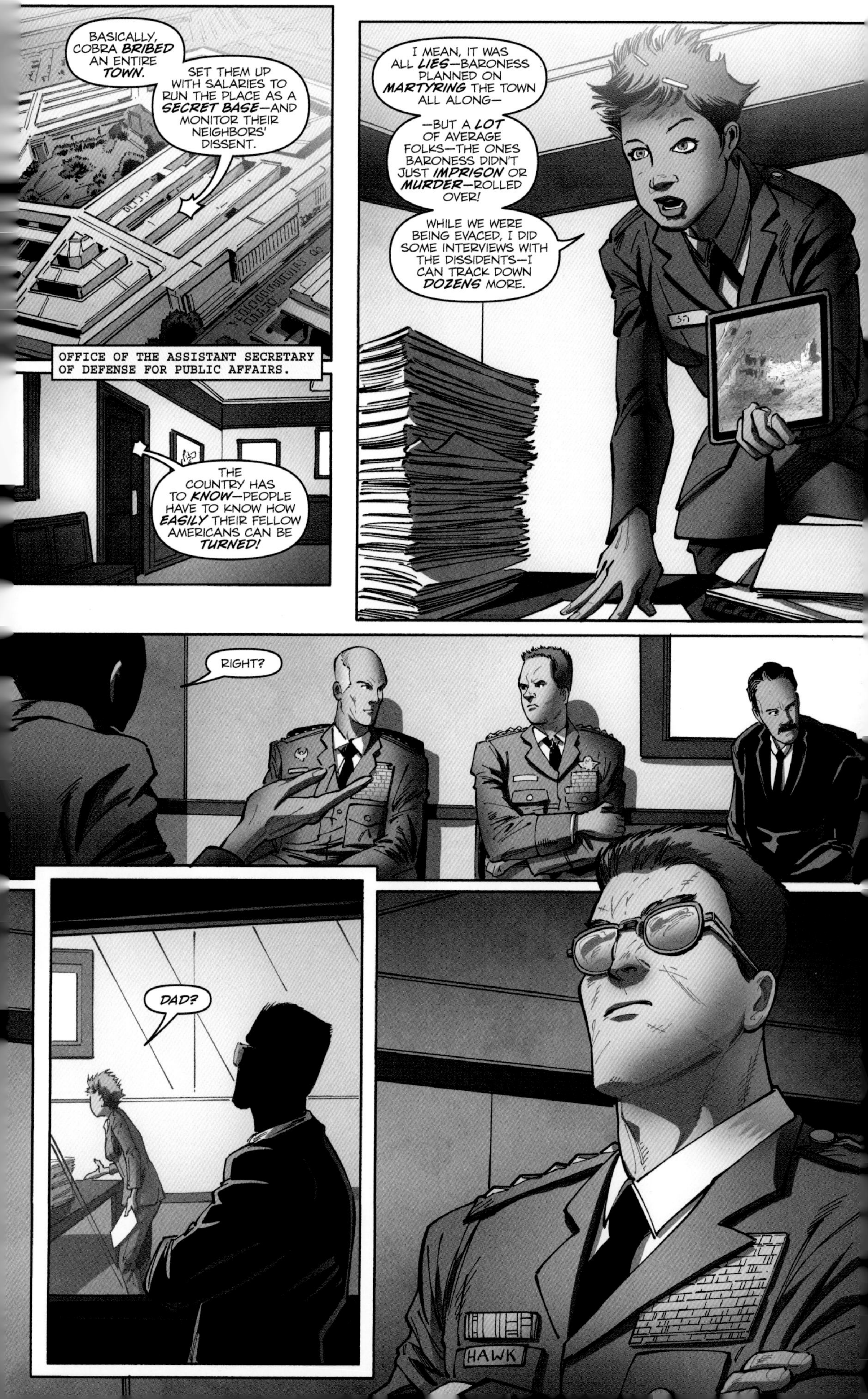
BASICALLY, COBRA BRIBED AN ENTIRE TOWN.
SET THEM UP WITH SALARIES TO RUN THE PLACE AS A SECRET BASE—AND MONITOR THEIR NEIGHBORS' DISSENT.
OFFICE OF THE ASSISTANT SECRETARY OF DEFENSE FOR PUBLIC AFFAIRS.
THE COUNTRY HAS TO KNOW—PEOPLE HAVE TO KNOW HOW EASILY THEIR FELLOW AMERICANS CAN BE TURNED!
I MEAN, IT WAS ALL LIES—BARONESS PLANNED ON MARTYRING THE TOWN ALL ALONG—
—BUT A LOT OF AVERAGE FOLKS—THE ONES BARONESS DIDN'T JUST IMPRISON OR MURDER—ROLLED OVER!
WHILE WE WERE BEING EVACED, I DID SOME INTERVIEWS WITH THE DISSIDENTS—I CAN TRACK DOWN DOZENS MORE.
RIGHT?
DAD?
HAWK

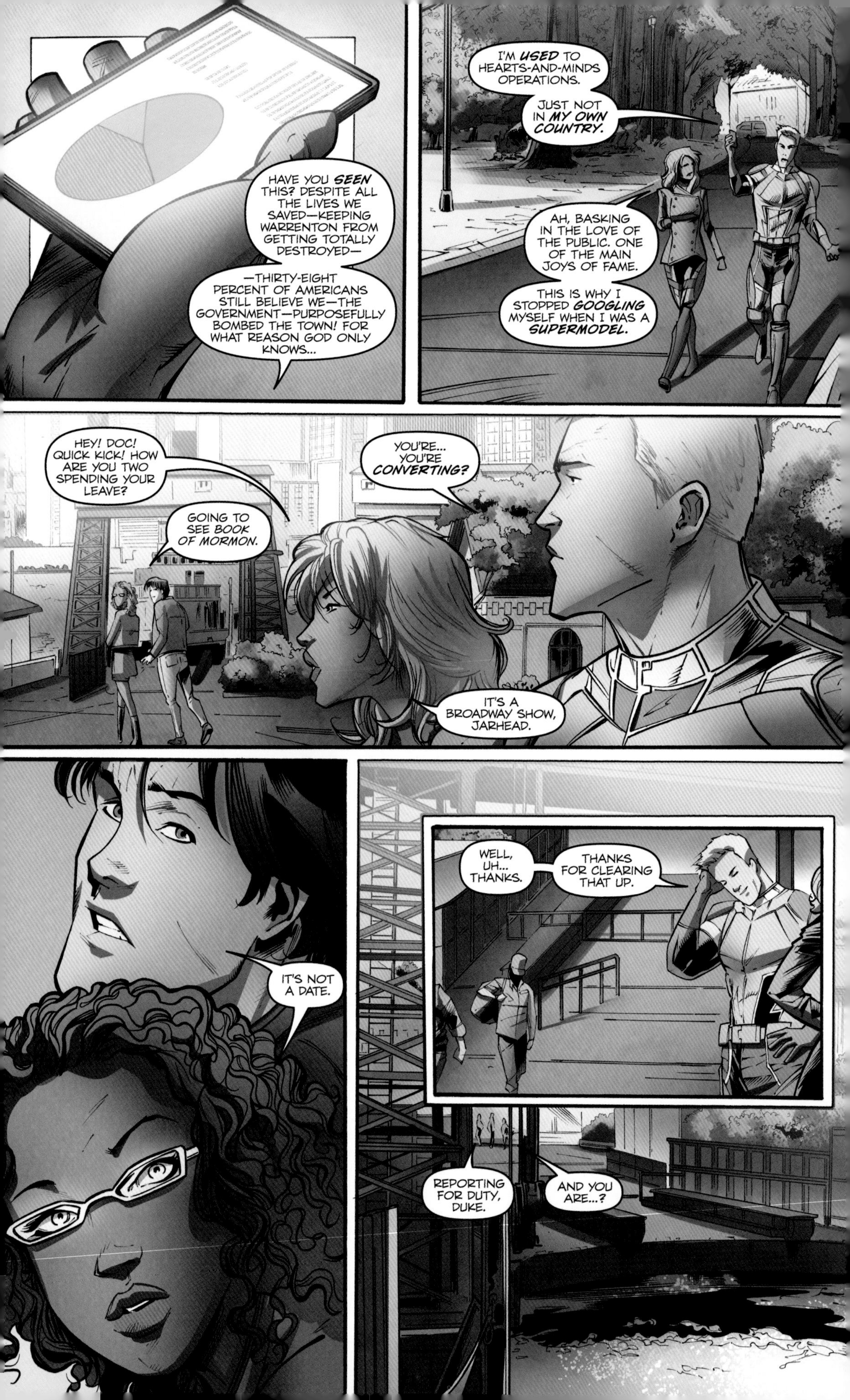
HAVE YOU SEEN THIS? DESPITE ALL THE LIVES WE SAVED—KEEPING WARRENTON FROM GETTING TOTALLY DESTROYED—
—THIRTY-EIGHT PERCENT OF AMERICANS STILL BELIEVE WE—THE GOVERNMENT—PURPOSEFULLY BOMBED THE TOWN! FOR WHAT REASON GOD ONLY KNOWS...
I'M USED TO HEARTS-AND-MINDS OPERATIONS.
JUST NOT IN MY OWN COUNTRY.
AH, BASKING IN THE LOVE OF THE PUBLIC. ONE OF THE MAIN JOYS OF FAME.
THIS IS WHY I STOPPED GOOGLING MYSELF WHEN I WAS A SUPERMODEL.
HEY! DOC! QUICK KICK! HOW ARE YOU TWO SPENDING YOUR LEAVE?
GOING TO SEE BOOK OF MORMON.
YOU'RE... YOU'RE CONVERTING?
IT'S A BROADWAY SHOW, JARHEAD.
IT'S NOT A DATE.
WELL, UH... THANKS.
THANKS FOR CLEARING THAT UP.
REPORTING FOR DUTY, DUKE.
AND YOU ARE...?

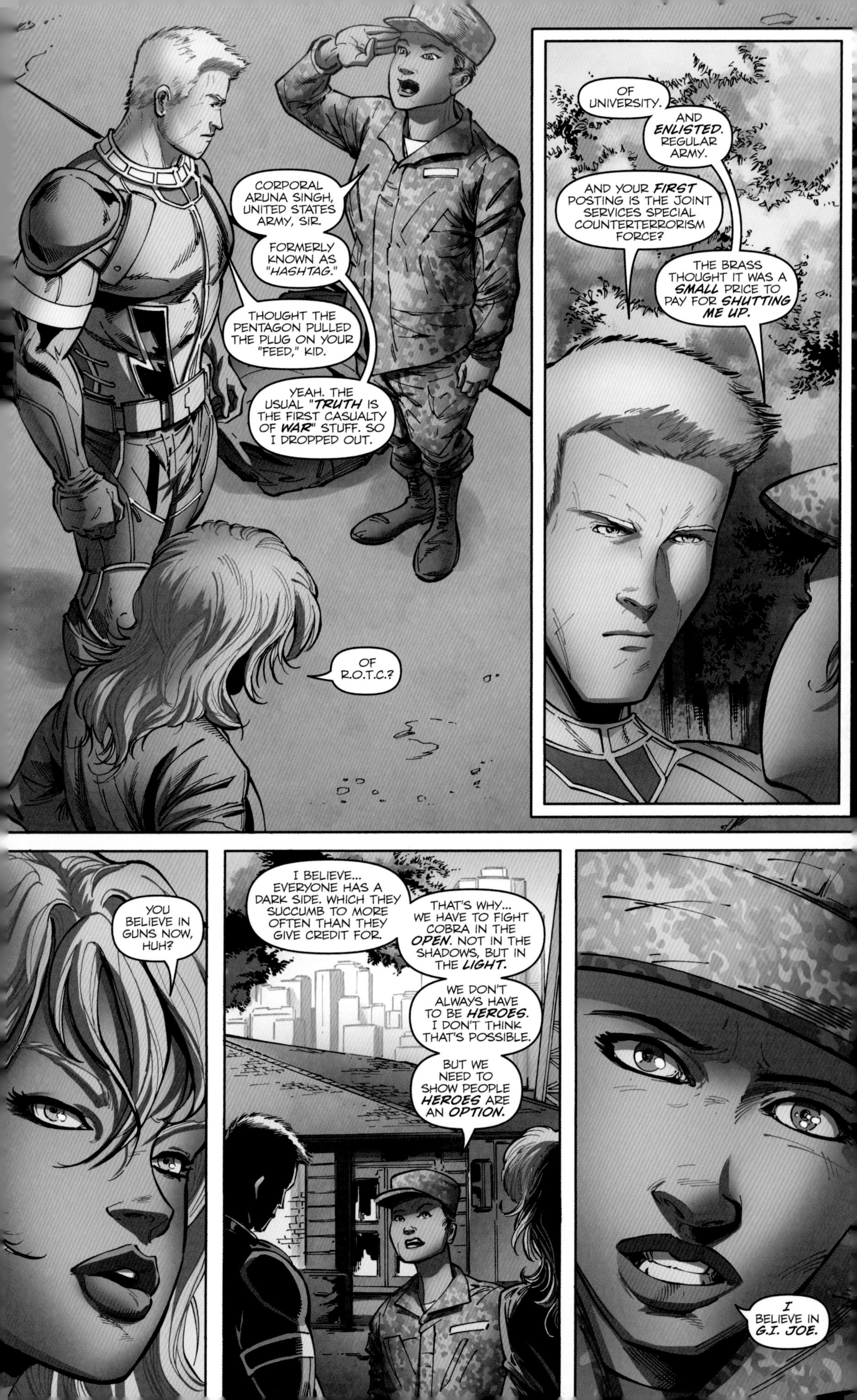
CORPORAL ARUNA SINGH, UNITED STATES ARMY, SIR.
FORMERLY KNOWN AS "HASHTAG."
THOUGHT THE PENTAGON PULLED THE PLUG ON YOUR "FEED," KID.
YEAH. THE USUAL "TRUTH IS THE FIRST CASUALTY OF WAR" STUFF. SO I DROPPED OUT.
OF R.O.T.C.?
OF UNIVERSITY.
AND ENLISTED. REGULAR ARMY.
AND YOUR FIRST POSTING IS THE JOINT SERVICES SPECIAL COUNTERTERRORISM FORCE?
THE BRASS THOUGHT IT WAS A SMALL PRICE TO PAY FOR SHUTTING ME UP.
YOU BELIEVE IN GUNS NOW, HUH?
I BELIEVE... EVERYONE HAS A DARK SIDE. WHICH THEY SUCCUMB TO MORE OFTEN THAN THEY GIVE CREDIT FOR.
THAT'S WHY... WE HAVE TO FIGHT COBRA IN THE OPEN. NOT IN THE SHADOWS, BUT IN THE LIGHT.
WE DON'T ALWAYS HAVE TO BE HEROES. I DON'T THINK THAT'S POSSIBLE.
BUT WE NEED TO SHOW PEOPLE HEROES ARE AN OPTION.
I BELIEVE IN G.I. JOE.

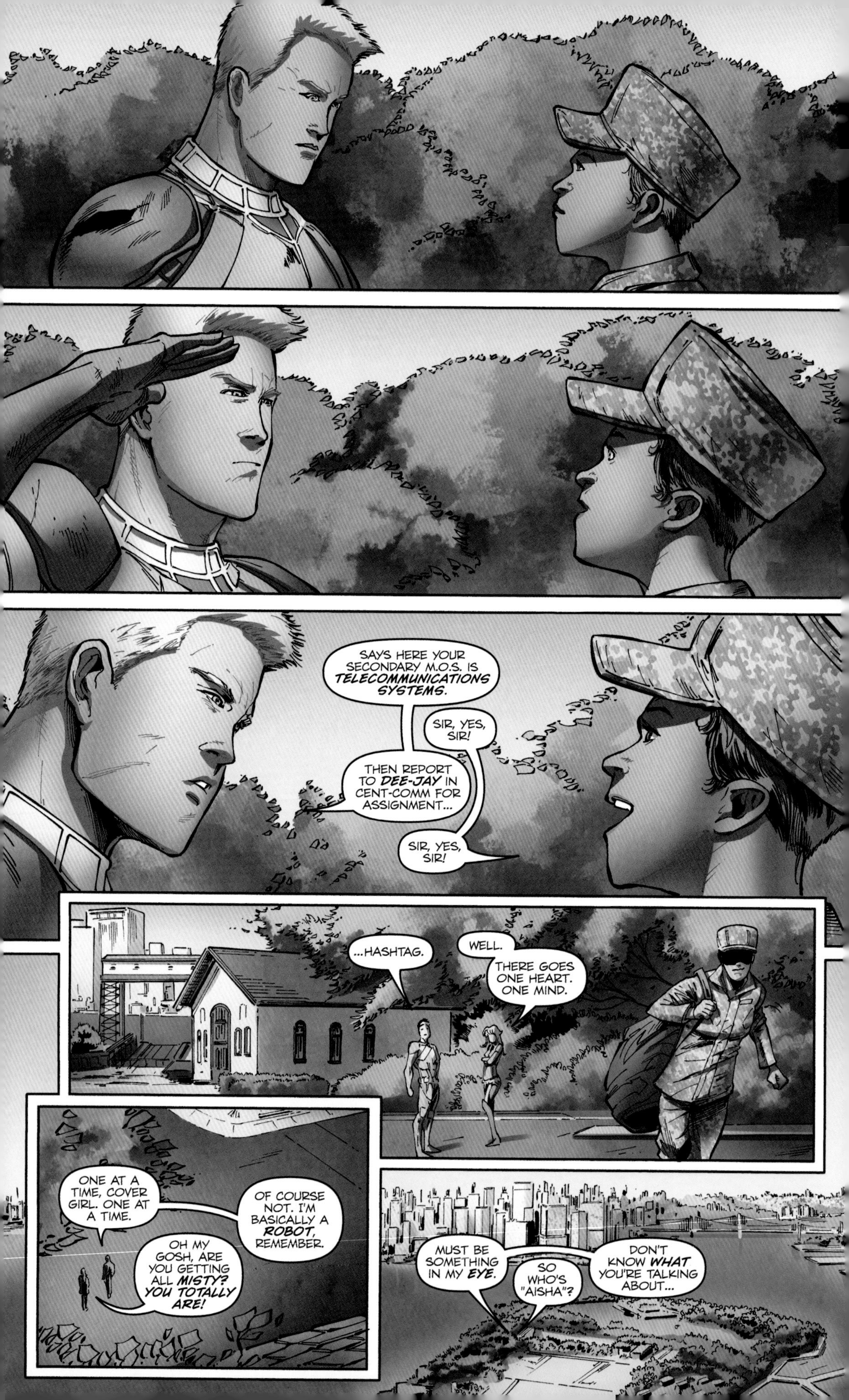
SAYS HERE YOUR SECONDARY M.O.S. IS TELECOMMUNICATIONS SYSTEMS.
SIR, YES, SIR!
THEN REPORT TO DEE-JAY IN CENT-COMM FOR ASSIGNMENT...
SIR, YES, SIR!
...HASHTAG.
WELL.
THERE GOES ONE HEART. ONE MIND.
ONE AT A TIME, COVER GIRL. ONE AT A TIME.
OF COURSE NOT. I'M BASICALLY A ROBOT, REMEMBER.
OH MY GOSH, ARE YOU GETTING ALL MISTY? YOU TOTALLY ARE!
MUST BE SOMETHING IN MY EYE.
DON'T KNOW WHAT YOU'RE TALKING ABOUT...
SO WHO'S "AISHA"?

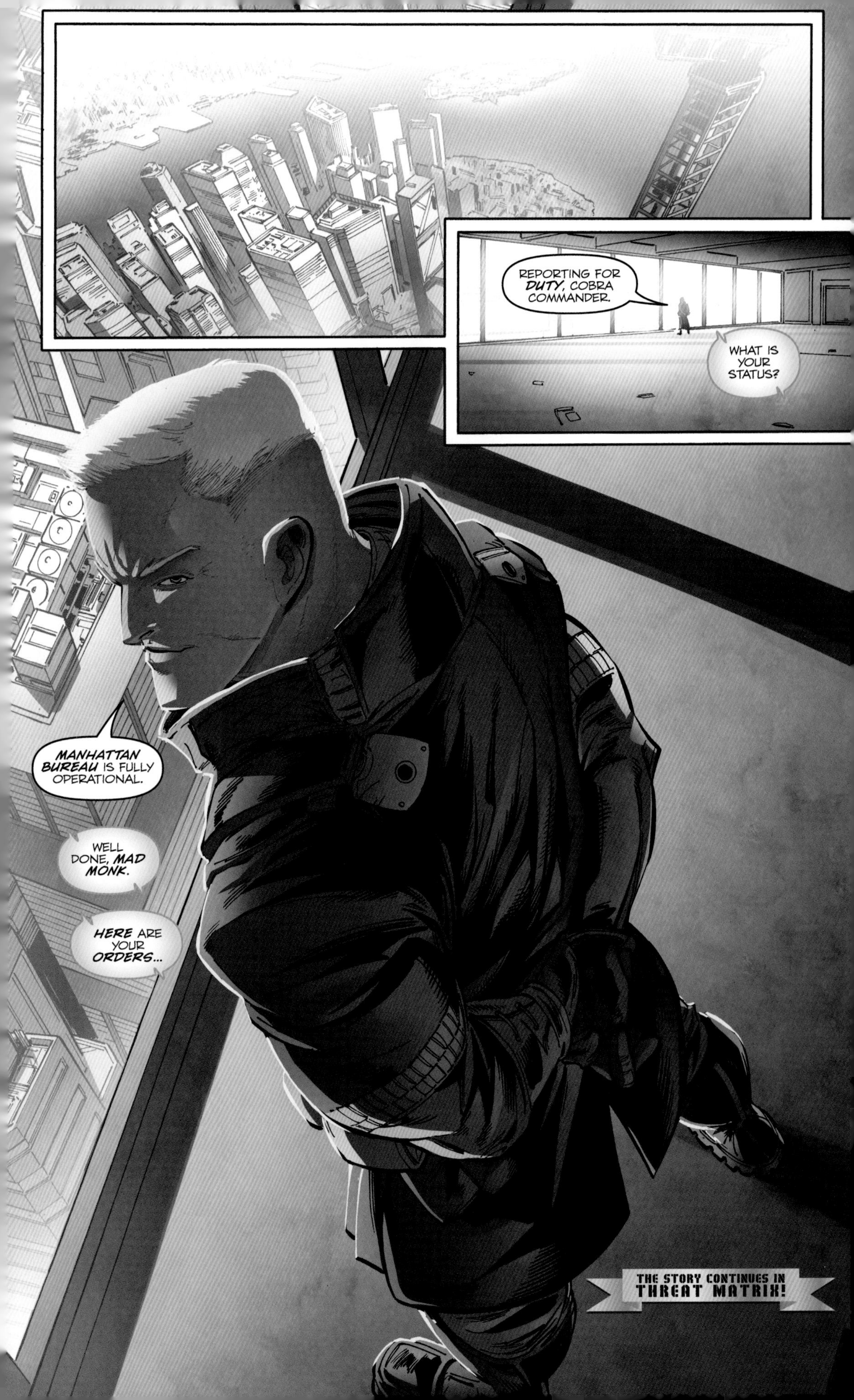
REPORTING FOR DUTY, COBRA COMMANDER.
WHAT IS YOUR STATUS?
MANHATTAN BUREAU IS FULLY OPERATIONAL.
WELL DONE, MAD MONK.
HERE ARE YOUR ORDERS...
THE STORY CONTINUES IN THREAT MATRIX!

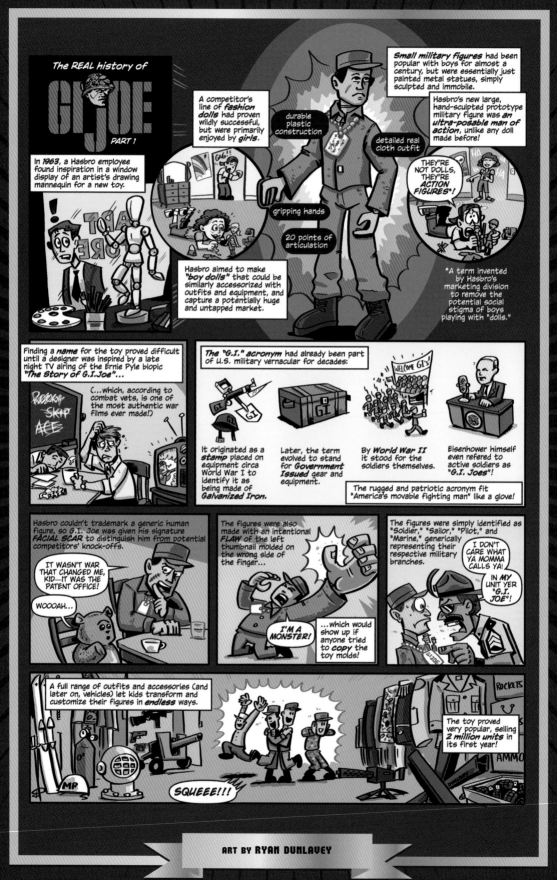

The REAL history of **G I JOE** PART 1

Small military figures had been popular with boys for almost a century, but were essentially just painted metal statues, simply sculpted and immobile.

Hasbro's new large, hand-sculpted prototype military figure was *an ultra-posable man of action*, unlike any doll made before!

A competitor's line of *fashion dolls* had proven wildly successful, but were primarily enjoyed by *girls*.

durable plastic construction

detailed real cloth outfit

In *1963*, a Hasbro employee found inspiration in a window display of an artist's drawing mannequin for a new toy.

ART STORE

gripping hands

20 points of articulation

THEY'RE NOT DOLLS, THEY'RE *ACTION FIGURES*"!

Hasbro aimed to make *"boy dolls"* that could be similarly accessorized with outfits and equipment, and capture a potentially huge and untapped market.

*A term invented by Hasbro's marketing division to remove the potential social stigma of boys playing with "dolls."

Finding a *name* for the toy proved difficult until a designer was inspired by a late night TV airing of the Ernie Pyle biopic *"The Story of G.I. Joe"*...

ROCKSEY SKIP ACE

(...which, according to combat vets, is one of the most authentic war films ever made!)

The "G.I." acronym had already been part of U.S. military vernacular for decades:

WELCOME GI's

It originated as a *stamp* placed on equipment circa World War I to identify it as being made of *Galvanized Iron*.

Later, the term evolved to stand for *Government Issued* gear and equipment.

By *World War II* it stood for the soldiers themselves.

Eisenhower himself even refered to active soldiers as *"G.I. Joes"*!

The rugged and patriotic acronym fit "America's movable fighting man" like a glove!

Hasbro couldn't trademark a generic human figure, so G.I. Joe was given his signature *FACIAL SCAR* to distinguish him from potential competitors' knock-offs.

IT WASN'T WAR THAT CHANGED ME, KID—IT WAS THE PATENT OFFICE!

WOOOAH...

The figures were also made with an intentional *FLAW* of the left thumbnail molded on the wrong side of the finger...

I'M A MONSTER!

...which would show up if anyone tried to *copy* the toy molds!

The figures were simply identified as "Soldier," "Sailor," "Pilot," and "Marine," generically representing their respective military branches.

I DON'T CARE WHAT YA MOMMA CALLS YA!

IN *MY* UNIT YER *"G.I. JOE"*!

A full range of outfits and accessories (and later on, vehicles) let kids transform and customize their figures in *endless* ways.

SQUEEE!!!

ROCKETS

AMMO

MP

The toy proved very popular, selling *2 million units* in its first year!

ART BY RYAN DUNLAVEY

The REAL history of G.I. JOE
PART 2

Hasbro continued to capitalize on the success of the world's first "action figure" with continuous new offerings of accessories to use with the figures kids already owned.

They made new models of the figures themselves with unique features—life-like hair, a range of ethnicities, and even ones that talked.

DUNLAVEY

In 1967, G.I. Joe went into space!

Amid the cultural anti-war backlash of the late '60s, Hasbro started to move G.I. Joe away from his military roots and rebranded the toys as the *G.I. Joe Adventure Team*...

...a rugged group of do-anything, go-anywhere adventurers and explorers!

In 1974 a slightly re-tooled G.I. Joe doll was given his famous *Kung Fu Grip*, allowing for more play possibilities. The revamped doll proved very popular, out-selling the original in its first year!

KUNG FU GRIP

New features quickly followed suit: *Eagle Eyed Joe* (whose eyeballs could move) was also a big hit with kids.

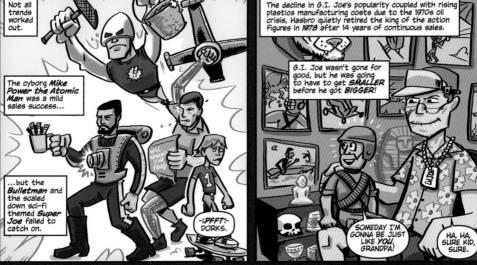

Not all trends worked out.

The cyborg *Mike Power the Atomic Man* was a mild sales success...

...but the *Bulletman* and the scaled down sci-fi themed *Super Joe* failed to catch on.

WILL ADVENTURE FOR FOOD

~PFFT~ DORKS.

The decline in G.I. Joe's popularity coupled with rising plastics manufacturing costs due to the 1970s oil crisis, Hasbro quietly retired the king of the action figures in *1978* after 14 years of continuous sales.

G.I. Joe wasn't gone for good, but he was going to have to get *SMALLER* before he got *BIGGER!*

SOMEDAY I'M GONNA BE JUST LIKE *YOU*, GRANDPA!

HA, HA, SURE KID, SURE.

ART BY RYAN DUNLAVEY

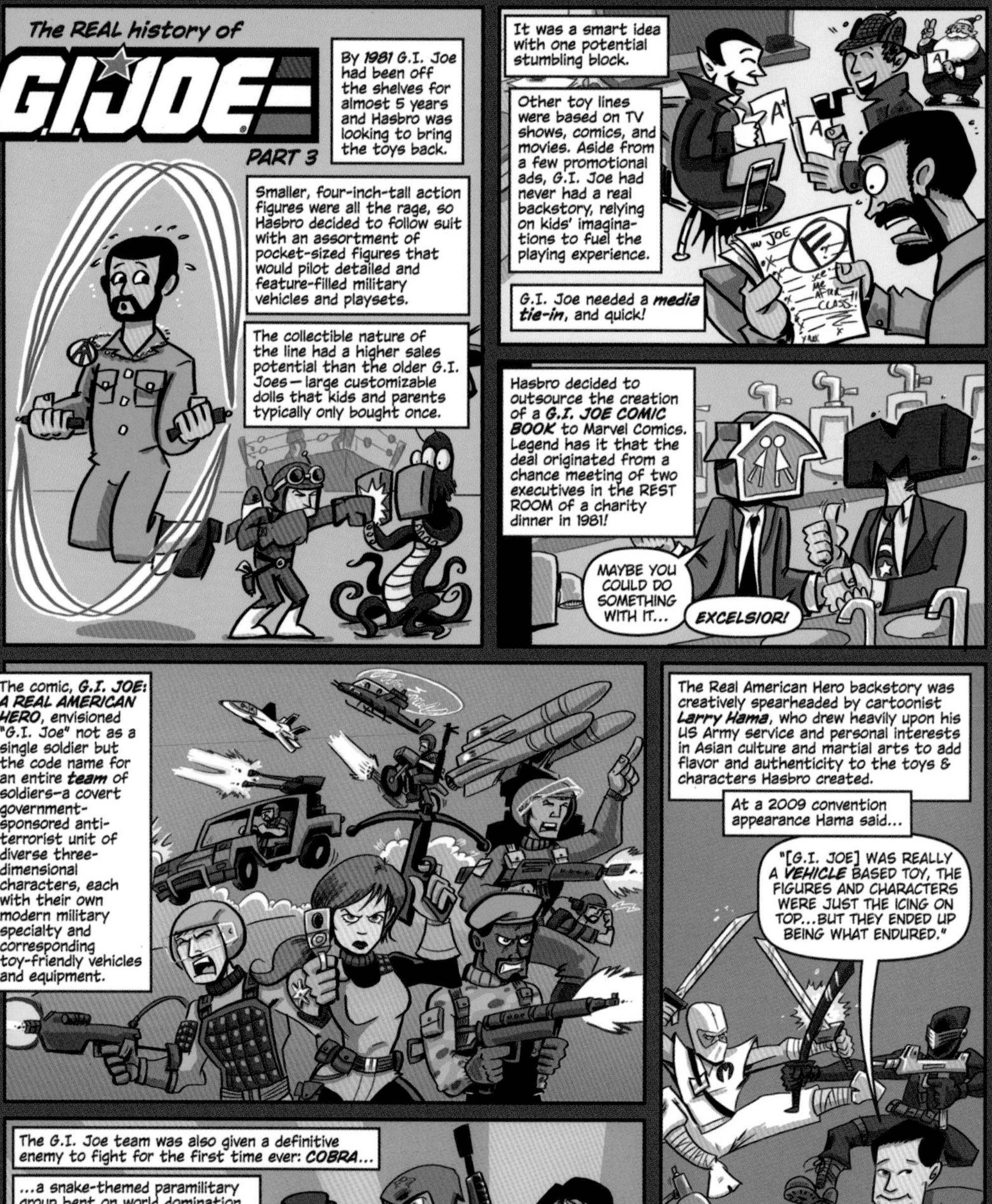
The REAL history of
G.I. JOE
PART 3
By 1981 G.I. Joe had been off the shelves for almost 5 years and Hasbro was looking to bring the toys back.
Smaller, four-inch-tall action figures were all the rage, so Hasbro decided to follow suit with an assortment of pocket-sized figures that would pilot detailed and feature-filled military vehicles and playsets.
The collectible nature of the line had a higher sales potential than the older G.I. Joes—large customizable dolls that kids and parents typically only bought once.
It was a smart idea with one potential stumbling block.
Other toy lines were based on TV shows, comics, and movies. Aside from a few promotional ads, G.I. Joe had never had a real backstory, relying on kids' imaginations to fuel the playing experience.
G.I. Joe needed a media tie-in, and quick!
Hasbro decided to outsource the creation of a G.I. JOE COMIC BOOK to Marvel Comics. Legend has it that the deal originated from a chance meeting of two executives in the REST ROOM of a charity dinner in 1981!
MAYBE YOU COULD DO SOMETHING WITH IT...
EXCELSIOR!
The comic, G.I. JOE: A REAL AMERICAN HERO, envisioned "G.I. Joe" not as a single soldier but the code name for an entire team of soldiers—a covert government-sponsored anti-terrorist unit of diverse three-dimensional characters, each with their own modern military specialty and corresponding toy-friendly vehicles and equipment.
The Real American Hero backstory was creatively spearheaded by cartoonist Larry Hama, who drew heavily upon his US Army service and personal interests in Asian culture and martial arts to add flavor and authenticity to the toys & characters Hasbro created.
At a 2009 convention appearance Hama said...
"[G.I. JOE] WAS REALLY A VEHICLE BASED TOY, THE FIGURES AND CHARACTERS WERE JUST THE ICING ON TOP...BUT THEY ENDED UP BEING WHAT ENDURED."
The G.I. Joe team was also given a definitive enemy to fight for the first time ever: COBRA...
...a snake-themed paramilitary group bent on world domination that was populated with its own set of quirky characters outfitted with a full complement of playsets and accessories.
Hasbro was understandably reluctant to make "terrorist" toys but Marvel insisted on their inclusion.
The Cobra characters proved very popular and the toys based on them would eventually represent over forty percent of the G.I. Joe toy line!
Hama would write almost all of the G.I. Joe comics and character bios during the "Real American Hero" era from 1982-1994. Hasbro even had one of the characters—Tunnel Rat—modeled in Hama's likeness!

ART BY RYAN DUNLAVEY

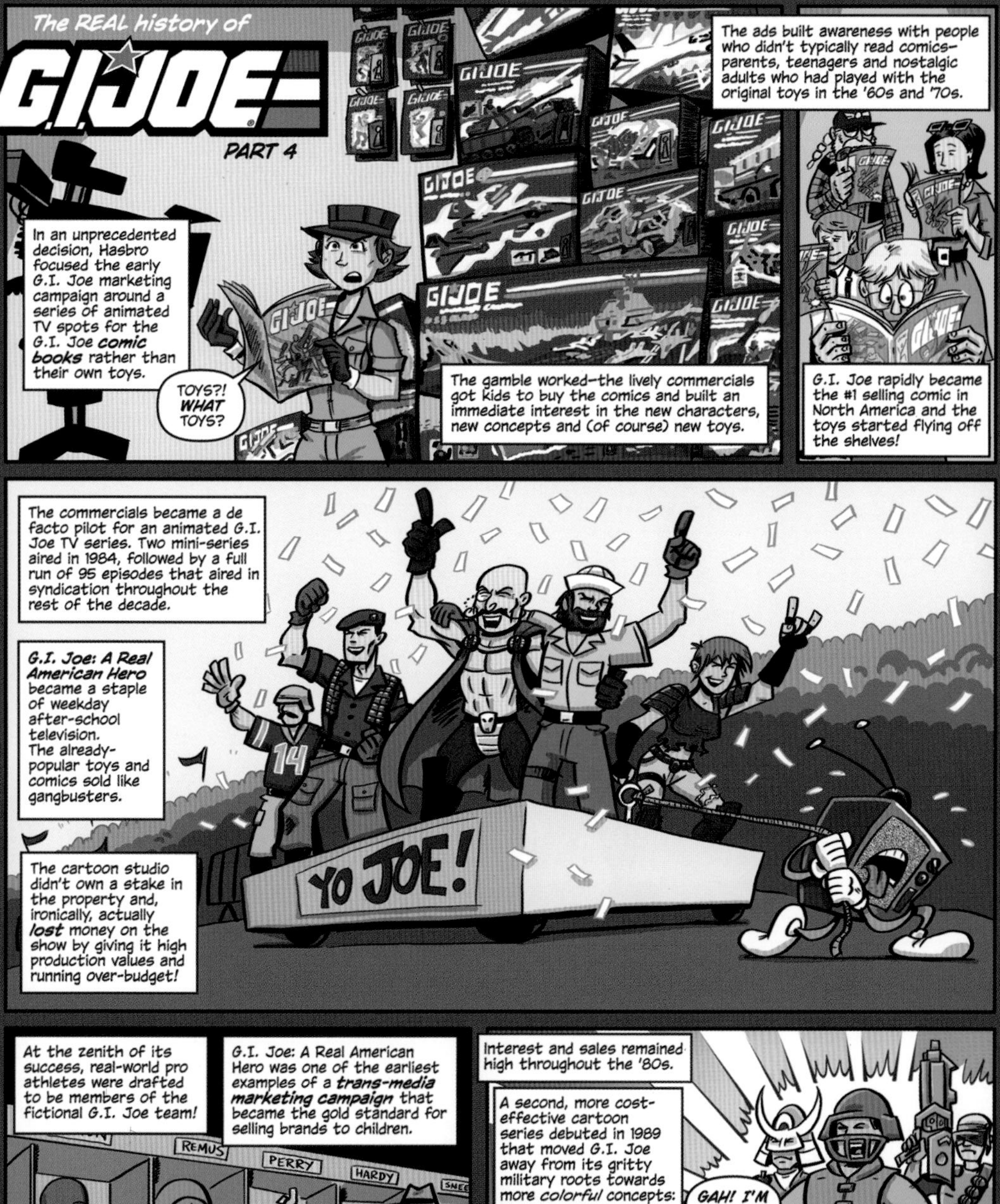

The REAL history of
G.I. JOE
PART 4
In an unprecedented decision, Hasbro focused the early G.I. Joe marketing campaign around a series of animated TV spots for the G.I. Joe comic books rather than their own toys.
TOYS?! WHAT TOYS?
The gamble worked—the lively commercials got kids to buy the comics and built an immediate interest in the new characters, new concepts and (of course) new toys.
The ads built awareness with people who didn't typically read comics–parents, teenagers and nostalgic adults who had played with the original toys in the '60s and '70s.
G.I. Joe rapidly became the #1 selling comic in North America and the toys started flying off the shelves!
The commercials became a de facto pilot for an animated G.I. Joe TV series. Two mini-series aired in 1984, followed by a full run of 95 episodes that aired in syndication throughout the rest of the decade.
G.I. Joe: A Real American Hero became a staple of weekday after-school television. The already-popular toys and comics sold like gangbusters.
The cartoon studio didn't own a stake in the property and, ironically, actually lost money on the show by giving it high production values and running over-budget!
YO JOE!
At the zenith of its success, real-world pro athletes were drafted to be members of the fictional G.I. Joe team!
G.I. Joe: A Real American Hero was one of the earliest examples of a trans-media marketing campaign that became the gold standard for selling brands to children.
REMUS
PERRY
HARDY
ARMORY
RESTRICTED AREA
DUNLAVEY
Interest and sales remained high throughout the '80s.
A second, more cost-effective cartoon series debuted in 1989 that moved G.I. Joe away from its gritty military roots towards more colorful concepts:
GAH! I'M BLIND!!!
MISSION ACCOMPLISHED, TEAM!
The flashy new G.I. Joes weren't quite as popular with the kid audience, and the future of the property seemed uncertain for the first time in a decade.

ART BY RYAN DUNLAVEY

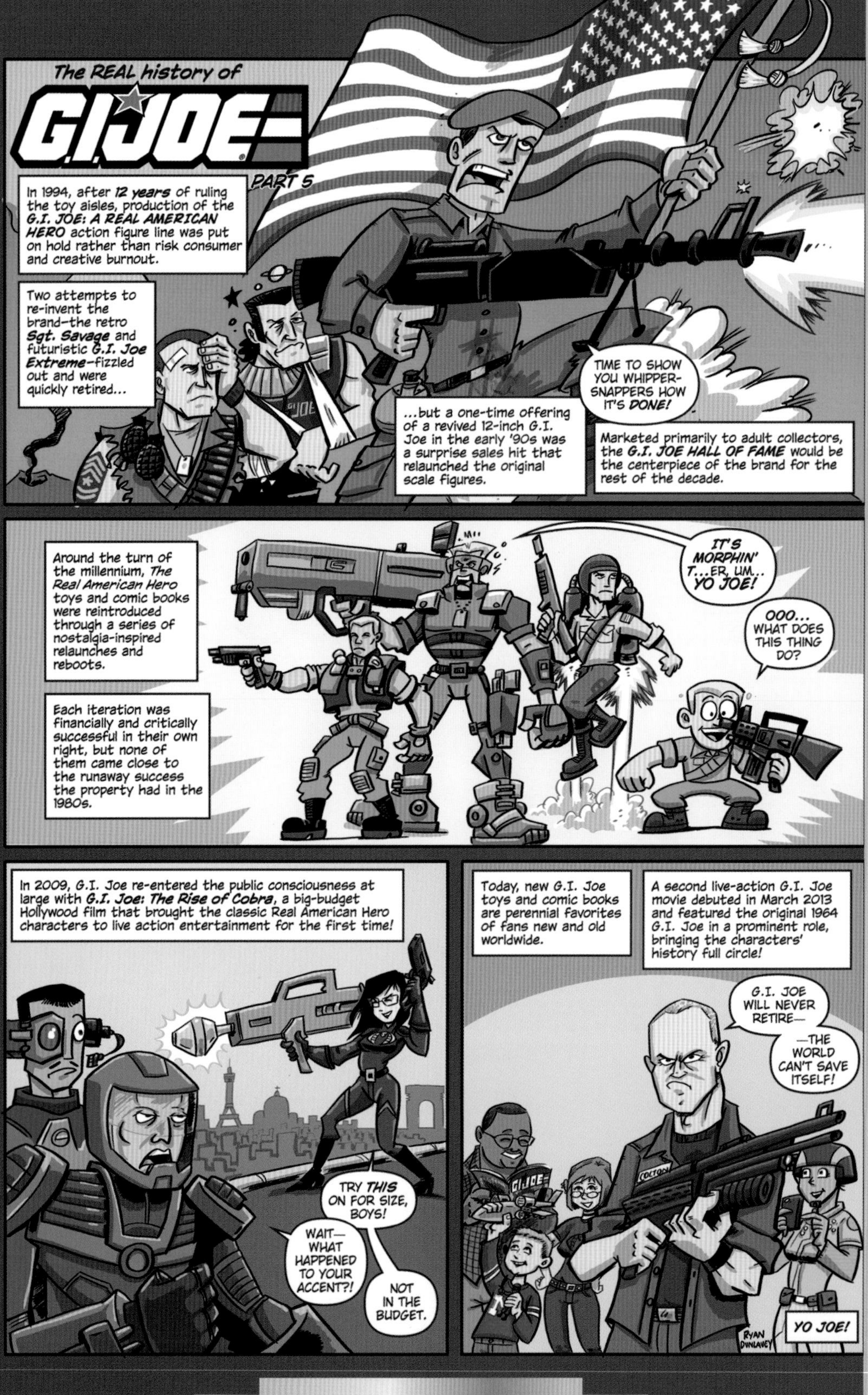
The REAL history of
G.I. JOE
PART 5
In 1994, after 12 years of ruling the toy aisles, production of the G.I. JOE: A REAL AMERICAN HERO action figure line was put on hold rather than risk consumer and creative burnout.
Two attempts to re-invent the brand—the retro Sgt. Savage and futuristic G.I. Joe Extreme—fizzled out and were quickly retired...
...but a one-time offering of a revived 12-inch G.I. Joe in the early '90s was a surprise sales hit that relaunched the original scale figures.
TIME TO SHOW YOU WHIPPER-SNAPPERS HOW IT'S DONE!
Marketed primarily to adult collectors, the G.I. JOE HALL OF FAME would be the centerpiece of the brand for the rest of the decade.
Around the turn of the millennium, The Real American Hero toys and comic books were reintroduced through a series of nostalgia-inspired relaunches and reboots.
Each iteration was financially and critically successful in their own right, but none of them came close to the runaway success the property had in the 1980s.
IT'S MORPHIN' T...ER, UM... YO JOE!
OOO... WHAT DOES THIS THING DO?
In 2009, G.I. Joe re-entered the public consciousness at large with G.I. Joe: The Rise of Cobra, a big-budget Hollywood film that brought the classic Real American Hero characters to live action entertainment for the first time!
TRY THIS ON FOR SIZE, BOYS!
WAIT—WHAT HAPPENED TO YOUR ACCENT?!
NOT IN THE BUDGET.
Today, new G.I. Joe toys and comic books are perennial favorites of fans new and old worldwide.
A second live-action G.I. Joe movie debuted in March 2013 and featured the original 1964 G.I. Joe in a prominent role, bringing the characters' history full circle!
G.I. JOE WILL NEVER RETIRE—
—THE WORLD CAN'T SAVE ITSELF!
YO JOE!
RYAN DUNLAVEY

ART BY RYAN DUNLAVEY

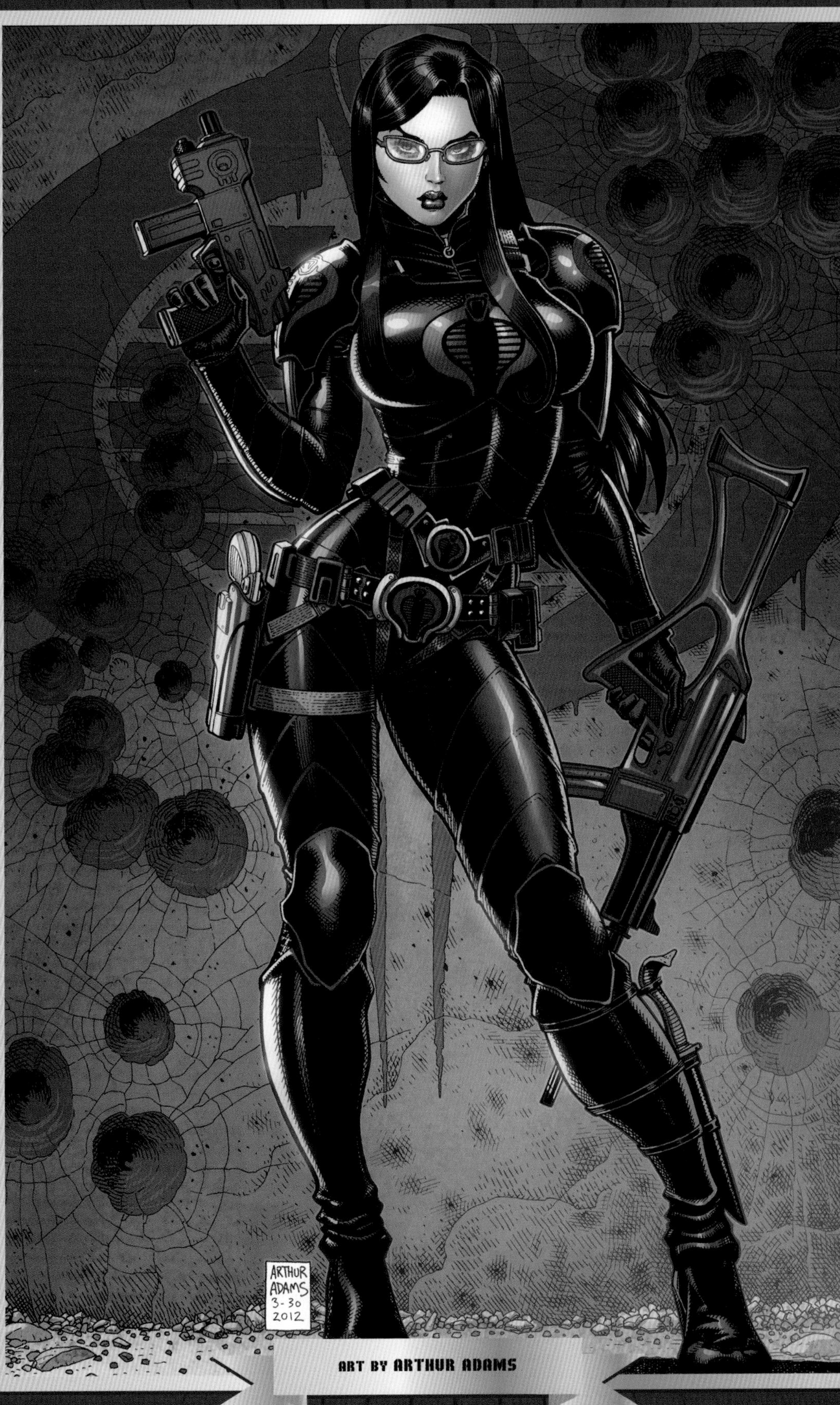
ARTHUR ADAMS 3-30 2012

ART BY ARTHUR ADAMS

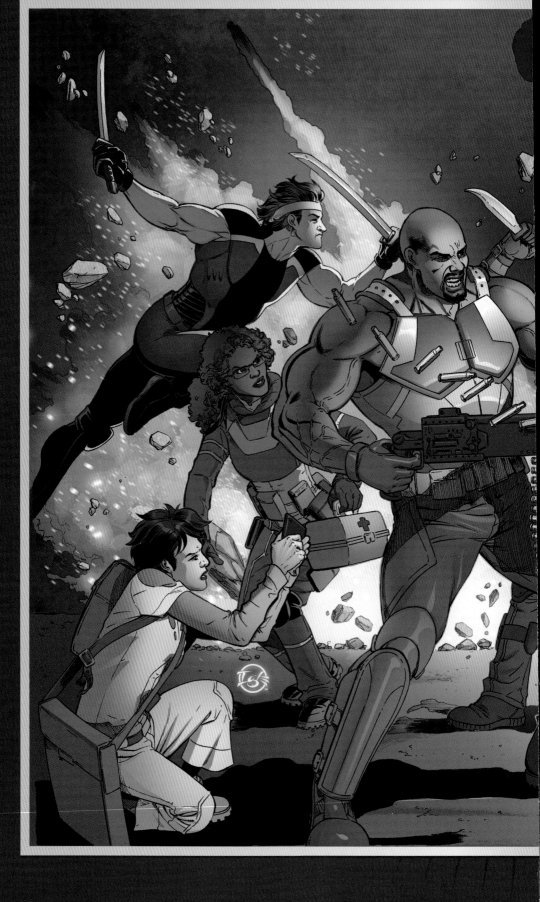

ART BY JAMAL IGLE
COLORS BY ROMULO FAJARDO, JR.

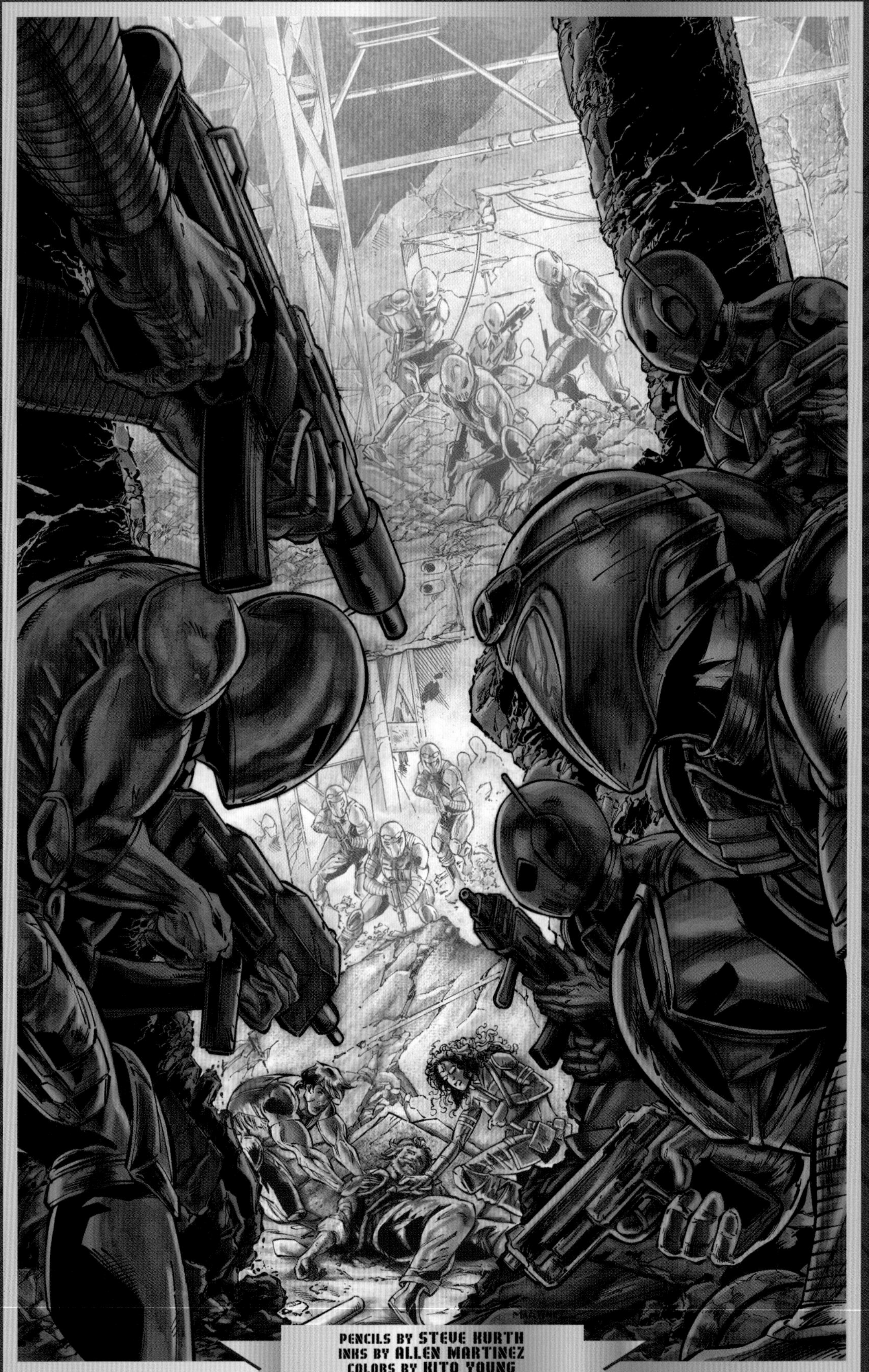
PENCILS BY STEVE KURTH
INKS BY ALLEN MARTINEZ
COLORS BY KITO YOUNG

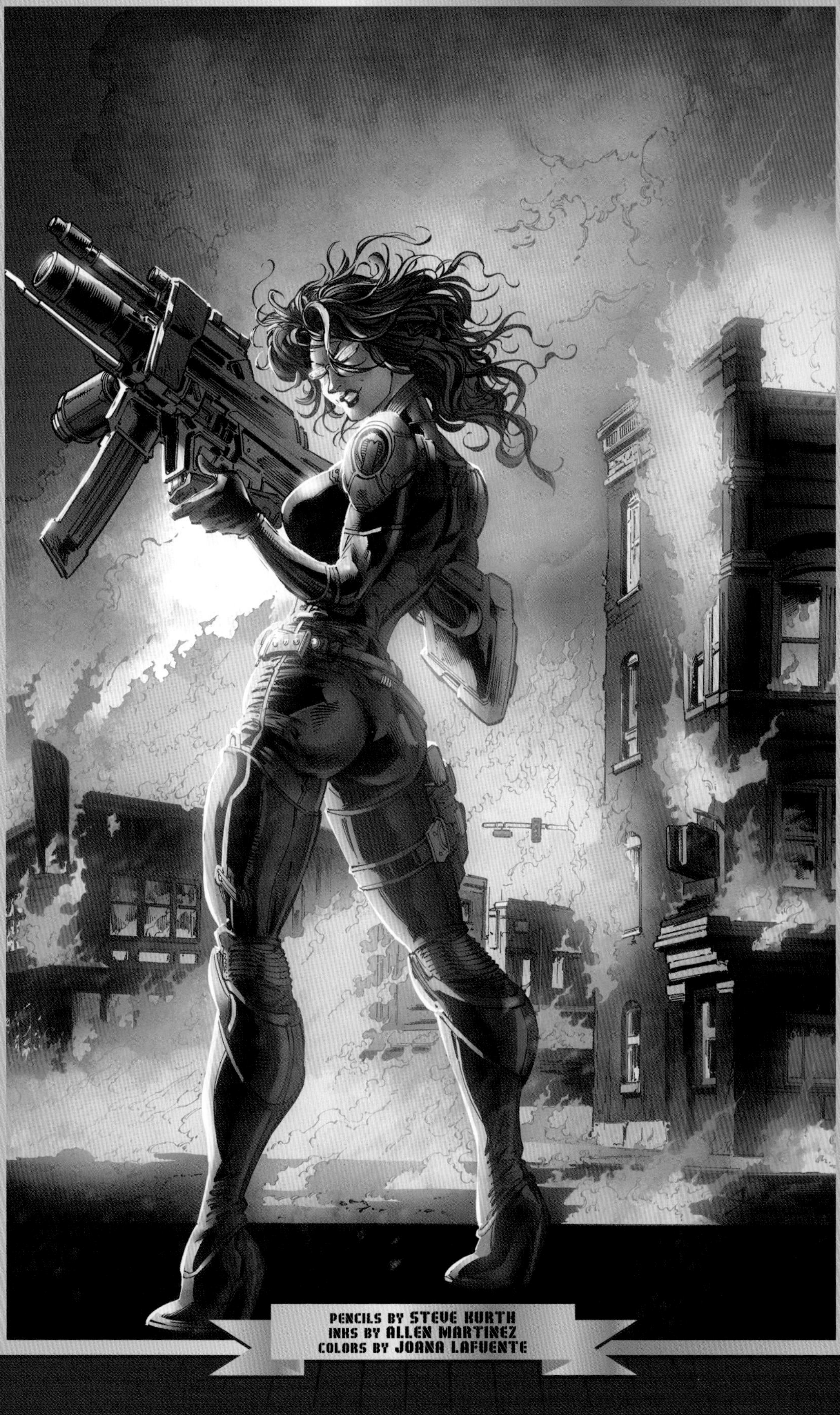
PENCILS BY STEVE KURTH
INKS BY ALLEN MARTINEZ
COLORS BY JOANA LAFUENTE

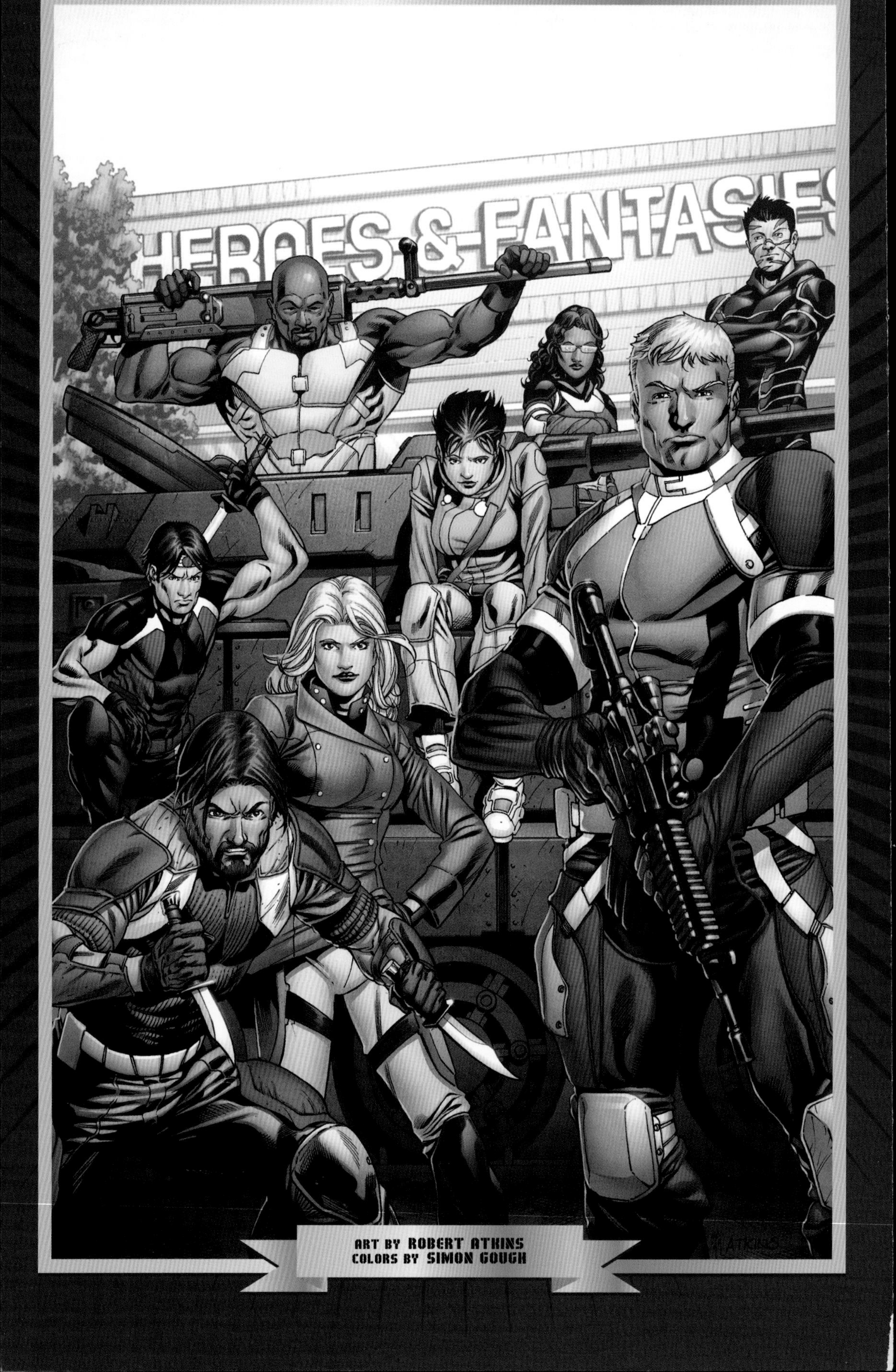
HEROES & FANTASIES

ART BY ROBERT ATKINS
COLORS BY SIMON GOUGH